The Great Breakthrough and Its Cause

The Great Breakthrough and Its Cause

Julian L. Simon

Edited by Timur Kuran

Ann Arbor
THE UNIVERSITY OF MICHIGAN PRESS

Copyright © by the University of Michigan 2000
All rights reserved
Published in the United States of America by
The University of Michigan Press
Manufactured in the United States of America
♾ Printed on acid-free paper

2003   2002   2001   2000   4   3   2   1

A CIP catalog record for this book is available from the British Library.

The manuscript for this volume reached the University of Michigan Press
only after the untimely death of its author. The efforts of the editorial
staff yielded some solutions to the multitude of puzzles posed by the
numerous incomplete quotations and sources in the book. Alas, some
could not be identified and we apologize for not giving due recognition
of sources and copyright holders for those quotations and sources that
remain unsolved mysteries.

Library of Congress Cataloging-in-Publication Data

Simon, Julian Lincoln, 1932–
        The great breakthrough and its cause / Julian L. Simon.
        p. cm.
        Includes bibliographical references.
        ISBN 0-472-11097-7 (cloth : alk. paper)
        1. Population — Economic aspects.   2. Economic development.
    I. Title.

    HB849.41 .S548 2001
    304.6 — dc21   00-059983

Contents

Figures

Tables

Foreword

Richard A. Easterlin

This book takes sharp issue with those who see the social and economic development of humankind as a gradual evolutionary process that is even now approaching finite limits. Its empirical focus is what is called Sudden Modern Progress, by which is meant the great advance in consumer welfare occurring in the last two centuries. The author presents a wide-ranging array of statistical time series documenting this discontinuity. These series embrace income per person, life expectancy at birth, the infant mortality rate, the literacy rate, urbanization, proportion of labor force in agriculture, and speeds of transportation and communication. Looking to the future, the author argues that conditions of life will continue to get better for most people, in most countries, most of the time, indefinitely.

The author's fundamental analytical concern is the cause of this great explosion in consumer well-being. His answer is the growth of human numbers and population density. He argues that had population numbers risen more rapidly than actually occurred, the "Great Breakthrough" would have occurred earlier; had they risen more slowly, it might not yet have occurred. The causal links in this theory are spelled out in chapter 2. At the center of the argument is a two-sided effect of population numbers — on the one hand, increased population and the multiplied interactions resulting therefrom promote the production of knowledge; on the other, population increase generates greater demand for the solution of problems of subsistence and survival. Chapter 3 presents empirical evidence in support of the theoretical argument.

Chapters 2 and 3 develop the volume's main thesis; chapters 4 and 5 address some counterarguments. Chapter 4 is concerned with alternative explanations that have been proposed for the sudden acceleration in progress, most notably, institutional changes. The author argues that such changes are, indeed, important for human progress but from a very-long-run perspective institutional changes are themselves a result of population growth. Chapter 5 seeks to refute two seeming counterexamples to the author's theory, China and India, that reached high population densities prior to the modern period without accelerated growth in consumer welfare.

This volume is a fitting capstone to Julian Simon's professional career. The economics profession has long labored under the weight of Malthusian doctrine, and Simon has been in the vanguard of those seeking to lift this burden. As handed down by John Stuart Mill in the mid–nineteenth century, Malthusianism sees the pressure of growing population numbers operating ineluctably to reduce productivity via the law of diminishing returns. Technological progress may forestall this outcome, but in the race between population and technology, population is inevitably the victor.

This doctrine, passed down in economics from generation to generation in increasingly sophisticated form, is sharply contradicted by the facts of the past two centuries, but economists, lacking a theory of technological change, have for the most part held with the diminishing returns relationship emphasized in the static theory of production and passed over the facts. Simon himself started out with this heritage as evidenced in articles written in the 1960s. As a result of studying the facts, however, he came increasingly to question the Malthusian view, and his 1977 work, *The Economic Consequences of Population Growth,* represents his first great break with this tradition. In that book, Simon sought to counter the population explosionist doomsday view by presenting theoretical and empirical arguments developed in articles published in the early 1970s that called into question the negative view of population growth. He put forward a thesis that a truly long-run view of population growth would find it to have beneficial effects and that most analyses were preoccupied with the short run, a period of three decades or less. This theme persists in his subsequent work and reaches its fullest development in this volume.

Meantime, the grounds on which population explosionists had been arguing were shifting, partly because of growing evidence of accelerating productivity growth in developing countries but partly because of the vigor and persistence of Simon's attacks. Population growth had initially been seen as an overriding obstacle to economic growth because of its supposed adverse productivity effects. But as country after country in the Third World began to exhibit unprecedented advances in living levels, the emphasis of the Malthusians gradually shifted to the environmental consequences of population growth—the notion, rooted again in Malthusian doctrine, that natural resources are limited and population growth depletes the Earth's natural resources. Simon responded, first, with a volume aimed at a general audience, whose title, *The Ultimate*

Resource, put forth boldly his positive view of population. This study incorporated the ideas of the 1977 volume and added new material addressing environmental concerns. This was followed with a coedited volume in 1984, *The Resourceful Earth;* a 1990 book, *Population Matters: People, Resources, Environment, and Immigration;* and, finally, a second edition in 1995 of *The Ultimate Resource.* His views on the environment stressed the adaptive processes of the economic system, that rising prices induced by incipient resource scarcities directed productive efforts to new resource discoveries and, most importantly, to technological innovations that increased the world's stock of natural resources by making economically feasible the exploitation of land, minerals, and the like, that had previously been unusable in production. Simon pointed to historical evidence of a long-term decline in the real price of resources, arguing that it would continue into the future. An article in *Science* presenting this view led to a now-famous wager with the leading population explosionist, Paul Ehrlich, and two other scholars with similar views on the likely change between 1980 and 1990 in the average real price of five metals—chrome, copper, nickel, tin, and tungsten. Simon won the bet hands down, and the Ehrlich group, when challenged to continue that or a similar wager, withdrew.

At the same time that Simon was trying to reach a more general audience, he was continuing detailed scholarly analyses of the effects of population growth. His studies of more developed countries were published in 1986 in *Theory of Population and Economic Growth;* of less developed countries in 1992 in *Population and Development in Poor Countries: Selected Essays.*

Julian Simon was not the only scholar arguing against the Malthusian and neo-Malthusian view, but there is little doubt that he was the most vehement, persistent, and articulate spokesman of the anti-Malthusians and attracted, in return, the most vigorous attacks. That his overall assault was successful is evidenced by the shift in views between the 1971 and 1986 National Academy of Science's reports on the effects of population growth. Although the 1986 report did not go as far as Simon in arguing for positive effects of population growth, it adopted a much more neutral stance than the predecessor report toward the supposed adverse effects of increased population.

Simon's assault on the gloom-and-doom theorists led him in time to a more general concern with the popular attraction to negative views of human progress in general, particularly in the media. In an effort to mobilize contradictory evidence, he organized and edited a 52 chapter volume, *The State of Humanity,* published in 1995, presenting the fruits of the work of over 60 contributors. Though overlapping his earlier coedited study, *The Resourceful Earth,* it went much beyond ecological concerns to assemble historical evidence on changes in living levels, life expectancy, the prevalence of slavery, education, agricultural productivity, food and nutrition, health, alcohol and cigarette consumption, suicide, and other measures of the human condition.

The present volume builds on much of what has gone before. Its empirical scope is the wide range of the state of humanity; its theoretical arguments draw on those presented in Simon's earlier studies; and it continues the theme of the importance of a long-run view. As is clear from what follows, in the course of his career, Simon evolved from preoccupation with the current effect of population growth in today's developing and developed countries to its impact on the whole of human history.

Personally, I think Simon is right here on both the facts and prognosis. The modern period does represent an unprecedented discontinuity in rates of social and economic development. Technological progress is occurring at, if anything, more rapid rates than ever before, and the prospect (failing political catastrophe) is for marked improvement in the material conditions of humankind throughout the world. Although I disagree with Simon's view of the preeminent causal role of population, I respect his analysis, and I strongly recommend this book for careful study of both the facts and theory.

Julian Simon died from a heart attack in 1998 at the age of 65, before this volume could be brought to full completion. We are fortunate to have this essay in its present form articulating his views. Simon was an energetic and creative scholar and, above all, a passionate and courageous fighter against great odds for the truth as he saw it. In all of his work he had the welfare of poor people at heart, and he saw his studies as contributing to human betterment generally. His statement in 1995 in the preface to the second edition of *The Ultimate Resource* is equally applicable here: "Poor people, as well as property of high social value such as natural habitats and valuable species, stand to gain the most from the public's being aware of the facts and concepts contained in this book, and from the policies of freedom and enterprise under the rule of wise laws that are the heart of the book's prescriptions."

Editor's Preface

Timur Kuran

The idea of including this book in the Economics, Cognition, and Society series of the University of Michigan Press emerged on a sunny day in September 1996, on a boat trip along the Danube. The outing had been organized for members of the Mont Pèlerin Society, which was meeting that year in Vienna. Julian Simon and I, invited speakers, were among those who enthusiastically joined the excursion.

As the Austrian landscape rolled before our eyes, we chatted for hours, with topic flowing into topic: medieval architecture, Turkish-Austrian relations in the age of Mozart, the direction of economics, ongoing advances in cognitive psychology, the art of persuasion, the economic effects of religion, and more. He was intrigued about a book I had just started to write on the role of Islamic law in the Middle East's successes and failures over the past fourteen centuries. "Will population play any role in your thesis?" he asked at one point. When he found out that it would not, we launched into a discussion about how population pressures influence the evolution of social institutions. Fascinated by his interpretations, I suggested that he write a book that would shed new light on economic history. Such a project was already under way, he said. "Would you be interested in seeing a partial draft?"

The manuscript that reached my desk two weeks later contained an early version of what was to become this book's first three chapters. Relying on an impressively diverse array of historical data, it built a well-documented and highly provocative case for optimism about the future of human civilization. The argument made the daily headlines trumpeting the ill effects of global poverty and inequality pale in comparison to the broader picture of spectacular material progress in recent centuries. Most of the people we now classify as "poor" live longer and enjoy more amenities than those we considered "rich" just a few centuries ago. This positive development was driven, the argument suggested, by population growth.

As it stood then, the manuscript left open the question of why some

highly populated countries are relatively poor, and why advanced regions with rapidly aging populations continue to produce most of the
world's technological and institutional innovations. If larger numbers
and higher rates of population growth are so conducive to economic
development, why have some of the South Asian countries with dense
populations and some African countries with explosive population
growth rates remained so poor? Julian recognized that the book would
leave too many issues open if such questions were not addressed directly. The fourth and fifth chapters present his efforts to identify the
reasons why we do not all share in prosperity to the same degree.

Over the following year we talked several times about the book's
progress. What turned out, sadly, to be our last meeting took place in
early January 1998, in Chicago, during that year's convention of the
American Economic Association. Between sessions we decided to walk
downtown. Julian had just come out of a session he considered "boring,"
so I joked that "perhaps the quality of the session would have been
higher if the AEA had more members." Taking me completely seriously,
he replied: "With more trained economists, more inefficiency-reducing
ideas would be produced. And some bright economist would come up
with a better mechanism for weeding out papers that say little."

At lunch, Julian was all ears. He wanted advice on how to make this
a book that even his persistent critics — people who had long ridiculed
his optimism and his emphasis on the economic benefits of population
growth — would view as an attempt at constructive dialogue. The fourth
and fifth chapters were important in this regard, as they would investi-
gate interactions between population and institutional factors that scholars commonly invoke in explaining why some societies advance faster
than others. This is where he would present mechanisms that researchers ought to consider in studying time periods of medium length — in my
case, a millennium and a half.

The heart attack that cut Julian Simon's life short struck a month
later, on February 8, 1998. Only 65, he had ambitious plans to launch
into new areas of scholarship. And he was continuing to work on this
book, which he called "my essay on economic history." He intended to
collect additional data to bolster various points. He planned to polish
the prose and sharpen key arguments. Most important of all, he wanted
to enhance the book's usefulness to potential readers from the poorest
parts of the planet and to those interested in their plight. His goal was to
leave them not only with the broad message that every region's long-run
trajectory points upward but also with sufficient details to illuminate
current problems.

What follows is an edited version of the manuscript that Julian Simon left behind. Loose notes and figures found on his desk have been incorporated into the text if it was clear where they belonged. A few paragraphs were completed on the basis of our conversations during the last two months of his life; a few others were extended to improve the flow or clarify the point being developed. Certain passages that were insufficiently developed and not essential to the overall argument had to be cut. I have tightened or rewritten many sentences, always trying to stay faithful to Julian's own style.

At the time of his death, Julian had not yet listed all the sources of the dozens of diagrams and tables that support the argument. Most of the missing references were identified through the painstaking work of Ellen McCarthy, Roxanne Hoch, Alja Kooistra, and Susan Whitlock of the University of Michigan Press; they also did a marvelous job checking quotations for accuracy.

Had Julian lived to carry the project to completion, it undoubtedly would have been even better documented, more polished, and most important, more detailed in its effort to address interactions between population and institutions. But we are fortunate that the manuscript was sufficiently complete to make a full argument. Even if the thesis does not convince everyone, at least it will be greeted as a valuable contribution to grand-scale economic history.

The Great Breakthrough appears at a time when the mechanism behind its main argument is no longer considered heretical. The most widely acclaimed new theories on the checkered progress of human civilization have tended to at least accommodate the finding that technology develops and social complexity advances fastest in regions with the largest and densest populations. No longer identified with a particular political ideology, this argument is starting to be viewed as common sense.

Ever optimistic, Julian was fond of saying that good ideas eventually catch on. I am sure that he would have seen the ongoing intellectual transformation as yet another hopeful sign of human progress.

Author's Preface

Multitudes of people, necessity, and liberty, have begotten commerce in Holland.
— David Hume, *Essays Moral, Political, and Literary*

The very understanding of the problems involved, let alone a theoretical formulation and solution, is hardly possible if we limit our view to one country or to a relatively short period of historical experience.
— Simon Kuznets, *Economic Growth and Structure —*
Selected Essays

Statistical data are emphasized because economic growth is essentially a quantitative concept. . . . [T]he economic growth of a nation may be defined as a sustained increase in its population and product per capita.
— Simon Kuznets, *Economic Growth and Structure —*
Selected Essays

The Method I take . . . is not yet very usual; for instead of using only comparative and superlative Words, and intellectual Arguments, I have taken the course (as a Specimen of the Political Arithmetick I have long aimed at) to express my self in Terms of *Number, Weight,* or *Measure* . . . leaving aside those that depend upon the mutable Minds, Opinions, Appetites and Passions of particular Men.
— William Petty

Year after year, in every empirical study I made concerning economic development, no matter the topic or the research design, country size and per capita income (a proxy for wealth and hence for technical level) turned out to be the dominant variables. Indeed, often these were the only variables that mattered. The same finding emerged in many others' studies that I reviewed. For a long time I therefore harbored the thought of editing into a coherent whole a variety of studies that hinges on these variables. But soon after I began this essay, I realized that it subsumes all of that research that was in fact its forebear.

Though this essay is about economic history, and offers an interpretation of it, I cannot claim to be a practitioner of the worthy profession of economic historian; no one can parachute successfully into such a demanding craft without serving a diligent apprenticeship. Therefore, I must pray of economic historians that they will be charitable toward my lapses in the use of their materials and methods as I try to be a conscientious consumer of their hard-won products.

Many quotations (perhaps too many), some quite long (and perhaps too long), are included in the text. An important reason for this is to show that the argument squares at most key points with the consensus of the great tradition of economic historians. Indeed, the essay may be thought of as mainly an arrangement of the data and theories of major economic historians into a larger framework than most have worked with but consistent with their great contributions.

Any essay that emphasizes a single element — as this essay emphasizes the sizes of populations and of their free, skilled subpopulations — runs the risk of both *seeming* to be simplistic and of actually *being* misleadingly monocausal. This is especially true where the single cause is the same phenomenon that has been at the heart of much of an author's prior work, as is the case with me. The only possible response is the content of the essay.

This has been a work of joy. As John Locke said somewhere, I hope that the reader has half the pleasure in reading it that I had in writing it. It is a wonderful era and society that enable a person not born into the nobility to have the time, freedom, and implements to engage in such an enterprise and even to get paid for doing so.

Author's Acknowledgments

This is a preliminary list of acknowledgments of the many gifts of time and thought that others have bestowed on me in the course of writing this short book. The order of the list is mostly chronological, and it is most certainly not in order of importance.

Eric Jones wrote me one of his characteristically long and searching letters in response to the first draft. He convinced me to peer more searchingly into several matters, but he also took the book sufficiently seriously that he gave me confidence to proceed with my first foray into the domain of economic history. I have also benefited from the advice of Colin Day, Timur Kuran, John V. Nye, and Gerald Scully.

CHAPTER 1

Introduction

The Basic Proposition

What was the rock-bottom root cause of the sharp break in living standards that occurred in the richer countries starting about 1750 or 1800? Why did the mortality rate, household consumption level, speeds of travel and communication, literacy rate, and other aspects of the standard of living leap above those in the previous centuries and millennia? Why are many of the world's population now long lived and endowed with much wealth and a high standard of living — and with an even larger proportion likely to enjoy these benefits in the coming decades — whereas very few people had those advantages 10,000, 2,000, 1,000, or even 200 years ago? What force(s) caused this extraordinary development to occur when it did — or ever — rather than centuries or millennia earlier or later? Figures 1 and 2 illustrate the central elements in material human welfare through the ages, in two different time frames.

If progress during the period since 1750–1800 is compared with the progress during any set of years before then, the difference is almost like night and day. One cannot pick a date in any other earlier century, or after 1800, about which one can make the same statement. The break seems to have been sharper for such socially and technically determined elements as the speed of transportation and the rate of literacy than for the demographic variables. (These observations do not refer to the ups and downs in the performances of single nations or in the comparisons of nations. Rather, these remarks refer only to the longest secular trend and to the "recent" break in that trend.)

Asked in other words, this is the central question for this essay: What conceivable difference in conditions in past millennia might have led to a major difference in when the breakthrough in material human welfare took place? Or seen in an imaginary forward-looking manner: If you were the chief of world economic development at some date 200,000 or 20,000 or 2,000 years ago, and endowed with all the knowledge that now exists in the world's libraries, what aspect of your situation would you have wished to be different than you then perceived it to be?

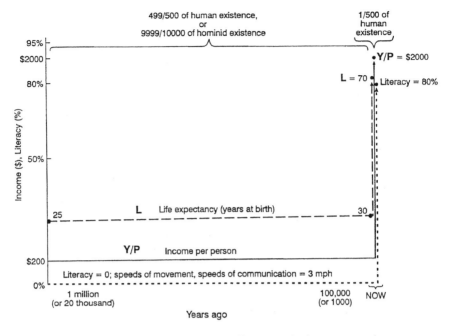

Fig. 1. Basic measures of human welfare over the long course of human existence (stylized)

Yes, the level of technology reached as a result of the accumulation of knowledge throughout human history is crucial. But what produced the accumulated knowledge?

The answer offered here is that the total quantity of humanity (and the nexus of human numbers with technology) has been the main driving force. Starting at any particular moment in the past, the length of time it took to reach the breakthrough into what will be called "Sudden Modern Progress" depended on the number of people endowed with intellect and training who lived thereafter, together with the amount of technology in existence at the particular moment about which the question is being asked. It follows that the only possible decisive difference that could have happened in the past would have been the introduction of knowledge of how to reduce epidemic disease — for example, knowledge of the transmission of cholera and typhoid fever by polluted water, of plague by rats and fleas, and of malaria by mosquitoes. With this knowledge in hand, steps could have been taken to reduce mortality even millennia ago; no complementary elements of technique or major capital resources were necessary, though lack of wealth would have kept

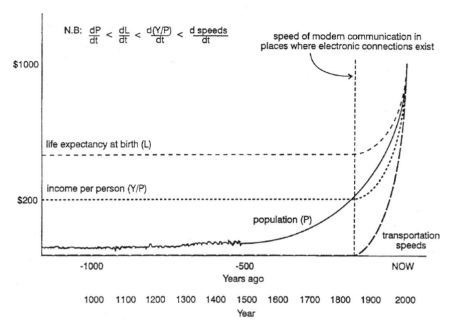

Fig. 2. Measures of progress during the millennium 1000–2000 (stylized)

improvement slow. This cannot be said of any other kinds of knowledge or interventions.

The theory offered here is the opposite of that offered by (e.g.) Eric Jones in his book *Growth Recurring*. When discussing non-Malthusian models of population growth (including my own work) he says that "[t]hey clarify some relationships, but by neglecting the institutional and political setting they leave the final outcome indeterminate" (1988, 129). The model offered here agrees entirely with Jones about the importance of institutions when one is considering periods of up to perhaps a century or two in length (and especially as short as a few decades). But when the horizon of the inquiry is extended to many centuries or millennia, the institutional and political variables are themselves quite endogenous and therefore wash out in the analysis.

It should be noted that the subject of this essay is *material consumer welfare* and not *productive capacity* or *productive knowledge;* this accounts for the very different shape of the kinked time path that is the subject of this essay from the more gradual time path of the subject of studies portrayed by such writers as Kuznets.

Two great questions arise frequently in discussions of long-term growth: explanation of the differential paths of China and Europe during the past half millennium and of the causes of decline of mortality in the past two centuries. Neither of these issues is central to the thesis put forth here. Nevertheless, both are examined at some length to ensure that the absence of such examination (and of possible answers to the questions) will not be seen as a fatal flaw to the argument provided.

Related Writings

Consumer Welfare Is the Subject Here

Expanding on the penultimate paragraph so as to avoid confusion: It is crucial that the subject here is different from that addressed by Simon Kuznets, Walt Rostow, Angus Maddison, and others who have written about what Kuznets called "Modern Economic Growth." (For a review of this literature, see Jones 1988.) Those writers focus on the *technical level* and the *production capacities* of a society — that is, the total potential output of a society and the outputs of particular industries. In contrast, this essay focuses on the *consumption levels achieved* by a society — that is, the material welfare of individuals within the society — as measured by such characteristics as the nutritional excellence of persons' diets and the opportunities of children to go to school. The level of material welfare shows a much sharper kink starting around 1750–1800 in advanced countries than do the production capacity and the knowledge base.

The difference in the concepts of production and consumption can be seen by comparison of the list of "characteristics inherent in modern growth" that Kuznets gives (in the course of his criticism of Rostow).

[A] high and sustained rate of increase in real product per capita, accompanied usually by a high and sustained rate of increase in population; major shifts in the industrial structure of product and labor force, and in the location of the population, commonly referred to as industrialization and urbanization; changes in the organizational units under whose auspices and guidance economic activity takes place; a rise in the proportion of capital formation to national product; shifts in the structure of consumer expenditures, accompanying urbanization and higher income per capita; changes in the character and magnitudes of international economic flows; and others could be added. Underlying all this are the increasing stock of useful knowledge derived from modern science and the capacity of society, under the spur of modern ideology, to evolve institutions which permit the exploitation of the growth potential provided by that increasing stock of knowledge. (Kuznets 1965, 213–14)

Kuznets does not even mention an increase in life expectancy, which is the foremost item in the list of characteristics of material human welfare (though this may be an oversight on his part; elsewhere he emphasizes decreased mortality as an important factor in growth). The difference between the concepts of production and consumption as used here can be seen in two interpretations of the same urbanization data shown in figure 3. The *total number* of people living in cities increased considerably in the centuries prior to 1750, which implies an increase in the number of persons available to produce physical goods and new knowledge, as well as constituting a larger number of specialized workers as a result of greater division of labor. Yet, since nonurbanized people tended to work in agriculture, the same *proportion* of people in the world as a whole remained in close-to-subsistence agriculture throughout those centuries.

Continuity and Discontinuity

There is another key difference between this essay and the works of the many worthy economic historians who have in recent decades addressed Modern Economic Growth. They have emphasized the continuity of progress leading up to, and through, the supposed industrial "revolution." They are certainly right that important processes of discovery proceeded in earlier centuries and millennia. But the data presented in this and subsequent chapters seem to show that, starting about the eighteenth century, the increases in rates of change of the most important magnitudes pertaining to human welfare (and even to productive capacity) are breathtakingly large. This recent period must therefore be seen as qualitatively different than any other period, even if it is continuous with them. As Mokyr put it, "In two centuries, daily life changed more than in the seven thousand years before" (Mokyr 1990b). Yes, "technological change did not begin with the Industrial Revolution. The difference between the period after 1750 and the period before was one of degree; but degree was everything" (52). Exactly.

Kuznets was uncharacteristically emphatic that the modern era is sharply different than all previous ages, though he noted that one's moral and aesthetic reaction may not simply be a celebration.

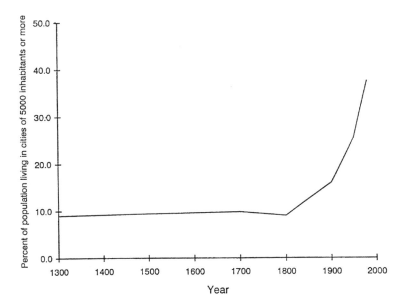

Fig. 3.   Urbanization in the world. (From Bairoch 1988, 495.)

[T]he modern economic epoch is the *first* in history with universal scope, i.e. with the capacity to reach and affect every corner of the earth, there is no historical precedent by which to judge the rate of spread in terms of world population.

Indeed, one could easily wax eloquent in support of both sides of the proposition. One could marvel that within the short period of less than two centuries, an exceedingly brief tag-end to thousands of years of human history, as much as a fifth to a quarter of mankind managed to attain overall levels of economic performance and per capita standards of living that are far higher than the highest enjoyed by even the most advanced people in the past; and one could argue that the rate of spread has been striking indeed, since its continuation for another four or five centuries would raise all of mankind to truly millennial levels of economic and material attainment. Or one could stress that, despite the enormous gains in science- and invention-based power of man to command vast resources and bend enormous natural forces to human ends, between three quarters and four fifths of mankind still suffer from low economic performance, and a large proportion of these from truly inadequate standards of living; and that, despite almost two centuries of spread, modern economic growth has failed to improve substantially the material lot of most of mankind—even if it has permitted a larger number to survive longer—so that they have fallen increasingly behind the small fraction of world population in the economically advanced countries.

These two positions are not inconsistent. (Kuznets 1966, 468, 469)

This essay also argues against Jones's contention that it was an accident that intensive growth did not continue in one or more of the places and periods where he earlier notes its presence but where it petered out.[1] Unlike Jones, I believe that it was impossible for any of those episodes to have blossomed into anything like the period of modern progress that we are now experiencing. This essay concludes that continued intensive growth was impossible for any earlier society because (1) it lacked the capacity to produce engines for mechanized agriculture and transport and hence could not markedly reduce the agricultural labor force; and (2) the infrastructure of mechanical skills was not of sufficient scale. Remedying these deficiencies was not possible until there had been major progress across a wide front of knowledge.

The main thrust of this essay may also be contrasted with that of Maddison's work, although it is consistent with his excellent data. He lists the following as the key elements in the "ultimate" explanation of growth.

In assessing the nature of capitalist performance, one can conduct the causal analysis at two levels—"ultimate" and "proximate." The investigation of ultimate causality involves consideration of institutions, ideologies, pressures of socio-economic interest groups, historical accidents, and economic policy at the national level. It also involves consideration of the international economic "order," exogenous ideologies, and pressures or shocks from friendly or unfriendly neighbours. These "ultimate" features are all part of the traditional domain of historians. They are virtually impossible to quantify and thus there will always be legitimate scope for disagreement on what is important. "Proximate" areas of causality are those where measures and models have been developed by economists and statisticians. Here the relative importance of different influences can be more readily assessed. At this level, one can derive significant insight from comparative macroeconomic growth accounts which try to "explain" growth of output, output per head, or productivity by measuring inputs of labour and capital, availability of natural resources, influences affecting the efficiency with which resources are combined, and benefits derived from transactions with foreign countries. (Maddison 1991, 10–11)

Maddison does not mention human numbers in his list; in contrast, this essay emphasizes *only* human numbers (together with technology). One reason for this difference is that Maddison aims to discuss development *within* the capitalist world in the past couple of hundred years, after the breakthrough into Sudden Modern Progress took place, whereas this essay seeks to explain why that breakthrough took place when it did.

Other Comparisons with the Literature

The general approach of this essay — in perhaps surprising contrast to Kuznets and Peter Bauer, who both made much of values, attitudes, culture, and the like (despite the headnote by Kuznets in the preceding) — will attempt to follow the course that is recommended by Petty and Kuznets in the headnotes and will leave those difficult-to-quantify concepts aside as much as possible.

My earlier writings have addressed the subject of this essay tangentially rather than directly. Predecessors in discussing the wide-ranging effects of population size and density whom I read and learned from include Colin Clark, Friedrich Engels, Alexander Everett, Henry George, Eric Jones, Simon Kuznets, Douglass North, and Alfred Sauvy. In addition, Harold Barnett, Ester Boserup, Friedrich Hayek, Simon Kuznets, and Theodore Schultz have all analyzed the effects of population on natural resources in a fashion consistent with the point of view here, and I drew much from them. (Robert Godwin's ideas about population growth were important historically, especially in triggering Malthus's work, but his writing does not seem to be in the same tradition as this essay.)

Conventions

The body of the text uses no special notation other than occasional designations for a few standard rough periods and dates, as follows: -1 mill = roughly one million years ago; $-80M$ = between 100,000 and 60,000 years ago; $-10M$ = between 8000 and 10,000 B.C.E.; 0 C.E. = 2,000 years ago (the beginning of the common era, or A.D.); 1000 C.E. — dates after that will be given in standard fashion such as "1750–1800,"

"1900," and "present"; a subscript with two digits separated by a hyphen refers to a period rather than a date.

Even in the footnotes, no mathematics other than substitution will be used, despite the algebraic notation.[2] And it must be emphasized that most readers have absolutely no need to consult the formal footnotes; the text is entirely self-contained without them. But that formalism helps prevent errors in the logic of the prose; the reader may or may not wish to follow the substitutions in the formalisms for the sake of improving his or her understanding.

Outline of the Argument

The advanced countries are rich now compared to the past and especially compared to any period before the last few hundred years. That is, the standard of living (1997) in the United States, Europe, and Japan is perhaps 20 times as high as the standard of living in Europe (1000 C.E.) and perhaps 10 times as large as the standard of living (1997) in India.

The most important and striking sudden change was in mortality, as seen in life expectancy (figs. 4 and 5) and in infant mortality (fig. 6). The subject of this essay is consumption progress rather than production improvement, and one may wonder whether the reduction in mortality is a producer gain or a consumer gain. This essay suggests that all consumer

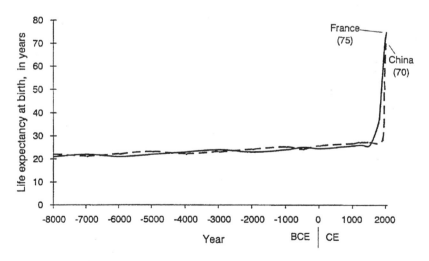

Fig. 4.   Trends in life expectancy over the millennia (stylized)

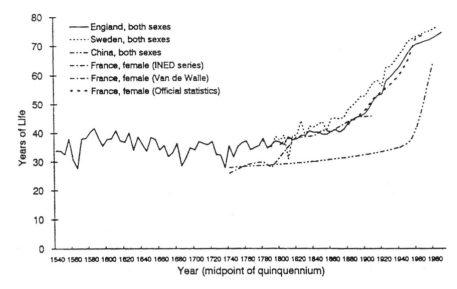

Fig. 5. Life expectancy at birth: England, Sweden, France, and China, 1541–1985. (Adapted from Lee 1979, 142; Preston 1995.)

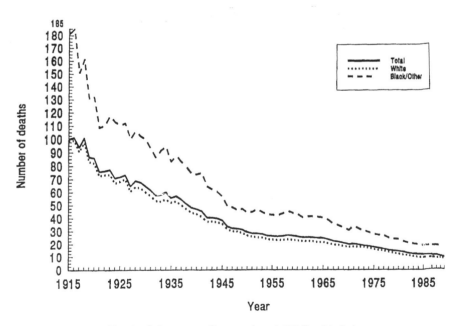

Fig. 6. Infant mortality rate (per 1,000 live births)

progress implies producer growth, though not the other way around. That is, improvements in health and wealth are improvements in the capacity of human beings to bring about material production, even though the influence of health has been surprisingly difficult to demonstrate statistically. The same process can be seen in a cross section of nations as of the 1950s, where expectation of life and infant mortality are plotted according to mean income (figs. 7 and 8).[3]

The material progress experienced by humanity was sudden.[4] The sharpness of the rise from a very low standard of living is demonstrated by the fact that even knowledgeable persons as late as the time of John Stuart Mill could not be sure that the large bulk of the population was better off in 1850 than in (say) 1800 or previous years. Mill wrote:

> Hitherto it is questionable if all the mechanical inventions yet made have lightened the day's toil of any human being. They have enabled a greater population to live the same life of drudgery and imprisonment, and an increased number of manufacturers and others to make fortunes. (Mill 1848, bk. 4, chap. 6, 756, corrected from quote in Abramovitz 1989, 323)[5]

And even with the benefit of hindsight, the probable gain even as late as 1850 is seen to be so slight that economic historians until recently were still at odds about whether or not there had been a gain (Hayek 1954; Fogel 1989).

The proximate cause of the higher present wealth is the present level of technology (as of 1997). But what was the cause of 1997 technology being what it is? Almost by definition, current technology is the sum of increments to knowledge in the past. These discoveries of the past were produced by people, and therefore the rate of discovery must have been influenced by human numbers. The cultural, political, economic, and social systems of the past were also a factor; some writers (e.g., Coale, correspondence, 1971) argue that the social system of (say) ancient Greece, rather than human numbers, has been the crucial factor. This essay argues, however, that those systems were themselves a function of human numbers together with the economic levels of past societies; this is one of its main points. (It will also be suggested that the glorious literatures that we attribute to ancient Greece and Israel may, in considerable part, be the results of a few gifted collectors and editors of the accumulated wisdom of the large numbers of humans who had lived earlier than they [see fig. 9] and that had been handed down orally, rather than specific, flesh-and-blood Greek and Jewish writers being the main authors. Such editing was doubtless an awesome achievement, but

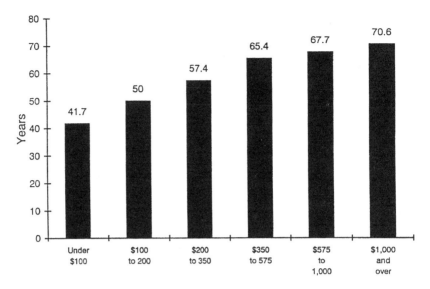

Fig. 7.   Life expectancy at birth by mean income, 1955–58. (From Kuznets 1966.)

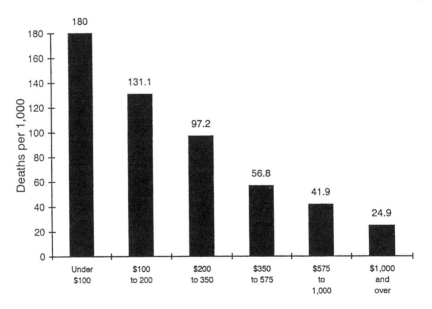

Fig. 8.   Infant mortality rate by mean income, 1955–58. (From Kuznets 1966.)

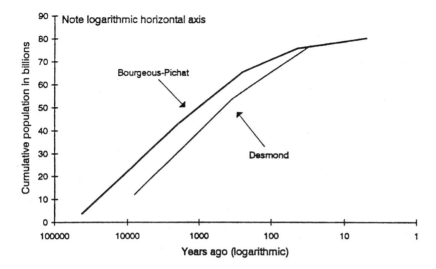

Fig. 9. Cumulative world population: 42,000 years ago to the present. (Adapted from Bourgeous-Pichat 1989, 90; Desmond 1975.)

certainly it was much less vast an achievement than authorship de novo would have been.)

An example of the evidence for the importance of the size of the population — or at least the size of the educated labor force — is the progress of nuclear fusion as a source of power for electricity. As of 1997, all agree[6] that the speed of technological discovery connected with nuclear power and other modern technology has been affected by government funding and by the number of skilled persons working in the field.[7] And government funding itself is mainly a function of income level and population size; the financial resources to support government funding for research derive only from productive work performed elsewhere in the economy. So population size and income (as well as education, which depends upon income) are the elements that account for the rate of progress in nuclear fusion technology just as elsewhere in science.

Why did the rapid[8] progress of the past two centuries not begin centuries or millennia earlier or not begin until sometime in the future?[9] Was there something special or critical about the particular population size or the level of technology starting after 1750–1800 that triggered the breakthrough into Sudden Modern Progress? Probably not. We must notice one crucial element, however: About that time both population size and the level of technique, as well as the standard of living, began to rise rapidly in the advanced countries, though population began to rise earlier; there was an unprecedented tripling (or more) of population within a century or two, the first such event in all the thousands of years of human history.

To repeat, the answer offered here for the observed discontinuity is that the size of the human population — as measured by both population density and total population size, together with the technology these people produced — is the root cause of the speed of progress.

To phrase this more operationally: If the world's population had not grown at all since (say) 10,000 years ago, or if population had not grown as fast as it did over the millennia, the material condition of humanity could not have progressed to its present state by now. To put it differently, if the rates of population growth had been different (and had resulted in lower total populations at various times) than actually were the case, the extraordinary phenomena of falling mortality and increasing income in the past 200 years would have happened later than they did, and if population had grown faster than it actually did, the Great Breakthrough would have occurred earlier than 1750–1800. Furthermore, *one cannot say this of any other variable unless a change in that variable would primarily alter human numbers* — as, say, a climatic change would have affected food production or the quantity of available energy would have improved survival probabilities. If there were not an associated effect on human numbers, such a change could have affected the amount of leisure and perhaps the mode of getting a living — for example, herding versus hunting — but would not have affected the speed of economic progress.

Perhaps the reader will consider this counterfactual: If the Library of Congress or the British Museum as of 1997 were to have been available at major urban locations in the year 100 C.E., would that have made subsequent progress much faster? I doubt it. Even bestowing a library of today's technical knowledge upon a small population in the past probably could not have led to rapid progress (except for knowledge of how to reduce mortality).

It is easy to overestimate the effect of the presence of knowledge on the occurrence of adoption of new techniques. The existence of useful but unused agricultural techniques was well documented by Boserup (1965), though one can argue that until population density increased the nonuse of those techniques was rational in many or most cases. But the lack of wheels in the Muslim world, perhaps because of the heavy use of camels, is harder to rationalize.[10]

Indeed, we know from the experience until recently of India and China and other poor countries until the late twentieth century that the existence of such knowledge can coexist with continuing lack of development.

Does that coexistence contradict the basic thesis of this essay? No; one can already see (as of the end of the twentieth century) the inexorable process of rapid modernization in these countries despite their having economic-political-social systems initially not well designed for such progress—systems that prevented the modernization from happening earlier (as indeed occurred earlier in Japan). And in turn the combination of human numbers and the existence of knowledge, together with the demand for the fruits of that knowledge that the awareness of the existence of that knowledge brings about, is (as of 1997) inducing huge changes in the economic systems so as to accommodate more rapid progress, as the thesis in this essay suggests; this has been the case most vividly for 700 million rural Chinese whose agriculture was essentially privatized starting in 1979, with astonishing results; see figure 10. Taken together, then, the evidence available as of 1997 concerning the poor though heavily populated countries is not inconsistent with the thesis offered here.

Nor would the intended adoption of any small set of new techniques have been likely to have made a difference, aside from mortality reducers. Most mechanical devices could not have been produced, as the ancient Greek steam-engine model illustrates. Only knowledge of the transmission of diseases such as plague and malaria could have made a difference, and that knowledge might well have come by way of an increase in human numbers, the central theme of the book.

How might one test the basic argument offered here? Two lines of evidence will be adduced to support the basic proposition: (1) correlations of population size and population density with the amount of knowledge production, wherein the demographic variable shows a leading relationship; that is, population growth came before the associated growth in knowledge; and (2) evidence that other relevant variables are mainly a function of population size and income level rather than the converse and therefore these other variables could not be the "original" cause. Also presented are some scraps of evidence that population size is not only correlated with knowledge production but also is the primary causal variable in that relationship. Theory and data that disprove the proposition that the "natural" availability of natural resources has been a crucial force also are adduced to help test the basic arguments.

One cannot disentangle from human numbers the effects of the human brain and its contents—call it human capital, if you will—any more than one can disentangle the effects of the human digestive or procreative anatomy from human numbers. It is not abstract numbers of

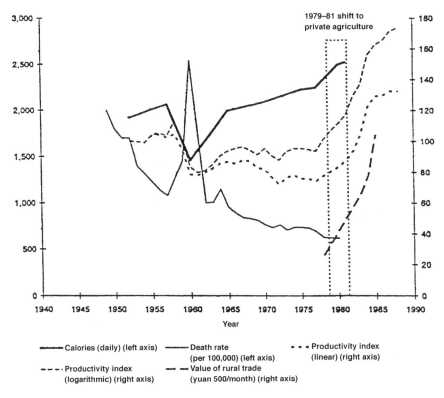

Fig. 10. Economic system, productivity, mortality, and nutrition in China, 1952–88

humans that are at issue but rather humans beings who eat, have sexual intercourse for both procreation and pleasure, and also think.

To return to the main line of the argument now, this essay will argue (in connection with the causal concept used here) that there is no nonbiological variable "deeper" than human numbers that one can point to as being responsible for the population growth that occurred, as one *can* point to population size, density, and growth as being responsible for the growth in income and the evolution of institutions and patterns of behavior that were necessary for the progress that occurred. That is, I will argue that unlike all other nonbiological variables, population growth is the *most* exogenous variable in the process—more like a "control variable"[11] than any other element in the system—at least until after the break into Sudden Modern Progress.[12]

This does not imply that in periods even as long as a century or two, political systems and institutions are determined completely or in large part by demographics or by such other endogenous variables as the standard of living. The political systems in Germany under Hitler, in Russia and China under Communist rulers, and in Hong Kong during the nineteenth and twentieth centuries must be considered accidents of history and quite unpredictable a decade or so before those regimes began. But before the fall of the Soviet Union, the general shape of the political systems in most countries of Eastern Europe to the west of Russia *if* the USSR were to break up *was* reasonably predictable, it would seem. And so, too, the general shape in coming decades of the political systems in Latin America (including Cuba) is predictable as of 1997. This is not a matter simply of countries imitating and converging to a common model but rather a matter of the voiced preferences of widespread public opinion in favor of democracy and (at least some) economic freedom. And the desire for economic freedom would seem to be, in part, due to comparison of the observable results of the different forms of political systems in operation since the Russian Revolution in 1917, results that arise predictably out of scientifically understood processes. These results seem as predictable as that (a) no society in the foreseeable future will exist in a state of anarchy for a prolonged period; and (b) adult sports teams of almost any kind, in any country, will always have captains either elected by the players or imposed by a coach or sponsor or "owner" of the team, because a team with no one to issue some instructions for common action will on average do worse than other teams in all known team sports. But the general political-economic system that now holds sway in Eastern Europe as of 1997 and that will increasingly hold sway in Latin America would not have been predictable for these countries even one century ago, let alone five or 10 or 20 or 40 centuries ago, even if one were to know that there would be sufficient instability in a country for a new form of political structure to emerge; furthermore, such a political system is not predictable now for any remaining group of nomads on Earth. It is in this sense, and this sense alone, that political system is determined by demographics, technology, the standard of living, and other endogenous forces. (There is further discussion of this matter subsequently in chapter 5.)

Many laypersons would say (and I agree with them) that the basic proposition stated here is entirely obvious: If there were no people there would be no human capital to create the knowledge that leads to progress, and hence there would be no progress. But this proposition is not at all obvious or agreed to in the view of many scholars, when speaking of long-run as well as of short-run progress. So this essay is not a demolition of a straw man.

It is a crucial element of the model stated here that population growth and density affect the structures of markets, law, tradition, and political institutions. If this had not been so, structures incompatible with an improvement in technology and the long-run standard of living could have remained in place indefinitely, thereby preventing further progress. It is therefore an important part of this essay — and perhaps its most important novelty — that it offers fine-structure evidence for this process of population-induced social change.

The complex web of relationships among (a) endemic and epidemic disease and knowledge of them; and (2) population density and total numbers also is an important part of the analysis.

The essay goes far out on a specific limb by suggesting that until the creation and development of one particular body of technology — the mobile nonanimal engine capable of powering agricultural work and land transport and drawing water — sustained intensive growth was not possible. And it seems likely that if there had been larger populations earlier (or later) than were the case, this development would have come earlier (later).[13]

One may wonder about similarity between the general viewpoint of Marx and the strong flavor of economic determinism in this essay. And there is indeed a resemblance, though the determined relationship here is between human numbers and the date of the breakthrough to Sudden Modern Progress, rather than between the economic structure and the social structure. In fact, it should not be surprising to assert the existence of such determinism given that — quite contrary to common belief — the longer the perspective, the easier it is to predict with respect to matters such as these.[14]

A Stylized Description of Human Progress

As a preview before launching into more systematic work, here is a stylized description of the long-run history of the process of human progress.

The first hominids came into being without any body of knowledge that they themselves created. But instinctive knowledge of how to survive was programmed into their genes, just as it is with every other species. And by observing other animals that happened to live within their ken, the early people may have learned additional techniques of gathering food and building shelters. Such imitations may have been the first sort of learning that is distinctively human in its cumulative adaptation to the world about us. (Someone has written that there seems to be a similar process of imitation among apes, but it is questionable whether the knowledge can be handed down from one generation to the next.) The hominids then increased their population, just as other successful new species increase their populations by spreading across territory into additional niches that will sustain them, pushing out other species (see E. O. Wilson's autobiography *Naturalist* [1995]). At some point — whether or not population had stabilized by then is unknown — new discoveries were made, perhaps including the knowledge of fire and of stone implements, the latter occurring at least two million years ago (Leakey 1981, 78). Each subsequent discovery improved the ability of our ancestors to survive and allowed numbers to increase faster than before the discovery; even simple stone tools must have had a large effect on the rate of population growth, as suggested in figures 11 and 12 (absolute growth rates and logarithmic size scales for the same phenomenon).[15] These first discoveries must also have speeded the discoveries of other inventions.

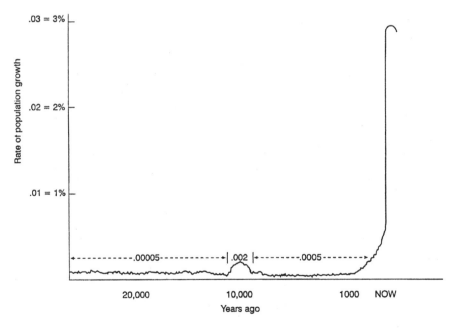

**Fig. 11.   Rate of population growth (*dP/P*) for 20,000 years (stylized).
(From Kremer 1993.)**

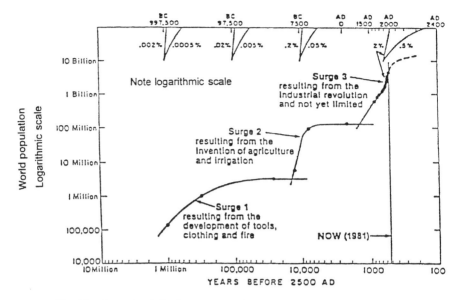

Fig. 12.   Growth of the human population during the past ten million
years. (Adapted from Deevey 1960; Tinsley 1980.)

Despite there having been almost two million years for hominoids
to increase their numbers, studies using genetic markers suggest that as
of about 65,000 years ago—only about twice as long as the cave paint-
ings were made in France—the human population numbered only perhaps 100,000. Because of climatic conditions, total population then sup-
posedly declined to perhaps only 10,000 persons before expanding again
("Research News," *Science,* October 1, 1993). This suggests that the
then-available technology could hardly provide even bare survival, implying that until then there had been very little progress in the vast
stretch of hominoid existence.

Again, could rapid economic progress have begun, say, 100,000 or
one million years ago rather than 200 years ago? Was it just an accident
that rapid progress *ever* began, and could that accident just as easily
have taken place many millennia earlier? It seems most doubtful that
any single event could have come along and made such a big difference—two million or 200,000 (or even 2,000) years ago. For example,
the early invention of nuclear power obviously is inconceivable. And
even had a nuclear reactor or an internal-combustion engine plus full
instructions been dropped onto Earth by Martians before the mid-
twentieth century, the material would have been less useful than a mete-

orite. Utilization of inanimate power had to wait on the accumulation of the nexus of human numbers and knowledge.

In the context of many thousands of years ago, it is clear that only a biological or environmental phenomenon that would have altered the nutrition and/or the rate of fertility and hence brought about a change in total population size — such as a major change in climate, or the appearance of a remarkable new easy-to-obtain food source, or a change in the human digestive system — could have altered the speed of economic progress through the millennia. But if numbers had been greater earlier on, there would have been more people to speed the process by inventing and developing new discoveries — for example, new ways of herding and cropping. Larger numbers also would have meant greater need for such improvements earlier on, which would have sped their adoption after invention in those cases where adoption is not immediately profitable (i.e., Boserupian population-push inventions).

Other kinds of forces than those mentioned previously could not have changed the rate of progress, I contend. The earliest hominids surely had elements of a social system in their genetic programs, just as do apes; for example, incest was undoubtedly practiced only infrequently, as among some other species of animals. Later on, the type of social system seems to have been determined by the nature of the life of hunting and gathering. Leakey (1981, 99) tells us that bands of a "magic number" of about 30 are found among nomadic groups everywhere. And while there might have been some variations in social system from one band of hominids to another, it would not have been possible for hominids to live with a modern form of social system that is consistent with modern rates of rapid progress — such as democracy over an area as small as hundreds or even tens of miles in each direction — even if someone had invented such a system; modern social-political systems could not be used until population and technology (and the standard of living) had increased many times over.

Would history have been very different if human numbers had remained what they were at the time of Athens's glory? This essay contends that humans would not have reached the technology and the standard of living we now enjoy — especially our unprecedented life expectancy, which began to lengthen rapidly only about 1750 — if our numbers had remained at the few hundreds of millions that existed at that time.

Jones (1988) points to periods of intensive growth in living standards in the past, in contrast to the more pervasive periods of extensive growth in human numbers, and he suggests that in some place(s) intensive growth might have continued if historical accidents had not occurred, especially in connection with political and social systems. This essay argues to the contrary that (1) intensive growth could not continue in the absence of mechanized farming; (2) the conditions for mechanized farming were not present until the nineteenth century; and (3) only larger populations at earlier times could have led to a faster rate of the broad advance of technology that made possible the appearance of farm machinery powered by steam, internal-combustion engines, and electricity. The absence of evidence of declining proportions of the population working in the agricultural labor force in any period prior to the modern period supports this view. Indeed, the agrarian labor force probably never was below 60 percent of total population anywhere in the world until perhaps 1600 in Holland. And as of 1880, half of the U.S. population still was rural.

Concerning the Suddenness of the Shift

It was suggested earlier that the change in rates of increase in the level of living was so great that the beginning of the modern period may be referred to as a "breakthrough," though with a very different sort of meaning than intended by the "takeoff" of Rostow; the phenomenon is here labeled "Sudden Modern Progress" (SMP). But there is no conflict between this notion and the views of Kuznets and of such later writers as Jones (1988) who emphasize the continuity between the pre- and post-1750 periods. Those writers address the quantity of available technology and the *capacity to produce,* which did not experience sudden acceleration. In contrast, SMP refers to *consumer and economic welfare;* herein the evidence of discontinuity — as seen earlier in figures 2, 4, and 5 — seems to be undeniable. Also, Kuznets et al. focused on shorter periods. The great transformations in the past two centuries, such as from high to low mortality, from employment mainly within agriculture to employment mainly outside of agriculture, from mostly rural to mostly urban living (see figs. 3–6 presented previously) represent such a quickening of the previous rates that it is indeed reasonable to call the process a takeoff, as I see it. Data on income per person in figure 13 make the same point.

For further evidence on the sharpness of the break, consider that the development of the first major advance in speed of land travel since the Romans built their roads was the railroad. Figure 14 shows the quantities of track in the various European countries through the nineteenth century into the twentieth. The world total quantity of track went from zero in 1825 and 5,490 miles in 1840 to 675,000 miles in 1920. Is this not a sudden breakthrough in the ability to travel?

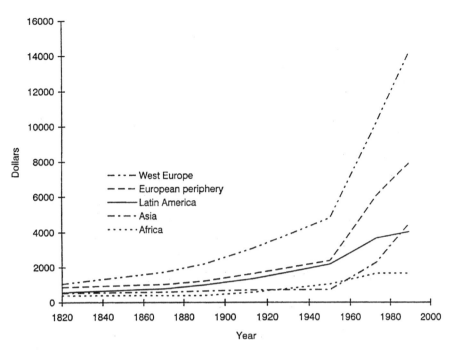

Fig. 13.   GDP per person by area. (From Maddison 1994.)

The breakthrough in communications progress was even more sharp. Fittingly, on an airplane I met a man whose family had started the Pony Express from Missouri to California. To my surprise, he told me that the entire operation lasted only for a single year. Then the telegraph came along, and in one moment it increased the speed of communication from the speed of a horse to the speed of light. Hence the Pony Express went kaput. Now e-mail, almost as fast as the speed of light itself, has spread across the globe in just a few years.

Consider our power to see and view. From 200,000 years ago until about the year 1100, the naked eye was our only instrument of vision. To fix a sight permanently, drawings were made on parchment, stone, or cave walls at least 30,000 years ago, but there was no further progress until a millennium or two ago when block printing was done on paper in China and perhaps batik printing on cloth in the Middle East. Then around 1100, eyeglasses and telescopes were invented; that was the entire progress in seeing until around 1540.

Then Gutenberg invented printing, so that drawn images could be

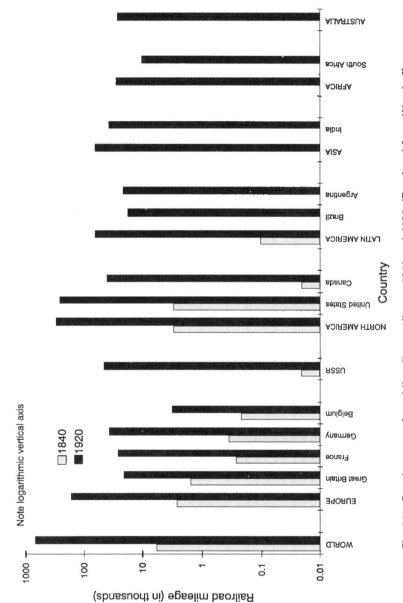

Fig. 14.   Development of world's railway mileage, 1840 and 1920. (Reprinted from Woodruff 1973.)

published widely. But that huge leap was the only one there was, though printing was improved with metallurgy and sped up with mechanical power. No more progress was made for almost another 500 years until the X ray at the turn of the twentieth century. Then human beings could for the very first time see below the surface of the human body and other bodies.

Humanity's capacities obviously have exploded since then: television, radar, electron microscopes, CAT scans, magnetic imaging, electron telescopes — ever further, ever deeper.

And for everyday use you can now see inside your own mouth on a television screen as the dentist works on you and into other apertures of your body, too, should you so desire. And if you live in a rich country, when the gas or water service crews come to your street they snake television cameras through the pipes without even marveling at the wonder of it all.

Other striking evidence on the sharpness of the breakthrough comes from the practice of medicine. Abraham Flexner, in the famous Flexner Report on medical education in 1910, commented (if memory and secondhand quotation serve me well) that in his judgment, as of that date in the United States, a random patient consulting a random physician for a random ailment stood only a 50–50 chance of benefiting from the encounter. And please note that that was the state of affairs after humans had been practicing the healing arts for tens of thousands of years.[16]

Another dramatic example comes from education: The majority of army recruits in Europe in 1830 were illiterate (fig. 15). Most of the people (two-thirds) born around 1930 in India are (were) illiterate as adults, as had been the case since time immemorial; of those born only 40 years later, only perhaps a small proportion (a fifth) are illiterate (see fig. 16). Figure 17 recapitulates this transition with a cross-national plot by income as of 1950. This crucial transition from mostly illiterate to mostly literate has taken place within the lifetimes of most readers of this esssay at the time of publication.

For anyone who already is a parent or expects to be one, a poignant sign of the progress in the past century is the decline in the probability that one's young child will die. The breakthrough may also be seen in commerce in Europe, as shown by the rise in exports from 1830 to 1910 in figure 18.

The apparent difference between this point of view and that of Kuznets (when rebutting Rostow) can perhaps be reconciled as follows: Kuznets and Rostow focus on the rates of change of productivity as a whole, which includes many aspects of an economy, and they restrict

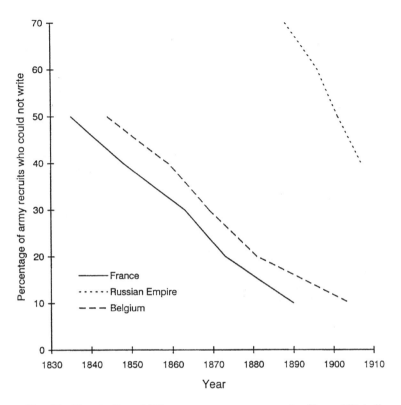

Fig. 15.   The decline of illiteracy among army recruits. (From Mitchell 1973.)

their attention to a single millennium or less—mainly the past three centuries. In contrast, this essay focuses on a few key measures of welfare such as life expectancy and includes in its scope of all the many millennia of human history.

Stylized figures 2, 4, and 5 (shown earlier), portraying the takeoff in consumer welfare, are drawn so as to dramatize the fact that population growth was the leading variable. In the earlier epochs the rate of growth of population was greater than the rate of growth of life expectancy, which in turn was greater than the growth rates of the speeds of transportation and communications and of motive powers. (In the most recent period, however, the rate of growth of population was less than the rate of growth of life expectancy, which in turn was less than the growth rates of the speeds of transportation and communications and of motive powers.)[17]

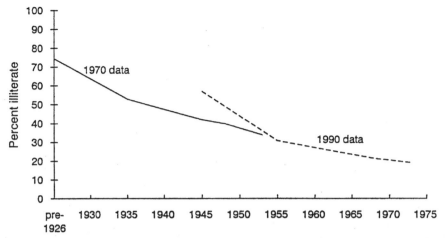

Note 1: The two lines represent estimates made from two surveys taken in different years, 1970 and 1990. Both provided estimates for the groups born from 1945 to 1953.

Note 2: UNESCO provides data on illiteracy rates among different age groups for the years 1970 and 1990. In this graph, the middle of each age range is represented as the birth year for the purposes of comparing 1970 and 1990 data and showing the overall trend. Example: the illiteracy rate among persons age 20-24 in 1970 (born 1946-1950) was 52.9 percent, represented above a point at 52.9 percent for 1948.

Fig. 16. Adult illiteracy, developing countries, by birth year, pre-1925–73. (From UNESCO 1990, table 3.)

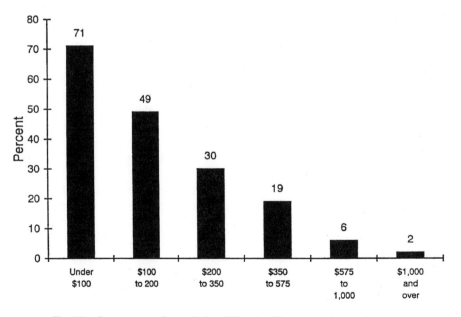

Fig. 17. Percentage of population illiterate, 15 years and over, by mean income, 1950. (From Kuznets 1966.)

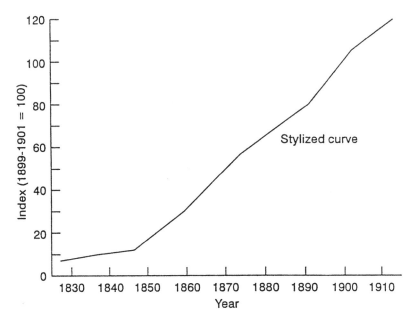

Fig. 18. Index of the annual volume of exports of European countries. (From Cameron 1989.)

I am not suggesting that conditions were uniformly bleak for all people. Surely there were improvements for some groups. De Vries asks us to consider the vibrant atmosphere in the major cities of Europe, and I quote extensively so that the reader will feel that this aspect of the matter has not been given short shrift.

In 1660 the postal officials of Amsterdam cooperated with it to organize a regular 56-hour horseback service to Hamburg and points north and east. In the same year Amsterdam inaugurated a service of twice-weekly mail boats to London. By 1670 the Republic was crisscrossed by a network of nightly mail routes connecting every city. In France the value of the postal monopoly rose from 1.2 million livres in 1673 to 8.8 million in 1777.

Street lighting spread in the major cities during the same period. Paris began to hang lanterns in 1667; by 1700, 65 miles of city street were illuminated, using 200,000 pounds of candles annually. In London a joint stock company, the Convex Lights Company, endeavored to illuminate city streets beginning in 1684. It is, perhaps, a reflection of the growing relative backwardness of the Mediterranean, that Venice acquired street lighting only in 1732.

Fire protection also had to be upgraded. The bucket brigades on which cities had relied since the Middle Ages no longer seemed to suffice in the great metropolises. The hand-powered water pump first used in Holland in 1668 spread to Paris in 1704. By 1723, twenty-two of the contraptions, capable of sending a jet of water to the upper floors of houses, functioned in the French capital while Amsterdam stationed seventy of them around the city.

These municipal services developed in societies where the standards of private comfort were also being upgraded. Among the well-to-do, leaded windows, French furniture, and tapestries were acquired while the use of carriages for movement about the cities became *de rigeur*. The need to use carriages was reinforced by the elaborate new fashions, for which the streets were far too muddy and filthy. Thus, by 1636 some 6000 private and public-hire coaches transported the rich in London, while the official estimates of coaches in use in Paris rose from 4000 in the 1630s to 20,000 by 1700. (De Vries 1976, 189, 190)

At times there also were glorious civilizations in Greece, Rome, Israel, China, and elsewhere. But for the overwhelming proportions of populations even at the most glorious of times, life was still no better than in times of yore, as may be seen in the data on literacy even in the Europe of the nineteenth century (fig. 15).

The rest of the essay attempts to support with theory and data the ideas sketched in the preceding paragraphs of this section.

A key aspect of the graphs in figures 4 and 2 is that they are drawn without apparent upward (or downward) limit. This is quite the opposite of the logistic curve that has been drawn so often in discussions of development and demography — especially with respect to total population growth and also with respect to technology.[18] The cause of the difference is that these graphs plot only the observed (or idealized-observed) data, whereas others superimpose a theoretical form; I remain agnostic about the appropriate form (though not without opinion).

The Meaning of *Cause*

The meaning of the word *cause* is complex in this context, and explicating it is part of the answer to the question. In brief, *cause* here will mean *most exogenous* cause — that is, *causing but not necessarily (though it may be) caused by* some other variable whose relationship with population is under discussion. The tests of such causality are as follows: (1) a high correlation; (2) an explanatory theory; (3) no "third" variables for which the variable in question is simply a proxy; and (4) few "side conditions" — ifs, ands, and buts. (For extended discussion of this concept of causality, see Simon and Burstein 1985, chap. 35.)

A solid demonstration of causation is not possible for the phenomena discussed in this essay. The most that can be done is to (1) show that the most prominent data are consistent with the central hypothesis; and (2) argue that the other influences that one might consider causes could not have been Sudden Modern Progress (SMP).

The Units of Analysis

Until the early part of the millennium starting 1000 C.E., the various continents (and perhaps the subcontinent of India) can be considered to have had separate civilizations and cultures, with little interchange of technology. Hence they may be considered separate units of analysis at that time. And the levels of technology and of consumption of these units at that time apparently were roughly in the same order as their population densities, in consonance with the basic hypothesis set forth in this essay.

At the beginning of the thirteenth century man's occupation of the earth was physically discontinuous. Dense centres of population which were strong and active were separated by huge spaces; these expanses either supported scattered groups of nomadic civilizations or remained as undisturbed sanctuaries. The human race presumably came from a single source, but was overcome by distance during its long prehistory; it split up and developed separate and autonomous cultures and civilizations. European expansion in the thirteenth to fifteenth centuries was only a chapter, albeit an important one, in a very slow process of emergence from these separate enclaves. . . .

. . . [T]he 120 million Chinese and the heavily populated India of the Indo-Ganges basin were separated by thousands of kilometres sparsely populated by private nomads. At the same time agricultural Europe's furthest outposts were still a thousand kilometres from the Urals. Therefore China, the Indo-Ganges plain, Iran, Anatolia, and the Slav agricultural settlements were at the edge of an enormous void of thirty-five million square kilometres with fewer than two million inhabitants. (Chaunu 1979, 52, 53)

But the separateness began to break down in the centuries after 1000 C.E. and even more so after 1200.

In the thirteenth century no civilization was aware of more than one-third of the world. The West's horizon embraced about thirty per cent of the land and four to five per cent of the seas. The Chinese horizon was somewhat more restricted, as was that of Egypt, the best situated part of Islam. The brilliant Central American civilizations of Teotihuacan or Maya Yucatan knew no more than one per cent of the world's land surface, and had scarcely any contact with the sea at all. The largest effective networks of communication, either in China or on the shores of the Mediterranean, never in fact covered more than two to three million square kilometres. The achievements of the thirteenth century were in depth and therefore at a local level only. The four centuries after Las Navas de Tolosa (1212) saw the slow but irreversible start of the process of breaking down the barriers between the different human civilizations. (Chaunu 1979, introduction)

Then the important interconnections between Europe and Asia began to deepen. Some crucial elements were already shared, especially the knowledge and practice of writing. Europe and Asia now came to share other crucial elements, especially mathematics and the Indian/ Arabic number system. Hence from that period forward, this essay will treat the Asian-European ecumene as a single element. Europe forged ahead, but this is no more exceptional than that one section of a country forges far ahead of another. (Further discussion of this specific observation will be found in chap. 5.)

Now a brief digression concerning the use in the previous paragraph of William McNeill's word *ecumene* to describe the Eurasan unit. There clearly was important technological interchange between Asia and Europe even as long ago as the sixth century C.E., when there is written record that "a system of nine digits and a zero, with place notation for the tens and hundreds, comes from Gujarat . . . AD 595" (Basham 1954, 495). And this knowledge became widespread throughout Eurasia by way of the Arabs. Similarly, printing and paper for writing apparently came to Europe from China, which had known them thousands of years ago. Is it not plausible that these techniques substantially affected the course of subsequent progress and that therefore the entire Eurasian unit should be considered together as the same unit of analysis? McNeill writes as follows:

[I]n the latter decades of the second century B.C., China consciously entered into regular contact with the other civilizations of Eurasia. Organized trade routes, both by land and by sea, soon linked the four great cultures of the continent. In addition, Eurasia's central sea of grass provided a third linkage. . . . Thus the Eurasian ecumene was closed as never before.

This event may be compared with the far more famous closure of the global ecumene in the sixteenth to eighteenth centuries A.D. . . . In the centuries between 200 B.C. and 200 A.D., the four major civilizations of Eurasia were very nearly on a par technologically and aesthetically. . . . (1963, 324, 325)

We may contrast this technological connectedness with that of the Americas. "The Maya of Central America had a vigesimal [twenties] numeral system with positional notation before this time [the regime of the Guptas, 320–550 C.E.]," writes Basham, who then added the crucial point: "but it had, of course, no effect on the world at large" (1954, 495, referring to Morley 1946, 274).

A digression: What is needed here to avoid confusion is a quantitative rather than qualitative sense of the word *ecumene*. Two magnitudes seem relevant: (1) The *proportion* of the new knowledge that they produce that is transmitted to other geographical areas within some given unit of time; we can consider whether that proportion going from (say) China to Europe in the year 1000 was 1 percent, 10 percent, or 50 percent (leaving the time units vague for now) and which of those proportions described the flow from Europe to China in 1600; I would guess that the latter proportion was much smaller than the former and that the proportion going from China to Africa in 1000 was less than the proportion going to Europe. The proportions prior to 1500 were great enough for McNeill and others to apply the word *ecumene;* whether they would still apply the term *after* 1500 I do not know. (2) The *absolute* magnitude of the flow per unit of time; I would guess that the absolute amount of technology flowing from Europe to Africa in 1850 was less than the absolute flow to China. Both the proportional and absolute amounts were sufficiently small that no one is likely to apply the word *ecumene* to the nexus of Africa and Europe.

It is possible that although the amount of knowledge transfer is substantial in both proportional and absolute measures, the living-standards gap between the two areas or countries may still increase; that is, divergence rather than convergence. This was the case with Europe and China after 1500 until recently. It also describes more closely the situation of the northern and southern states of the United States from

1865 to at least 1900; the North and the South diverged yet clearly were part of the same "ecumene." Or, the absolute transfer can be small and yet there can be a convergence, as probably was the case with Europe and Asia prior to 1500, because the proportion was large. Therefore, nothing said here about the past need be inconsistent with the expectation of convergence in the twenty-first century in national consumption levels throughout the world. And it does not imply that one is working both sides of the street to sometimes consider the entire world population as the relevant unit — an ecumene — and sometimes consider individual continents or countries as being the relevant units on the grounds that the differences among them are greater than the similarities. I hope for a bit of indulgence from the reader as the analysis shifts back and forth among units of analysis, without full justification in each case.[19]

To return to the main line of the argument: This perspective helps this essay to deal with the vexing matter that China and India lagged behind Europe even though their population sizes and densities were greater, as will be discussed at length in chapter 5.

Second Thoughts, Doubts, and Disclaimers

In order to make the main argument both clear and provocative, it is stated quite starkly. I hope that the reader will understand, however, that the central argument is not meant to be literally true. The date of the final emergence of Sudden Modern Progress certainly could have been different by hundreds or thousands of years if chance had intervened in some earlier time by altering some regimes or institutions or climate or biological environment (disease or animal). But the stark statement should accomplish an important additional purpose: providing a framework against which one may try out other formulations and explanations. For example, this framework might lead the institutionally minded reader to ask: Is there any possible institutional regime other than that which is here assumed to have existed (based on our knowledge of modern hunters and gatherers) that could have led the early bands of hunters and gatherers to have progressed more rapidly than they actually did? Could stronger links among scattered bands of hunters and gatherers have affected the rate of progress? I would argue "no," but if others might argue "yes," the ensuing discussion might be enlightening.

Another example: The advances in knowledge and technique made in Europe during the several hundred years starting in perhaps 1500 C.E. almost surely were unaffected by the size of the populations in India and

China. One might argue *either* that this calls into question the basic validity of the argument of this essay *or* that with suitable modification the argument still stands as well as if the inconvenient facts of the Indian and Chinese populations did not exist.

And a third question among the many others that might be put forward: Is it true, as this essay implies, that advances in England would have been slower if, starting perhaps in 1750, the population had been smaller than it was? Study of patents in England during the years 1541 to 1850 suggests that this is so (Simon and Sullivan 1989). And in her article "The Industrial Revolution in Great Britain" (1973), Deane says that

> the transformation . . . is made up of a set of interrelated changes in (a) economic organization, (b) technology and (c) industrial structure, associated with (as both cause and effect) *a sustained growth of population and total output.* (1973, 161; italics added)

She then specializes the argument to agriculture when she writes that

> wealthy landowners started . . . to experiment with new crop rotations, new agricultural machinery and new strains of livestock, or to consolidate their estates into more economical units, or to enclose wastes and commons and put them under crops or livestock. They were attracted to do so in part . . . by the rising price of food which was associated with *increasing population, and growing urbanization.* (202)

Deane also emphasizes the importance of the size of the population as a key element in the scale of the economy.

> There is nothing distinctive . . . about the elements. . . . Few of the changes which made up the industrial revolution that gathered momentum in England in the latter part of the eighteenth century . . . were unprecedented changes. . . . What distinguished the British experience in the latter part of the eighteenth century from all previous epochs . . . was that the changes concerned developed together, and on a scale that was sufficiently far-reaching and pervasive to set off a continuing and cumulative process of change and growth. . . . *It was the sheer scale and persistence of economic change that was new.* (162–63; italics added)

On the other hand, the effect of human numbers on progress *since* the start of the irreversible period of Sudden Modern Progress is not a central issue here. Rather, the main question addressed is the extent of the influence of numbers on why it did not happen 1,000 years earlier or 1,000 years later.

The plan of the essay is as follows. Chapter 2 presents the theory in prose and graphs (and in simple notation in footnotes), except for the process by which an increase in population eventuates in an increase in resources, which is briefly presented here but developed in more detail elsewhere (Simon and Steinmann 1981), not only in graphic form but also in algebra and simulation. Chapter 3 reviews the skimpy time-series and cross-sectional evidence on the relationship of the population to the rate of economic growth in the long run, and it asks about the possibility that variables other than population could explain the observed long-run economic growth; at best, these data make a prima facie but not a compelling case for the theory. Chapter 4 digresses to explore one particular topic that has been at the root of thinking about population economics for 3,000 years: the relationship of numbers of people to supplies of natural resources. Chapter 5 presents evidence on the relationship of population to the structural factors that affect the rate of economic progress; this section is the heart of the essay. Chapter 6 offers conclusions based on the body of evidence.

Various sections draw heavily upon my earlier work on the subject of population growth; this essay may therefore be thought of as part of an evolutionary process in knowledge development, rather than invention de novo.

CHAPTER 2

The Theoretical Framework

The thesis of this essay is that higher population densities, and larger total populations, in individual societies and on Earth altogether, were *necessary* conditions for progress. The extent to which they were *sufficient* conditions depended in the past upon the natures of the societies at the time.[1]

The appropriate form for the inquiry is to ask: What would have been an effect of a major change in some specified variable x at some time in the past? For example, what effect would there have been if the Anglo-Saxon legal system had somehow been transmitted to North American natives in the year 1000? Would this have caused their economic and demographic growth to be very different than it actually was?

The theory offered here asserts that there would *not* have been a major effect, because the rates of growth were dictated by the states of the variables that are the key conditions of readiness for growth, to wit: (1) the nexus of total population, together with (2) the stock of knowledge and (3) the level of the standard of living. By contrast, some anthropologists argue that the agricultural revolution was brought about (at least in important part) by "the elaboration of complex social systems among the late hunter-gatherers," rather than mainly as a result of "technology and demography" (Leakey 1981, 205). As will be explained subsequently, however, the view expressed here does not conflict with the view of Kuznets and others that the political-economic system is crucial to determining the extent to which technology is exploited.

A thought experiment that corresponds to this theory — and only a thought experiment is possible because we do not have a sample of other human histories to explore statistically or worlds to study experimentally — might be conducted with the following hypothetical scenario: If the course of population size had been at all points (say, half or double) what it actually was, Sudden Modern Progress would have occurred later (or earlier) than it did. But the same cannot be said of any other variable. And another thought experiment: If some authority had instituted a regime of taxing every rural family 20 percent of its output and then giving back that tax as a subsidy for more children, farmers would have had to work harder (and perhaps shift to more labor-intensive technology) in order to produce more sustenance for the original family as well as for the added offspring. According to the hypothesis offered here this increase in population growth would have resulted in faster progress in the standard of living over the centuries. A biological shift that would have increased population growth by, for instance, reducing nutritional requirements would serve the same purpose.

An alternative theory that I consider relatively less compelling is that the invention of new knowledge *by itself* would raise the standard of living. For example, if starting in the year 1000 societies had somehow decided to educate a much larger number of people and then put them to work in knowledge-producing pursuits, would that have raised the rate of progress of the living standard? Surely there would have been some increase in progress, but how much? The work of Boserup (1965) together with my analysis of inventions into those that are and are not immediately adopted without appropriate demand conditions (1977, chap. 8; 1978b; 1992, chap. 3) shows that some newly invented knowledge can remain dormant for a long time if demographic conditions are not appropriate for its adoption at the time; hence the gain in knowledge would not necessarily be converted into an increase in progress.

What would people have done in earlier times with a larger quantity of education? Would it have led to a faster growth of productive knowledge? Most evidence points to negative answers. Consider that the Jewish houses of study, from 2,000 years ago until the present, did not produce material progress. (On the other hand, Christian Cistercian monasteries did so.) Physical and biological scientists born in poor countries, and even social scientists, often find it much easier to do research in advanced countries than in their own; the infrastructure and professional context seem to matter enormously, as the record of Nobel Prizes indicates. And it is likely that the development of a chronometer good enough for navigation was impossible much earlier than its actual invention because of the absence of necessary technology, such as sufficiently accurate machine tools. (On the other hand, an increased quantity of education must *somewhat* increase the likelihood of increased discovery and progress.) This murky topic needs more thought, perhaps in the light of knowledge of the economics of education.

A secondary and related thesis suggested here is that a society's income level (or wealth level, because the two variables are nearly interchangeable in this context) is the second most important determinant (after population) of important material and technical variables such as health, knowledge, physical and social mobility, and communications. This secondary thesis will not be developed here, however.

Conceptual Frameworks and the Time Horizon

The appropriate conceptual framework for the analysis of the effects of population depends crucially upon the length of horizon and upon the level of economic development (which for the aggregate in the long run correlates with the historical date). Appropriate diagrams or sets of equations mapping the system that produces goods and services must differ greatly depending upon the span of time under consideration. These are some of the relevant possible frameworks.

1. For the *very short run* in a *subsistence* society, the framework of Malthus (fig. 19) is appropriate; the arrival of more mouths, or a deterioration of natural conditions, leads to diminishing returns in agriculture and reduces the amount to eat for the average person. For the very short run in a *developed* economy, the appropriate framework is a system of equations that may have hundreds of variables and thousands of connections, as seen in the spaghetti-like large-scale multisectoral models used for short-run forecasting by consultants to government and business. In these short-run models for both subsistence and developed economies, the stock of technology and the nature of institutions — and sometimes even the size of the labor force — are considered fixed.[2]

2. *Somewhat longer-term* models treat physical and human capital as variable. The growth of technology usually is considered to occur at a constant rate. The structures of political institutions, law, work behavior, and tradition are considered to be fixed, while the income level and the size of the labor force are important variables in such models.

3. An *even longer-run model* of a *subsistence* society allows for the nonconstant endogenous introduction of new technology. The alternative frameworks of the long-run dynamics of Malthus (quite different from the short-run Malthusian model mentioned previously) and of the Boserup analysis for subsistence agricul-

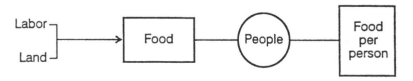

Fig. 19.   The static Malthusian model

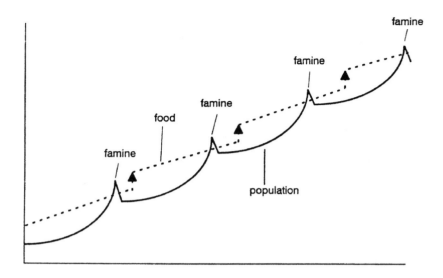

Note: arrowhead indicates the effect of lucky spontaneous invention

Fig. 20. Malthus-Ehrlich-newspaper-television vision of population and food

ture are shown in figures 20 and 21; these models are complementary rather than opposing. For *developed* economies, the
recent crop of endogenous-growth models (see the pathbreaking
article by Phelps [1966]; and my own work on endogenous knowledge in connection with population growth [1977]) makes technology endogenous, but these models do not include some of the
variables included in the shorter-run models. The endogenous-
growth models include only income, population, and knowledge
as independent variables, and they consider the structures of law
and tradition only peripherally if at all. Population growth may
or may not be endogenous in this sort of model (see fig. 22).

4. The *longest-run model*—the basis of this essay—considers population growth at the earliest date in the dynamic system to be the
sole exogenous (or most endogenous) variable; tradition, the
structure of law, and other institutions are endogenous variables
in this model along with the standard of living, technology, and
subsequent population growth. As will be seen, from such a
model one can deduce that if biological or climatological elements had caused the rate of population growth to be faster than

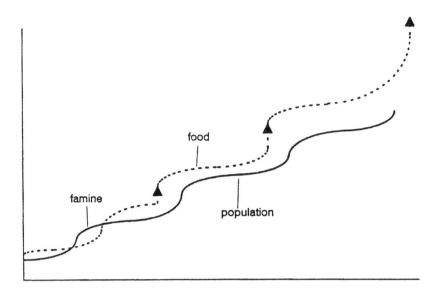

Note: arrowhead indicates the effect of lucky spontaneous invention

Fig. 21.   Barnett-Boserup-Clark-Schultz-Simon vision of population and food

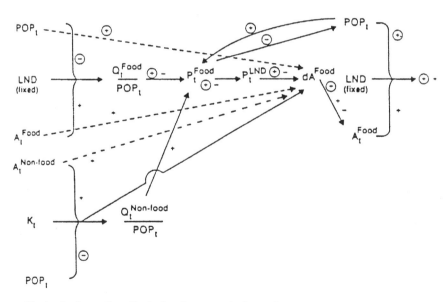

Circles indicate the effect of an increment of people,
uncircled effects are those of an increment of technology,
and dashed lines indicate long-run effects.

Fig. 22.   Population and technology in the intermediate run

it actually was, humanity would have had greater numbers than actually existed at various times in the past. Moreover, each stage of development — including the present stage of high material culture and low mortality — would therefore have been reached centuries or millennia earlier (see fig. 23).

The Model Specified More Precisely

The aim of the model is to help examine the proposition that population size (and hence the rate of population growth) controlled the rate of economic progress throughout history and that exogenous alteration in no other variable along the way could have dictated the long-run path of progress and the date of reaching the Sudden Modern Progress period. The purpose of specifying a series of relationships is to explore the conditions that must have held for this to be true — that is, to reveal what could and could not have caused the dynamics to be consistent with the overall hypothesis. Such a model should make explicit the full structure that is being assumed — what is included and what is excluded at any moment. The model will be stated in prose in the text and written in formal equations in the footnotes; the formalism in this case is a device to help discover the necessary relationships (and a device to state the theory precisely), rather than a device for proof.[3]

The following statements of relationships aim to be plausible hypotheses but not obvious truths. Though some reasons for their plausibility are adduced in this section, more solid evidence to support their validity comes only in later sections.

If an element is included in the following discussion (and in the accompanying equations), that variable is deemed to be important; omitting an element does not imply, however, that it has no effect at all but rather that it is *relatively* unimportant. For example, social institutions at all times surely have had some effect on fertility and perhaps on mortality, and hence on population growth. But in most premodern periods, population growth has been *largely* exogenous, except with respect to climate and disease. This is so, even though since perhaps 1700 the rate of change of population has been a function of income level (along with other factors), and in more recent times it has become a function of many economic, political, and social institutions.

The Earliest Period

Let us start with the earliest population size and growth rate: The number of human beings alive at the earliest date that ought to be considered

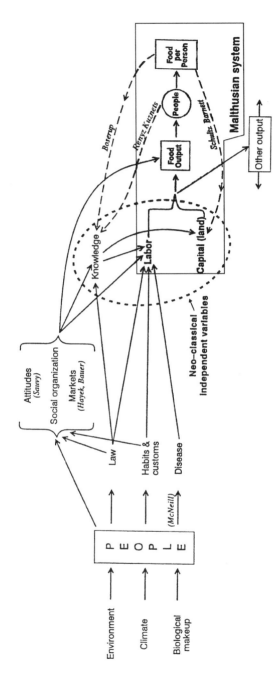

Fig. 23. Very-long-run full-adjustment model

(prior to the discovery of fire and the invention of stone tools) was not a function of human-invented technology or society[4] but only of earlier climatic conditions and the inborn human reproductive and survival mechanisms.[5] This does not imply that those people had no technical knowledge or social organization but rather that there had not yet begun a process of cumulative learning from hominid experiences.

The growth rate of population in earliest times was affected not only by the number of couples in the childbearing ages but also by the conditions for survival; more people constituted greater protection against animal depredation.[6] Population must quickly have attained the minimum level necessary to avoid species extinction even in the presence of substantial variability due to climatic shifts and perhaps epidemic disease, or else one of the dips in the cycle would have finished us off. (As noted earlier, however, genetic archaeology has suggested that population in the world was still sufficiently small that we were seriously vulnerable to extinction about 65,000 years ago.) Technology is not mentioned in this discussion because the knowledge affecting health was still in an unevolved state, being much the same as the knowledge that dogs and children utilize nowadays in keeping clear of moving vehicles; apparently there is no cumulation of such knowledge from generation to generation. Leakey (1981, 117) says that the same kinds of tools were used for a million years and more, which suggests no cumulation of knowledge.

Warfare among human bands will be ignored here and henceforth, because it probably did not have a decisive effect and also because there is little or no knowledge of its effects at earlier times.

The Earlier Course of Technology

It seems reasonable to assert that the initial stage of human technology was a function of our genetic endowment plus imitation of animals.[7] Hence the first increments to knowledge were a function only of the supply side (human numbers in their role as inventors) and the demand side (human needs for inventions to fill survival needs), because the original stock of human-generated technology was zero.[8] The first important increments to knowledge probably were fire, tools of stone, and the information that the absence of sexual intercourse and the practice of coitus interruptus prevent births. Readers may offer other suggestions (especially about social knowledge), and the list may well change as genetic biology teaches us more about controls exerted by our biological endowment.

In every period, people are both suppliers of new technology out of their imaginations and demanders of new technology, especially as their numbers increase and new needs therefore emerge. But because the two aspects of population always accompany each other, there will not be any further notice taken of this distinction in the discussion or in the equations.

Natural Resources
After centuries of speculation about the matter, there now seems to be agreement among economists that there is no observable relationship between an objective measure of the value of a group's natural resources and that group's economic progress (except perhaps in the case of Eskimos). One of the earliest to assess the situation correctly was Kuznets (1957–60, 31). Hayek (1960, chap. 2) provided a very full understanding of the process of increasing the availability of natural resources, as part of the economic underpinning for his work *The Constitution of Liberty.* The underlying idea that resources become more available rather than more scarce as development occurs was perhaps first shown (for the case of farmland) by Theodore Schultz in an astonishing 1951 essay and then was proved by Barnett and Morse (1963) for all other natural resources. All of those writers taught that the amount and value of a particular natural resource are functions of the available knowledge about how to put the resource to use.[9] One part of the explanation of this startling anticommonsensical idea (at least, for the case of land) is that people migrated from places that were poorly endowed relative to their current technology (such as mountain heights) to places that were better endowed (such as lowlands).

Physical Capital
In the decades since World War II, economists have learned that physical capital (other than natural resources) is much more a result of technology and wealth than the converse. There is little reason to think that this was much less true in early times.[10] The preexisting stock of human-produced capital matters because a new stock of capital is not built de novo each day — which is the very nature of productive capital. But deterioration and depreciation take place sufficiently rapidly so that the carryover can be considered negligible in the long run. Hence there is no reason to believe that the stock of physical capital imposes a long-lasting constraint upon future progress.

Periods after the Earliest Period
The level of technology that we assume existed when humankind first emerged as a species perhaps a million years ago was the basis for the

first human inventions. The extent of the invention and technical change was, it was assumed earlier (and in equation (2b)), influenced by the population size at the beginning of the period and thereafter. It follows that the level of technology that existed perhaps 60,000–100,000 years ago was a function of the original population and technology.[11]

Further development of technology probably was affected by population growth in the past (as of then), the amount of land per person, and human needs for food. Hunters and gatherers each need several square miles of land to fill their stomachs, and an increase in people implies either migration, invention, or both.[12]

Now we begin to see the outlines of all the subsequent analysis. We notice that the same elements—the population sizes in each period and the current density per unit of land—are the only elements in the relationships. And later we shall see that this continues to be the case as other contemporary elements fall out of the analysis as the relationships for the various past periods are combined.[13] (The importance in the earliest times of imitation of animals, and of our genetically programmed technology, must have diminished rapidly, and both factors hence can be ignored in subsequent discussion.)

After the earliest period, the stock of accumulated knowledge, along with human numbers and needs, must have begun to affect the rate of knowledge acquisition. Population density also was a factor (see equation (2d)) though it is an open question whether, for example, the aborigines of Australia invented very little technology simply because of their small numbers or whether their low density was also a factor. The answer does not matter for the rest of the essay, however.

As equation (2d) indicates, population growth also matters because it affects the perceived demand for new solutions to economic problems. Early rates of growth in human numbers were low compared to modern rates, however, so the change would be harder to perceive. But as shown in the biblical story of Abram and Lot, the perception of population pressure can eventually occur.

It is an open question whether political and social institutions affected the change in technique and technology before, say, 5,000 years ago. Was Egypt the intellectual leader that it was because of its numbers and density alone, or did its political-social structure have an influence? The Incas and Mayas also built pyramids when their numbers rose, probably with a political system quite different than that of Egypt, though it may be that the differences in structures among poor and less developed nations do not differ greatly, despotism probably being the rule most of the time in most places. Additionally, Wittfogel (1957) made the argument that in places where large water-control systems fitted the environment, the structure of society was heavily influenced by those conditions. This observation does not depend on those parts of Wittfogel's analysis that have not worn well with the years.

Greece and Rome may or may not illustrate the importance of the political and social system upon the rate of growth of knowledge. However, I do not know of studies that resolve this issue.

The causal relationship set forth in the preceding and in equation (2d) for the path of technology development probably held much the same until the past millennium, when the political and economic system clearly began to matter greatly—as, for example, in the differing histories of China and Europe (about which more is said in chap. 5).[14] David Hume ([1777] 1987) put it as follows: "Multitudes of people, necessity and liberty, have begotten commerce in HOLLAND" (113) and "It is impossible for the arts and sciences to arise, at first, among any people unless that people enjoy the blessing of a *free government*" (115). Kuznets argued the same point.

> [E]ven among the European countries nearest and most closely allied historically to pioneering Great Britain, entry into modern economic growth may have been delayed, awaiting major required political and institutional changes. If we then add the element of *"Stadluft macht frei*—City air makes free," the process may be viewed as: More people, more cities, more free people, more knowledge. (Kuznets 1966, 472)

Social Institutions
Whatever the details of social organization at the earliest times that we may call human—perhaps a million years ago—it seems reasonable to assume that little or no change took place for eons,[15] because the social organization of our earliest ancestors was dictated by the conditions of survival into which humankind emerged. This Marx-like economic determinism is shown by the commonality of the size of the community. There were perhaps half a dozen families or 30 people (the "magic number" mentioned earlier) in all observed nomadic groups (see Cameron 1989, 21; Leakey 1981, 99).

Social organization surely changed from (say) the $-10M$ period to the 0 c.e. period but not as a result of the prior social organization. Rather, I would argue, institutions evolve to fit physical and economic circumstances with little influence of previous social organization and knowledge.[16] This crucial assumption is justified by casual observation of the relative ease with which a few people can de novo create a new form of commune (though it may not last very long) and even entirely reorganize an entire society in a relatively short period of time, as Marxists and their successors have shown (though this is not to say that either group operated without knowledge of earlier forms). Hence the social organization in the period from $-10M$ is omitted from the determinants of the social organization around the year 0 c.e. (5b)).

The absence of the influence of the prior social organization is necessary to be consistent with the hypothesis that it is population and technology that are the crucial driving and cumulative forces. If the prior states of social organization were included in the relationships, there would be a chain of lagged causation running from early social organization to later population size that is inconsistent with the central hypothesis. Incidentally, the revealing of this kind of explicit connection is the sort of contribution that the formalism in the equation can make in this context.

Markets are a particularly telling example of institutions being determined mainly by contemporary population and other current conditions; past conditions have relatively small lagged effects in determining markets.[17] The black markets that arise everywhere in response to opportunity illustrate how powerfully markets respond to current conditions. And data on the distributions of retail outlets in communities of different sizes (see fig. 24) illustrate how the opening of markets is a remarkably predictable function of population size, holding income and other institutions constant. Of course some markets, such as the insurance market at Lloyds in London, have a slower cycle of life, but it is not slow compared to changes in population density in various countries.

Population growth is not included in this statement about markets (equation (6)) because over a long period of time during which there is slow growth, it is the experience of the actual numbers, rather than of the increment in them, that is likely to affect social organizations. This may be less true in modern times when growth is sufficiently fast to be perceptible.

Perhaps the econometrician's "error term" should be included in this discussion of social organization (equation (6)) to indicate that vagaries of history and human personality influence human organization. But these vagaries probably were not important from the perspective of tens of thousands of years.

Later Population Growth

In periods earlier than the past few centuries, the amount of population growth (the absolute increment, rather than the rate) was relatively unrelated to social institutions or even to the level of wealth. Rather, it

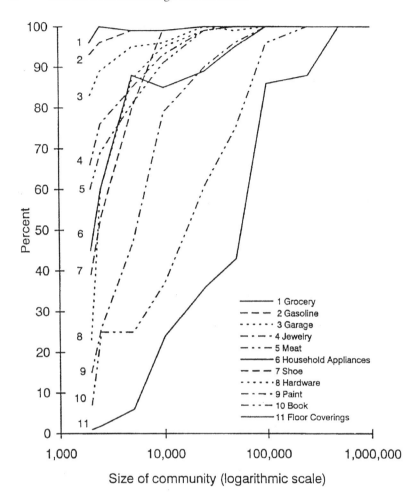

Fig. 24.   The relationship of community size to range of retail stores available in the United States, 1930s. (From Keyes 1942, 67.)

was a function only of current population size, the level of technology, and the disease level.[18] In more recent times, however, the amount of population growth has also been affected by the level of income and the characteristics of social institutions.[19]

The disease level is a function of prior population densities, as McNeill (1977) has convincingly shown. In periods up to around 1750, no social factor other than the present density of population (and hence past population sizes) affected disease levels, along with geography.[20] In more recent periods, income (wealth), technology, and the social system also came to influence the disease level.[21]

A substantive discussion of disease in connection to population size and density may be found in chapter 5.

Income and Wealth

The levels of income and wealth (together with the standard of living) come into the story relatively late because, as Jones (1988) documents, continuous intensive growth was rare or nonexistent until recently. The fruits of most technological gains ended up in extensive growth — keeping more people alive at the level of subsistence agriculture. This may have been due in part to the insufficiency of types of consumer goods that could be produced cheaply enough to make it worthwhile for farmers to produce more food to trade for them and also to the lack of roads to markets; hence the proportion of labor in agriculture remained high, rather than falling as is necessary for intensive growth.

Concerning income, when that concept becomes more recognizable in the periods starting about 1750, we can say that the income level is a function of current technology, population size, institutions, the disease level, and capital.[22] Physical capital might be excluded from this relationship (equation (8a)), but others will disagree.

Education is absent from this relationship (equation (8a)) and has not been mentioned so far. From any point of view, education was not an important factor in early periods. And in later periods it is so closely related to income and wealth that special mention would be redundant.

For the breakthrough period starting in 1750, physical capital was undoubtedly not a crucial element.[23] Given that, except for population size, all of the elements in the relationship (the variables in equation (8b)) have earlier been seen to be reducible to functions of current or previous population sizes, we can state that, as of 1750, current income depended only upon current and earlier population sizes.[24]

Analysis of the System on Relationships

Examination of the relationships discussed up until now shows that only for population size and technology is there a chain of influence between currently dated states and the earliest-dated states of those variables. The last relationship mentioned just previously (equation (8c)) corresponds to the basic idea of this essay that population size is the highest-order endogenous variable and the only variable that, if it had been different during certain (long) periods, would have resulted in a different date for the breakthrough into SMP. For all other variables the determinants are contemporaneous or recent, and current states are linked to the earliest states only through population size and the technological level. This reflects the theory proposed here.

The necessary empirical work implied by the aforementioned set of relationships (the structure of the equations), to which we shall return in chapter 3, calls for showing that (1) the "modern" surge of population size began earlier than the surge of the consumption variables; (2) (absolute) changes in population and the (absolute) changes in technology moved together and were intertwined in mutual causation over the ages; and (3) population size and also perhaps the technological level heavily determine the nature of current institutions (including markets), but there is no strong causation in the opposite direction. This empirical work constitutes the substance of later chapters.

Two intuitive checks upon the validity of the preceding set of relationships would include the following.

1. If the line of homo sapiens had begun 10,000 years later (or earlier) than it actually did, would one not expect the breakthrough of modern progress to have occurred 10,000 years later (or earlier) than it actually did? If one would not think that way, why not? Regrettably only a thought experiment is possible on this point, because there has been only one such historical episode.

2. It is no longer in doubt that the political-economic structure is the most important influence on the rate of economic growth *over the course of a few decades;* many analyses of large sets of nations (see Przeworski and Limongi 1993 for a review of 18 major studies) and the comparative experience of North versus South Korea, East versus West Germany, and China versus Taiwan (see Simon 1987b and tables 1–5) show this unmistakably. Przeworski and Limongi state flatly: "[E]veryone seems to agree that secure property rights foster growth" (51).[25] I am as firm a believer in this proposition as any economist, and it is crucial in my analysis of the relationship of fertility and the rate of natural increase to economic development.

Institutions in the Present Model: A First Cut

The role of political-economic institutions in this model certainly is one of the more difficult issues that must be grappled with. So we will take it up in several places, starting here.

TABLE 1. Population Density and Growth, Selected Countries, 1950–83

	East Germany	West Germany	North Korea	South Korea	China	Taiwan	Hong Kong	Singapore	Russia	United States	India	Japan
Population per sq km, 1950	171	201	76	212	57	212	2,236	1,759	8	16	110	224
% change in population												
1950	1.2	1.1	−7.8	0.1	1.9	3.3	−10.4	4.4	1.7	1.7	1.7	1.6
1955	−1.3	1.2	3.5	2.2	2.4	3.5	4.9	4.9	1.8	1.8	1.9	1.0
1960	−0.7	1.3	3.0	3.3	1.8	3.1	3.0	3.3	1.8	1.7	2.0	0.9
1970	−0.1	1.0	3.0	2.4	2.4	2.2	2.2	1.7	1.0	1.1	2.2	1.3
1983	−0.3	−0.2	2.1–2.6	1.4–1.6	1.3–1.6	1.8	1.5	1.2	0.7–0.9	0.9	2.1–2.2	0.6

Source: Population per sq km: UNESCO 1963, 12–21. Percentage change in population: U.S. Department of Commerce 1978; United Nations 1984.

TABLE 2. Real Income per Capita, Selected Countries, 1950–82

	East Germany	West Germany	North Korea	South Korea	China	Taiwan	Hong Kong	Singapore	Russia	United States	India	Japan
Real GDP per capita												
1950[a]	1,480	1,888	n.a.	n.a.	300	508	n.a.	n.a.	1,373	4,550	333	810
1960	3,006	3,711	n.a.	631	505	733	919	1,054	2,084	5,195	428	1,674
1970	4,100	5,356	n.a.	1,112	711	1,298	2,005	2,012	3,142	6,629	450	4,215
1980	5,532	6,967	n.a.	2,007	1,135	2,522	3,973	3,948	3,943	8,089	498	5,996
Real GNP per capita												
1950[b]	2,943	2,943	193	193	n.a.	417	1,053	n.a.	n.a.	7,447	217	649
1960	n.a.	3,959	n.a.	473	n.a.	429	979	1,330	n.a.	8,573	220	1,403
1970	6,584	6,839	556	615	556	868	1,807	2,065	4,670	10,769	219	4,380
1982	9,914	11,032	817	1,611	630	2,579	5,064	5,600	5,991	12,482	235	9,774

Source: Real GDP per capita: Summers and Heston 1984. Real GNP per capita: IBRD 1980. GNP deflator: Council of Economic Advisers 1986, table B-3.

Note: n.a. = not available.

[a]Figures for real gross domestic product (GDP) per capita are based on 1975 international prices.
[b]Figures for real gross national product (GNP) per capita are based on 1981 constant U.S. dollars.

TABLE 3. Life Expectancy and Infant Mortality, Selected Countries, 1960–82

	East Germany	West Germany	North Korea	South Korea	China	Taiwan	Hong Kong	Singapore	Russia	United States	India	Japan
Life expectancy at birth												
1960	68	69	54	54	53	65	65	64	68	70	43	68
1982	73	74	65	68	67	73	76	73	69	75	55	77
Infant mortality												
1960	39	34	78	78	165	32	37	35	33	26	165	30
1982	12	12	32	32	67	18	10	11	28	11	94	7

Source: IBRD 1985, 260–61.

TABLE 4. Industrialization and Urbanization, Selected Countries, 1960–82

	East Germany	West Germany	North Korea	South Korea	China	Taiwan	Hong Kong	Singapore	Russia	United States	India	Japan
% Labor force in agriculture												
1960	18	14	62	66	n.a.	n.a.	8	8	42	7	74	33
1980	10	4	49	34	69	37[a]	3	2	14	2	71	12
% Urbanized												
1960	72	77	40	28	18	58	89	100	49	70	18	63
1982	77	85	63	61	21	70[b]	91	100	63	78	24	78

Source: Labor force in agriculture: IBRD 1985, 258–59. Urban population: IBRD 1985, 260–61.
[a]Figure for 1978.
[b]Figure for 1980.

TABLE 5. Education and Consumption, Selected Countries, Various Years

	East Germany	West Germany	North Korea	South Korea	China	Taiwan	Hong Kong	Singapore	Russia	United States	India	Japan
Higher education enrollment												
1960	16	6	n.a.	5	n.a.	n.a.	4	6	11	32	3	10
1982	30	30	n.a.	22	1	n.a.	12	10	21	56	9	31
Newsprint per person												
1950–54	3.5	5.1	n.a.	0.6	n.a.	0.9	4.3	n.a.	1.2	35.0	0.2	3.3
1982	9.6	21.5	0.1	5.8	1.2	n.a.	16.4	32.1	4.5	44.1	0.4	24.0
Telephones per 100 population												
1983	20.6	57.1	n.a.	14.9	0.5	25.8	38.2	36.7	9.8	76.0	0.5	52.0
Autos per 100 population												
1960	0.9	8.2	n.a.	0.1	0.005	0.1	1.0	4.2	0.3	34.4	0.1	0.5
1970	6.7	24.1	n.a.	0.2	0.018	n.a.	2.8	7.2	0.7	43.9	0.1	8.5
1984	18.9	41.3	n.a.	1.1	0.010	3.1	4.6	9.3	3.9	55.5	0.2	22.8

Source: Higher education: IBRD 1985, 266–67. Newsprint: UNESCO 1963, 400–409. Telephones: U.S. Department of Commerce 1986, 845. Automobiles: Motor Vehicle Manufacturers Association of the United States various years.

Note: n.a. = not available.

Consider the pairwise comparisons of the Koreas, Germanies, and Chinas in table 1. The very fact that after living under different economic structures for at most a few decades the members of the pairs of countries that emerged from the *same* earlier pre–World War II political-economic structure arrived at such *different* economic results from each other suggests that after a few decades there is little *continuing* effect of the structure. Much the same can be seen in comparisons involving the two parts of the Karelian peninsula that were Finnish prior to World War II but were split between Finland and the USSR after World War II. For still another example, one might compare adjacent cities in Austria and Czechoslovakia that had similar economic standards before World War II but were very different by the late 1980s when Czechoslovak socialism ended. That the countries of Eastern Europe may take two or three decades to catch up to where they would have been in the absence of their Communist interludes cuts both ways — both *fully* two or three decades and *only* two or three decades. It is the latter interpretation that is relevant here.

The point of the preceding discussion is that the political-economic structure can be, and often is, quickly altered by various events. A factor that is so malleable is not a good candidate to be primary determinative variable in the very-long-run system under consideration.

Stating as clearly as possible the viewpoint of this essay regarding the relative roles of demography and institutions is crucial if the essay is to make itself understood. To this end, consider North's statement.

> The cumulation in the stock of knowledge has largely been irreversible throughout history, but human economic progress has not; the rise and the decline of political economic units, not to mention entire civilizations, are certainly indisputable. The contrast makes clear an important point — *it is the successes and failures in human organization that account for the progress and retrogression of societies.* (1981, 59; italics added)

North is certainly right in what he says about *societies.*[26] But the subject of this essay is not *societies* but the *human enterprise.* And it is not rise and fall that is the subject here but rather the timing of the one-time emergence into Sudden Modern Progress about 1750–1800. With respect to that event, the human organization of Europe at the time certainly was important. But the human organizations that operated in earlier times may be considered to be like epochs in the weather; they mattered at the time, but substituting any one of them when it was not present, or removing one that was present, probably would not have mattered much to the long-term outcome because of the very "cumulation in the stock of knowledge" that North properly considers "irreversible," especially after the invention of writing and secure libraries.

The evidence on the convergence of standards of living among the advanced countries in the past century, and also in recent decades (see Baumol, Blackman, and Wolff 1989), fits this point of view, too. So do the rapid advances of many countries that started at low income levels and had long been living with non-Western political-economic structures — such as Japan in the nineteenth century, Hong Kong and Singapore after World War II, the Cantonese southern portion of China starting sometime in the mid-1980s, and Mauritius starting in the 1980s.

Still another line of relevant evidence is the trends for many countries surrounding such great disasters as the black plague and World War II. In the former case, population grew faster after the disaster than before it, until the (absolute) change in population regained its former long-run trend line. In the case of World War II, Brems's diagrams (see figs. 25*a* and 25*b*) show how the economic losses induced by that period were soon erased by fast economic growth in various countries, the rate of change in income level soon returning to its long-run trend. It is as if there is a "warranted"[27] underlying rate of growth that not even natural and social catastrophes interfere with for longer than a relatively short while.

A last piece of general evidence is the history of national leadership in the present millennium. Until at least 1400, China was ahead in technology and perhaps in the standard of living as computed by Maddison (1982, 6) and as indexed by the level of urbanization as estimated by Bairoch (1988) (in part for Asia as a whole) (see fig. 26). Later, Holland had the lead from about 1500 to 1820, then the United Kingdom until 1890, and finally the United States, according to Maddison (1991, 30, 31; see figs. 27*a* and 27*b*). In a "mere" few hundred years political-economic structures changed, the leading countries fell from leadership, and economic glory was buried in the sands of time. Why then should one think that the introduction of a different political-economic structure at some point in history might have been decisive in altering *forever* the speed of progress throughout history? In contrast, a substantial continuing change in population growth or in numbers at some earlier time would certainly have continued to affect population numbers in all subsequent periods and presumably other outcomes.

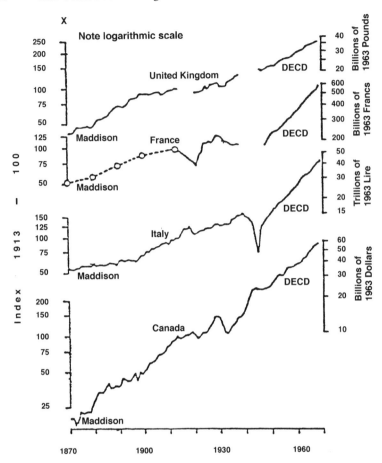

Fig. 25*a*.   Gross national product, United Kingdom, France, Italy, and Canada, 1870–1970. (From Brems 1980.)

Population and Knowledge: The Theory of the Nexus

The most complex analytic issue — though it need not cause difficulty for the rest of the analysis — concerns the relationship between the causal roles of population and knowledge. They are the only two variables about which one can reasonably claim that if its stock had been much lower (higher) than it actually was in period t, the state of humanity would have been vastly poorer (richer) than it actually was in period $t + x$. All other variables, such as the stocks of private physical capital and prime farm-land, are likely to be replaced rather quickly if there is a sudden catas-

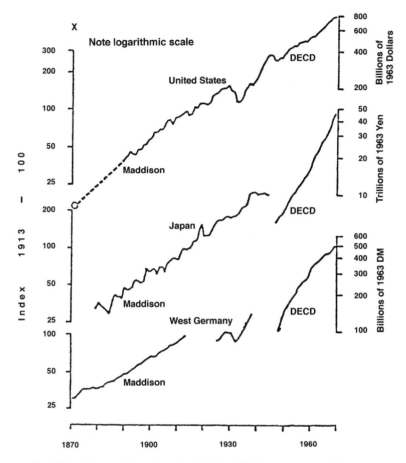

Fig. 25b. Gross national product, United States, Japan, and West Germany, 1870–1970. (From Brems 1980.)

trophic loss. Population size and the level of technology are less variable. But can anything much be said about the relationship of population size and technology to each other?

We surely can say that the rock-bottom causal element of long-run human progress is the *combination* of population size and technology. But it makes as little sense to ask which is the "original" cause as asking whether the chicken or the egg is more fundamental.[28] Even the earliest humans could not have survived and grown without such technology as fire and cutting tools; yet the knowledge of these techniques came from human beings.

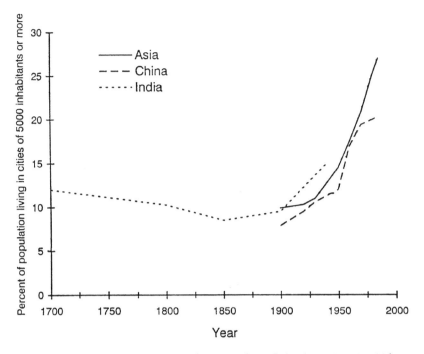

Fig. 26. Urbanization in Asia. (Adapted from Bairoch 1988, 400, 430.)

Indeed, the interpenetration of population size and technology is confirmed by the fact that history consists of both the Boserupian "population-push" and the Malthusian "invention-pull" processes, with causation running *from* one of these two forces in one case and *to it* in the other. (Simon 1977, [chap. 8], 1978a, and 1992 [chap. 3] provide geometric and arithmetic theories for these two processes, together with extensive historical examples.)

The key point is that no *other* element was as essential as the combination of knowledge and human numbers — not institutions, law, physical capital, or natural resources. Humankind could live in a variety of settings of these other variables. And it could produce some livable forms of them when they were completely absent. Not so with technology and population size.

The difference between progress in the group of continents consisting of North America, South America, Australia, and Africa and that consisting of Europe, Asia, and Middle East exemplifies the complex nature of the relationship between our two primary forces. Let us address

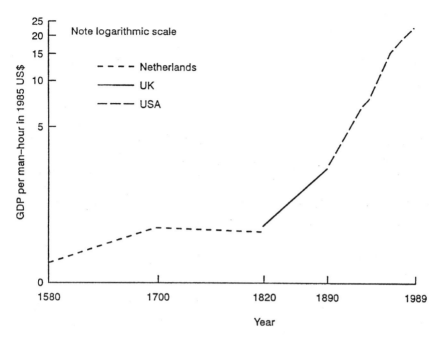

Fig. 27*a*. Locus of productivity leadership, 1580–1989 (logarithmic scale). (From Maddison 1991, 31.)

the matter by asking whether the state of knowledge might have determined population density in those various continents or the converse? A positive answer to either form of this question would raise doubts about the main argument offered here.

Elucidating this issue strengthens the argument of this essay rather than calling it into question, however. The first human inhabitants of the Americas whose settlements have been found apparently arrived about 10,000 B.C.E. via the Bering Strait ice bridge during the Ice Age (McEvedy and Jones 1978, 271; some more recent reports put the crossing much earlier, but the difference in dates does not matter much in the present context). Both population size and density remained below the levels in Europe from then until 1492 when Europeans arrived in the Americas (even more so if Asia is considered part of an ecumene; see figs. 28*a* and 28*b*). And agriculture in the Americas began only about 5,000 years ago, compared to between 10,000 and 11,500 years ago in the Near East and China respectively (Leakey 1981, 201; *Science,* January 17, 1997, 309, for China).

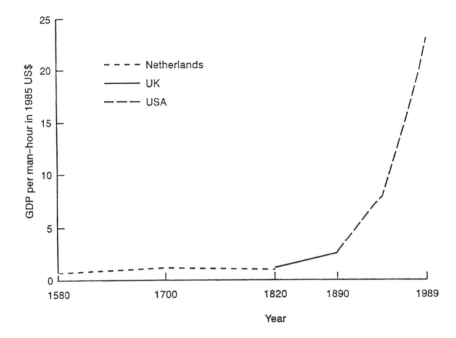

Fig. 27b. Locus of productivity leadership, 1580–1989 (linear scale). (From Maddison 1991, 31.)

It seems reasonable, then, that Mayan-Incan society was *not* on the brink of going the way of Europe but was a millennium or two behind them. One view is that it was not until the fifteenth century that "Mexico and Peru had reached a cultural stage equivalent to the Near East of 2000 B.C. and . . . had achieved comparable population densities" (Mc-Evedy and Jones 1978, 272), though 1990s' deciphering shows that the Mayas had a picture language as early as 100 C.E. (*Economist,* December 21, 1996, 56), but that was several millennia after Assyria developed a language. The isolation of the Americas from the ecumene of Europe and Asia prevented the former from participating in the sequence of progress in the latter continents.

The case of Africa is a bit more puzzling because, relative to the Americas, it was less separated geographically from Eurasia. But there is plenty of evidence that there existed little intellectual contact between Europe and sub-Saharan Africa prior to the arrival of the Portuguese explorers in the middle of the second millennium of the present era.

Kremer (1993) suggested that "holding constant" the various land

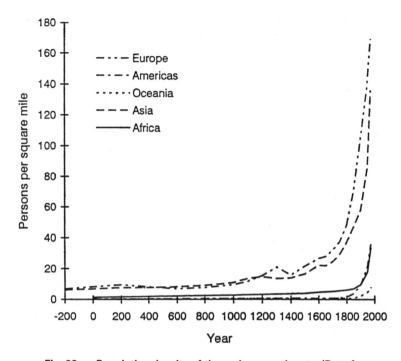

Fig. 28a. Population density of the various continents. (Data from McEvedy and Jones 1978.)

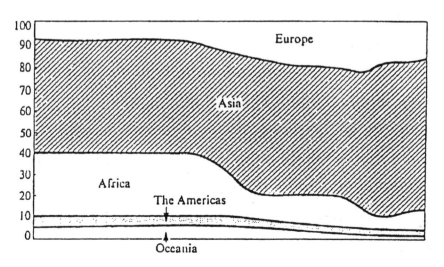

Fig. 28b. World population from 10,000 B.C.E. to 500 C.E. (From McEvedy and Jones 1978.)

areas by looking at population densities rather than numbers alone strengthens the comparison of the rates of their developments (which he measures by population size itself). And the numbers he thereby produces do indeed give a sense of the process proceeding in similar fashion in the two landmasses, though following different starting dates.

Departing from Kremer's procedure, one might define an aggregated variable such as total person-years lived (life expectancy multiplied by births) and compute this magnitude between such significant events as the first appearances of homo sapiens and the birth of agriculture, between agriculture and smelting, and so on, for the various land areas (holding density constant in some fashion) to examine for regularity across the landmasses.[29]

Derek de Solla Price showed many time series pertaining to the amount of new knowledge being produced as measured by the number of scientific journals, citations, and the like, during the past four or so centuries (see figs. 29a, 29b, 29c, and 29d). All series agree in showing that there has been at least a proportional rise in knowledge production as population has risen. The trends in the numbers of books published in the United States are illuminating.[30] There was an increase from 2,676 in 1880 to 36,071 in 1970 and 53,380 in 1983. Further analysis of such data might determine the portion of the knowledge differential for which population size is responsible; one could then calculate a residual for which income level may be said to be responsible.

Casual inspection suggests that over the past five centuries, citations in technical journals have become more recent, on average, though I know of no systematic study.[31] This may be taken as evidence that the quantity of recent knowledge available to researchers has increased with the passage of time.[32] The trend may be a function of increasing population size as well as technological improvements.

Several concepts are available for approximating the cumulative amount of creative potential until a given date. As a first approximation, one might plot the cumulative number of lives lived beyond the age of 25 (or better, the number of years of life 25–65) until chosen cutoff dates. A second approximation: lives lived *outside of agriculture* (or in cities) beyond the age of 25 until the cutoff dates. A third approximation: the weighted number of lives until the age of 25, outside agriculture, and *literate.* A fourth approximation: the weighted number of lives until age 25, outside agriculture, literate, and *above subsistence income.* A fifth approximation, and an estimate for one date, comes from Price, who wrote that (as of about 1961), "some 80 to 90 percent of all scientists that have ever been, are alive now" (1961, 107). This fifth measure is a very different sort of concept and estimate than is the total number of people

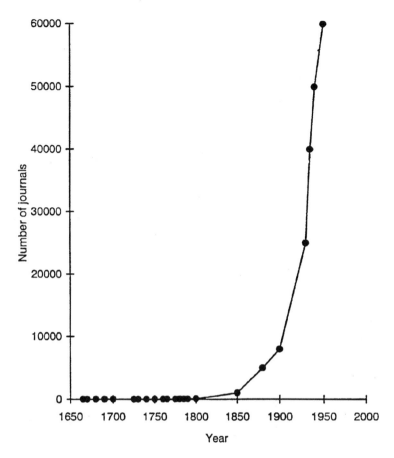

Fig. 29*a*.   Number of scientific journals in the world, 1650–1960 (linear scale). (From Price 1961, 97.)

who have ever lived. In addition, it may be more compatible with rates of progress through the ages, though it would not be sensible to make scientific discovery too dependent on people labeled "scientists" in the past.

According to Price (1961, 107), each working scientist produces about three technical papers in a lifetime, a number that has remained essentially constant over the years. His finding squares with the cross-national finding of a constant output of science with population and income held constant (Simon and Love 1978). While the number of papers may not be proportional to the amount of knowledge, Price's discovery does suggest an interesting constancy in *time and effort input*,

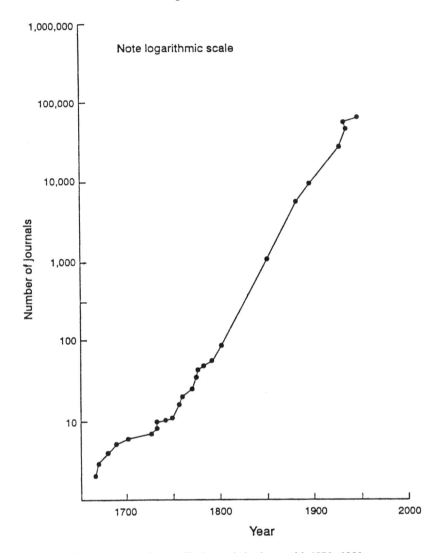

Fig. 29*b*.   **Number of scientific journals in the world, 1650–1960 (logarithmic scale). (From Price 1961, 97.)**

which makes it plausible to treat the number of persons creating knowledge as an index of total knowledge production.

One may wonder why the rate of human invention (controlling for other factors) is what Price has found it to have been. We do not have an answer — at least not yet. But there are many other unknowns. We do

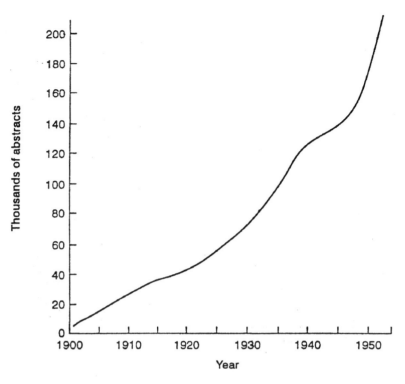

Fig. 29c. Number of "physical abstracts," 1900–1960 (physics and electrical engineering). (From Price 1961, 103.)

not understand why a baby should begin to walk after perhaps ten months rather than two months or two years, or why the murder and suicide rates lie within particular ranges. One can hope that in the future much more will be known, but the absence of an explanation at present does not render the observed rates meaningless or useless.

Summary

Though it may not yet be possible to say much about the mechanism that controlled the timing of development in the past, nowadays we can do so rather well with respect to the future. A competent director of research and development (R&D) in an industrial firm is able to make reasonable estimates about how long it will take for a given team to produce an

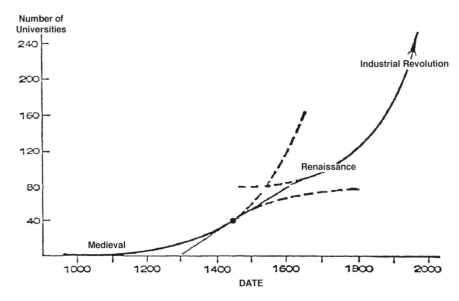

Fig. 29*d.* **Number of universities founded in Europe. (Adapted from Price 1961, 114, 115.)**

engineering solution to a given problem in biology, mechanical engineering, and the like. And he or she will give different estimates depending upon the number of R&D teams working on the problem, showing the influence of population size on the rate of development.

One would, of course, like to relate rates of growth and the overall pattern of growth to specific numbers of people. At the present state of knowledge that is clearly impossible, just as it is impossible to state how many straws it takes to break a camel's back. But structural analysis might eventually provide some qualitative estimates for both the camel's back and the problem at hand.

Retrodicting the Date of the Breakthrough

It may be objected that no reasons have been given for the breakthrough of Sudden Modern Progress occurring at the date when it did. Though that is so, it does not imply that the objection is critical. For eons, and perhaps still until now, physicians could say that pregnancy takes nine months, but they have not been able to provide a description of the mechanism that makes it that long rather than eight months or 10 months or even two months or 20 months. Yet this observation by physicians has been extremely useful in family planning and other preparations. For another example, consider why it takes about as long as it usually does for a person to learn to drive well enough to pass a driving test. To be sure, there is much variation among persons. But driver-training curricula can be completed within known periods with fair predictability, though it is doubtful that anyone could give a detailed analysis of why the human learning system requires exactly that much time.

Furthermore, the comparison of the time patterns of the major technical innovations in the various continents provides a sense of regularity in the historical record, rather than the accidental picture that Jones sketches. And if there *was* regularity in developments prior to the breakthrough itself—that is to say, a process that is knowable and explainable rather than stochastic—it suggests that the timing of the breakthrough, too, was determined by the previous events in a fashion that will eventually become understandable rather than remaining an accident of rulers and regimes.[33]

The beginning of this essay hypothesized that, starting at any particular moment in the past, the length of time it took to reach the modern breakthrough depended on the number of people who lived thereafter, together with the amount of technology in existence at the particular moment about which the question is being asked. This is quite analogous to the time required to reach a solution to an engineering problem in an R&D laboratory. Indeed, it is a function of the number of qualified people who go to work on the problem, together with their initial body of knowledge.[34] Just as a skillful director of the laboratory can predict this length of time with some accuracy, so the greatest of science-fiction imaginers of various past eras might have been able to forecast the breakthrough of Sudden Modern Progress with some accuracy, though the enormity of the leap probably hindered such imagination until before 1600 or 1650.

Lack of ability to retrodict the date of the breakthrough need not be permanent, just as the lack of ability to explain why pregnancy in humans takes nine months need not be permanent. Biologists may eventually be able to elucidate the various mechanisms that build up at rates that, altogether, lead to a pregnancy of nine months, just as a construction engineer can now clearly explain why it will require a given number of months to complete a given structure with specified inputs. Perhaps one can estimate that in the Americas the breakthrough might have taken place about 3000 or 4000 c.e. if those continents had continued to live in isolation, given the lags between them and Europe in population and in the onset of agriculture.

Perhaps at some future date it will be possible to specify the mechanism more closely with respect to the breakthrough date—how many people are required to produce how much knowledge at which points, which in turn was necessary input to produce further amounts of knowledge later on. Ecologists can predict the arrival of new species on an island a given distance from the mainland and the rate of spread of a species across an island of a given size. Similarly it should be possible to determine the rate of spread of the human species across the face of the Earth. It may eventually be possible to say something meaningful about the length of time required to achieve major new inventions in various periods. Note that people burned firewood from the discovery of fire, perhaps two million or 200,000 years ago, until perhaps 500 years ago, and even until the present in some places. (The matter of where one looks to date the adoption of innovations always is problematic). Then there was perhaps a 300-year period of coal use. Then perhaps 100 years for the age of oil. Then perhaps 50 years for nuclear fission until fusion. The acceleration is awesome—and perhaps predictable, too.

Concerning land transportation: For eons, walking and some riding of animals were the only modes of human movement. Then came the paved road for wheeled traffic of the Romans—a huge innovation but an innovation that then fell into disuse; the discarded Roman road that ran from Jerusalem to Jericho was again used in the twentieth century until its replacement in the 1970s. This phenomenon of great discoveries falling into disuse seldom happens now.

Starting in the early 1800s the railroad was sovereign for perhaps 100 years. Then the internal-combustion engine and road traffic ruled transportation for some decades. Then came the airplane and not long thereafter space travel; the pace of the major innovations predictably sped up.

It should be possible to retrodict certain lines of invention that led to near discontinuities; for example, it should be possible to retrodict the development of a chronometer accurate enough for long ocean voyages from the history of improvement in accuracy of timepieces over the ages. In particular, one can imagine that a person armed with the information in David Landes's book *Revolution in Time* pertaining to periods prior to 1400 should have been able to predict the subsequent development of that chronometer. Indeed, we now predict future technical developments with some probable accuracy, from minor engineering changes to major discoveries such as nuclear fission and fusion, as well as travel to, and the populating of, the planets and beyond.

Consider the case of agriculture—certainly the most important case in all respects, largely because it dominated almost every economy in the world, including the richest, until perhaps 1600, when it constituted more than 50 percent in the most developed countries and closer to 90 percent in most countries. One can go beyond the *sequence* of developments and connect the *timing* of the sequence with population density. Boserup (1965) has plotted the progression from hunting and gathering to slash and burn, then long fallow, then short fallow, and so on, all the way to three-course agriculture and beyond. Each shift can be related to a particular population density because (at least in Eurasia and perhaps in Africa, too) the knowledge necessary for the next stage is usually available (which may not be true for Australia and other isolated places, which makes for interesting side developments in the story). The time necessary for increase from one density level to the next is predictable from the conditions for population growth and from the growth rate itself. Hence the actual number of years necessary to complete the various stages in this progression is reasonably predictable.

Shelter and clothing constituted the other main constituents of consumption budgets before the advent of modern living. Shelter making still has not achieved multifold increased productivity in most places. And speeded-up clothing manufacture did not arrive until the middle of the current millennium.

If it were possible to do with the historical analysis of energy and metalworking what could be done with agriculture, one could retrodict their developments reasonably well, including elapsed times. James Burke's *Connections* (1978) discussed the diminishing lengths of time between major advances in metalworking in exactly this fashion.

The periods between major advances in medicine have certainly become shorter and shorter. Moreover, the times between the onset of a new epidemic or a newly discovered ailment and the prevention or cure of the disease have decreased dramatically; striking evidence lies in the history of the appearance of AIDS in the early 1980s and the discovery of drugs to fight the disease with some success, beginning in the late 1980s.

All of the foregoing in this section squares with both the expanding knowledge base and the increasing numbers of people, the latter affecting the progress through both the supply and demand mechanisms. The quickening of the tempo in each area of discovery is a regularity that encourages one to think that the date of the breakthrough into SMP should someday be much more comprehensible than it currently is.

The Importance of the Infrastructure of Skills

Burke (1978) and Cameron (1989, chap. 8) describe vividly the evolution of the basic discoveries in the technology of modern machinery and its fuel sources, an evolution that shows beyond the shadow of a doubt that no modern invention could have sprung fully formed in earlier times. Each one had to await the development of proper machine tools and other elements of production, which were in turn stimulated by the demands of the evolving knowledge. As noted earlier, the development of a chronometer accurate enough for navigation had to await the necessary technology, including sufficiently precise machine tools.

North makes this point vigorously.

[T]echnological developments are interrelated. The innovative ideas in Leonardo da Vinci's magnificent notebooks could not be realized without complementary developments in engineering, physics, and chemistry. Pasteur's discoveries were made possible only by complementary developments in optics, which produced the microscope. Technological developments, then, are built upon the prior accumulation of knowledge, which shapes the subsequent direction of inventive activity. (1981, 16–17)

North mentions Rosenberg 1976 and David 1975 as corroborating this connection.

Mokyr also emphasizes this point in several contexts: "One explanation of the absence of discontinuous breakthroughs between 1500 and 1750 is that although there was no scarcity of bold and novel technical ideas, the constraints of workmanship and materials to turn them into reality became binding" (1990a, 35); and

Which elements were responsible for making the Industrial Revolution possible in the late eighteenth century and not a century or two earlier? One factor surely must be the existence of a small but vital high-precision machine tool making industry. We have already mentioned the firm of John Wilkinson that made the cylinders used by Watt. It is only a mild exaggeration to say that Wilkinson and his colleagues made the difference between Watt and Trevithick on the one hand and Leonardo da Vinci on the other. (68; see also 68 ff.)

Not all improvements in technology depended on the broad advance of knowledge. The increase in seed yields over the millennia, for example, must have been quite independent of other improvements, at least until the twentieth century. But at the same time, the striking fact that seed yields showed sharp improvement during the twentieth century — though not as great as the gain in (say) speed of land transportation —

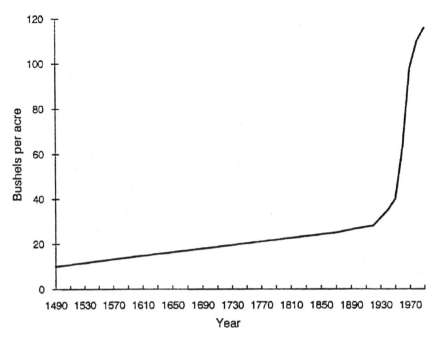

Fig. 30a. North American corn yields 1490–1990. (From Grantham 1995.)

suggests that the forces present in the modern period can have a huge effect on seed yields, too (see figs. 30*a* and 30*b*).

Was There an "Epochal Invention"?

Kuznets (1966, 286) suggested that the greatest invention of all was the "epochal innovation" of systematic inquiry. So did Usher.

The most decisive innovation was the introduction of systematic experimentation. This mode of inquiry is in evidence at every turn, sometimes incidentally, sometimes as a protracted search for specific formulas. The phenomena of percussion and recoil were studied. Experiments were made with falling bodies and a formula for the acceleration was suggested. The strength of struts and girders was studied with reference to variations of length and cross section;

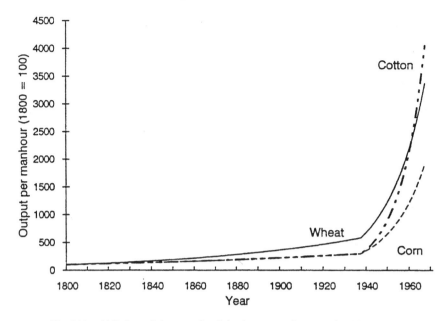

Fig. 30*b*.   U.S. farm labor productivity in corn, wheat, and cotton, 1800–1967. (From Grantham 1995.)

differences between single members and composite members were also determined. (1988, 109)

Usher gave a date for the epochal innovation.

The more sophisticated formulations of the primary principles thus invited the application to the mechanical sciences of the experimental methods whose necessity in physics had long been apprehended as a matter of abstract principle, especially by the Averroists in Italy. (1988)

CHAPTER 3

Evidence on the Long-Run Progress-Population Connection

The structure of relationships described in chapter 2 suggests the following line of empirical analysis: (1) Show that the "modern" surge of population began earlier than the surge of the consumption variables. (2) Show that the (absolute) population and the (absolute) level of technology moved together and were intertwined in mutual causation over the ages. And (3) show that population size (and also perhaps the techniques in use) heavily determines current institutions (including markets) and also that causation in the opposite direction is very weak. Thus, this chapter will review evidence on the long-run relationship of population size to the growth of per capita income, productivity, knowledge, and related variables. One objective is to show how all these variables generally moved in the same direction, with population moving earlier than the others. The lack of any precise data and the consequent absence of ups and downs in the series prevent any explicit statistical exploration of causality, however. Chapter 3 also contains discussion of the possibility that variables other than population could explain the observed long-run economic growth.

Population Size and the Standard of Living

Here follow some time-series and cross-sectional data on the relationship of population *size* (as distinguished from growth rates and density) to income growth. These data make a prima facie case for the theory that a connection exists between those variables, but the case is *only* prima facie and not compelling. To make a persuasive case requires the remaining chapters of this work.

Time-Series Evidence Relating Population to Living Standards

The first set of time-series evidence is stylized figures of population size, the (absolute) change in population, income per person, and the change in income per person, drawn for the very long run.

To begin with population, for the longest period of human existence as a species—from (say) two million years ago until (say) 6,000 or 7,000 years ago—population growth was very slow (see fig. 11 in chap. 1). Hence, population size and density remained low. The rate of population growth might be described by a straight line if plotted semilogarithmically, but such a plot would obscure the fact that the rate of early growth was infinitesimal.

The most striking aspects of the stylized population-size curve in fig. 31 showing total population for the world at various dates for the past 10,000 years are the rapid recent increases (1) in the richer countries since the eighteenth century; and (2) in the poorer countries in the second half of the twentieth century. Taken together, this rapid increase is a wholly unprecedented event, and it is the most important development in the history of humankind from the standpoint of both economics and noneconomic welfare. The graphs of life expectancy and population size (figs. 4 [in chap. 1] and 31) bear some resemblance to each other, but population has increased by a much larger proportion over the years.

Another perspective is offered by Deevey's idealized figure 12 (chap. 1). Here the logarithmic scale reveals the rapid increases in population starting with the onset of the agricultural, industrial, and postindustrial "revolutions." The tool-using and toolmaking revolution initiated the rapid rise in population around a million years ago. The aid of various implements "gave the food gatherer and hunter access to the widest range of environments" (Deevey 1960). But when the productivity gains from the use of primitive tools had been largely exploited, the rate of population growth fell.

The next rapid jump in population started perhaps 10,000 or 12,000 years ago when people in China and the Middle East began to keep herds and cultivate the earth, rather than simply foraging for wild plants and game. Once again the population growth rate abated after the initial productivity gains from the new technology had been exploited, and population size settled down to a near plateau, as compared with the rapid growth experienced for a while. The known methods of making a living constituted a constraint to further population growth once the world's population reached a certain size.

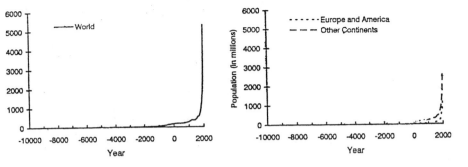

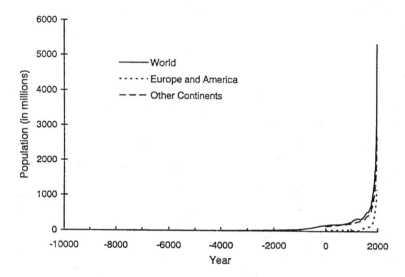

Fig. 31. Population from 10,000 to present. (Adapted from Kremer 1993, 683; McEvedy and Jones 1978.)

The sharp rise and subsequent fall in the rate of population growth suggest to many that the present rapid growth — which began perhaps 300 or 350 years ago, in the 1600s — may taper off again when, or if, the gains from the explosion of industrial and agricultural knowledge that followed the "industrial revolution" begin to dwindle. And population size may again reach a near plateau and remain there until the occurrence of another "revolution" due to another major change in technology, society, or psychology. Of course, the current knowledge revolution may continue without foreseeable end, and population growth may or may not continue as long as the revolution does or even beyond the revolution. (I foresee no "final" plateau, preposterous as that seems to many demographers, but there is no evidence to back one's belief in other directions.) Either way, in this long-term view population size adjusts to productive conditions rather than being an uncontrolled juggernaut.

Regarding economic progress: During most of the past millennia, economic progress was very slow or nonexistent. This is proven by jobbing backward; one spreads total growth over a long period of time, which implies a very low average rate, though it is difficult to find meaningful indicators (see fig. 32). As Kuznets puts it: "[G]iven the state of human knowledge in the earlier period, potentialities for economic growth were narrow" (1965, 8).[1]

Evidence from the modern period (figs. 33 and 34) demonstrates that economic growth in the developed countries has been faster in more recent decades than in more distant decades when population was smaller (see the work of Abramovitz and David in Abramovitz 1989; Maddison 1991; Fellner 1970; and Meguire in correspondence, August 1993, the latter finding that the U.S. data do not square with the other

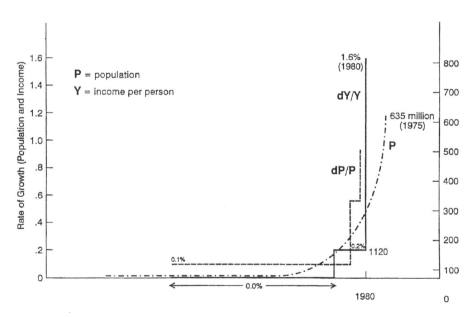

Fig. 32. Growth of population and income in Europe. (Adapted from Maddison, McEvedy and Jones 1978.)

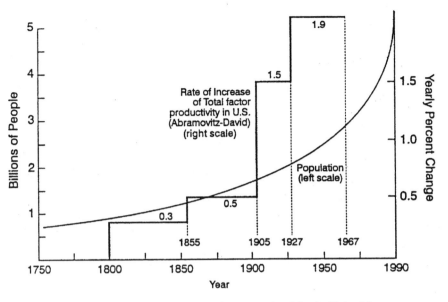

Fig. 33. Rate of increase of total factor productivity in United States.

countries' data, though it is logically necessary that growth now be faster than [say] 200 years ago.)

To recapitulate, it seems clear that sometime after 1000 or 1500 C.E. total population began to rise in Europe and in the world and also that individual consumption did not begin its rise until about 1750. Hence we can say that the former variable preceded the latter.

The *rate* of population *growth* (or mortality or life expectancy at birth, its almost-equivalents in the historical context of fairly stable fertility)[2] is a separate matter, however. Life expectancy is perhaps the most meaningful measure of economic progress through the ages, because of its intrinsic importance and also because many reliable data are available. It increased only very slowly from the minimum level at which the species could be sustained rather than going extinct. Figure 1 (chap. 1) is the stylized diagram of life expectancy over the past ten millennia, and figure 5 (chap. 1) portrays the past couple of centuries. We would like to know whether the rates of growth of population and of life expectancy increased considerably before the rate of consumption growth did so.

Kuznets thought that the population growth rate rose earlier than did growth in personal income.

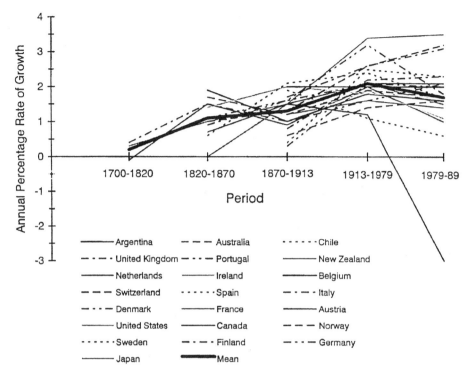

Fig. 34a. Growth rates of output per person, by period, various countries (Adapted from Moore 1993, table 5–1.)

There is a suggestion (in the record of the United States before 1840, of Sweden before the 1880's, even of Great Britain before the 1820's) that the acceleration in the rate of growth of population is initiated before that in growth of per capita income: the swarming of population, to use the demographers' term [more a biologist's term than a demographer's], is such that despite the technological changes the rise in total income can barely keep up with or only slightly exceeds the increase in numbers. It is only with some lag, as the high rate of population growth becomes stabilized or begins to decline and as the process of industrialization gets into full swing, that a significant increase in the rate of growth of per capita income is attained. This early phase, rapid rates of growth of population and total income but not of per capita income, is in many ways crucial. To this phase belong the early shifts in structure of the economy, away from agriculture and toward industry. It is in this

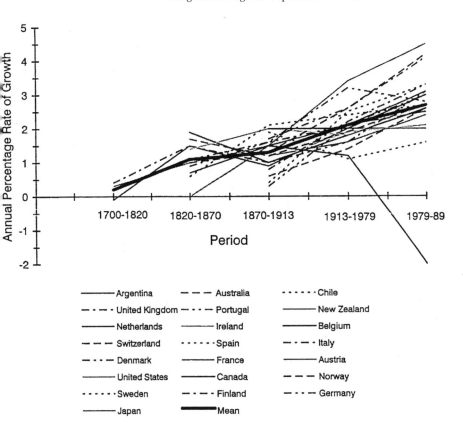

Data for period 1979-1989 incremented by 1 percent for each country in accord with possible adjustment to Consumer Price Index in the United States.

Fig. 34*b*. Growth rates of output per person, by period, various countries; incremented by 1 percent, 1979–89 (Adapted from Moore 1993, table 5–1.)

phase that rapid adjustments must be made to the changing conditions constituted by the differential impact on the several classes of population swarming and of the technological changes made possible by the same factor that made for larger numbers. (1965, 21)

Time Order and the Inference of Causality

The previous paragraphs asserted that population size increased earlier than did economic progress and other variables. To bring out this point, the stocks of population and of other variables are indexed as equal at present numbers in figure 35 (a device for standardizing). It then is seen that the rise of population has been at a slower rate in the later period, and at a faster rate in the earlier period, than the standard of living and the other variables to be shown later. And while a comparison of a stock versus a rate is difficult to make meaningfully, the size of the total population, or perhaps the rate of population increase, certainly seems to have grown more slowly than the speed of transport and communication, computing capacity, and the like. All these admittedly vague comparisons suggest that population size was a leading variable, which gives it some presumption of being the causal force.

Cross-National Evidence Relating Population and Living Standard

A work tradition that began with Rostas (1948) shows that when pairs of countries are compared, growth in productivity is higher in those industries in which more is produced. This association between higher production and higher population, ceteris paribus, suggests that higher population leads to higher productivity increases (see figs. 36a and 36b).

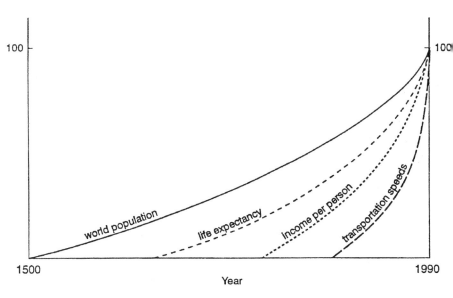

Fig. 35.   Rises of key measures relative to present sizes, 1500–1900 (stylized)

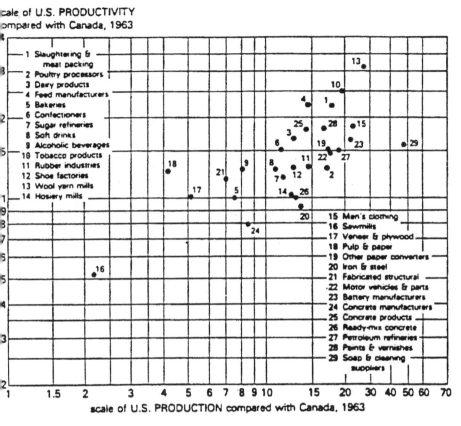

Fig. 36a. Scale of U.S. productivity compared with Canada, 1963.
(Adapted from West 1971, 18–22.)

The Rostas-tradition findings seem to show a process of learning by doing. This squares with the time-series data on learning by doing in particular industries, a phenomenon that is very clearly a function of population size. Higher population size implies higher demand, which implies higher volume, which implies more opportunities for learning by doing, which implies more learning and higher productivity. Indeed, the entire history of humanity may be thought of as the concave-upward envelope of concave-downward individual learning-by-doing functions, as in figure 37.

Cross-national comparison of the data for recent decades reveals that higher population density is correlated robustly with a higher rate of

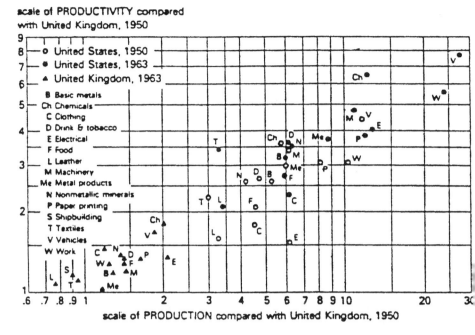

Fig. 36b. Scale of productivity compared with United Kingdom, 1950. (From Clark 1967, 265.)

economic growth (Simon and Gobin 1980; Kelley and Schmidt 1995; see figs. 38*a* and 38*b*). And another set of data shows that the rate of scientific productivity is proportional to population size, holding income constant (fig. 39).

Population and the Growth of Technology

Getting more specific about measures of progress now: The next set of evidence concerns the bivariate relationships between population size and such other variables as technology and physical productivity over the period for which at least some data exist to check for causality.

Agricultural Technology

A long-run measure of the stock of agricultural technology — perhaps the most important kind of knowledge at the early stages of economic

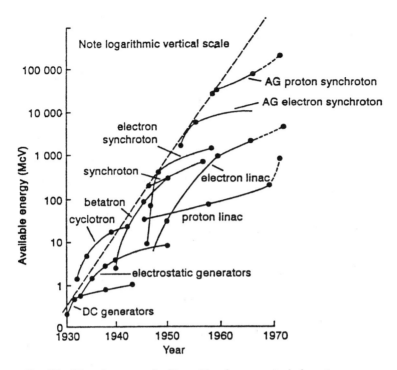

Fig. 37. "Envelope curve" of transition from one technique to another: Energy machines. (From Rescher 1978, 177.)

development—is the number of persons that a single agricultural worker can feed. The complementary variable is the proportion of the labor force that works in agriculture. Throughout human history that proportion has encompassed nearly the entire labor force. But around 1600 this proportion began to decline in the richest countries, and it now stands at less than 2 percent in some affluent countries, as shown in figures 40, 41, and 42. The decline has unmistakably begun in the poor parts of the world such as India, too.

A closely related measure of agricultural technology (as indicated by agricultural productivity per person) is the price in labor time of a given quantity of food. Figure 43 shows that since 1800 this price has fallen in the United States by a factor of perhaps 20 (Simon and Sullivan 1989, Simon 1981).

A measure of technology related to productivity per person is productivity per unit of land—that is, the amount of land employed to feed an average person. Figure 44 shows that the quantity of land needed to

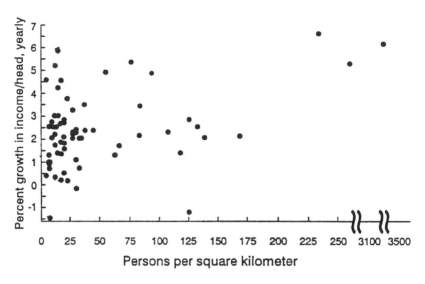

Fig. 38a.   Bivariate relationship of population density and per capita income growth. (From Simon and Gobin 1980.)

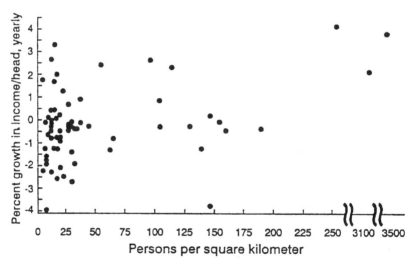

Fig. 38b.   Relationship between population density and income growth after allowance for population growth. (From Simon and Gobin 1980.)

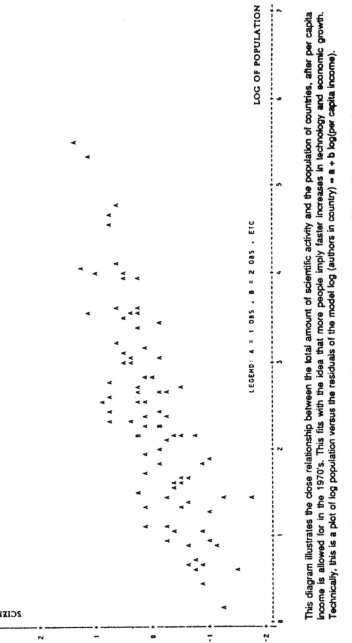

This diagram illustrates the close relationship between the total amount of scientific activity and the population of countries, after per capita income is allowed for in the 1970's. This fits with the idea that more people imply faster increases in technology and economic growth. Technically, this is a plot of log population versus the residuals of the model log (authors in country) = a + b log(per capita income).

Fig. 39.   Relationship of scientific activity to population size. (From Simon 1978a.)

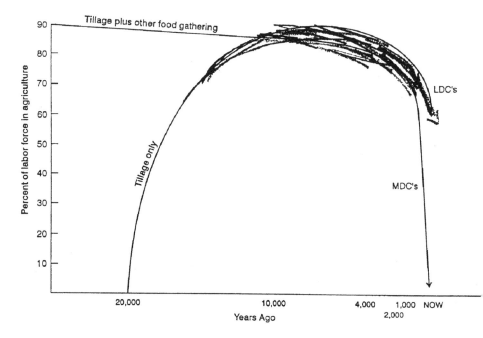

Fig. 40. Proportion of labor force in agriculture (stylized)

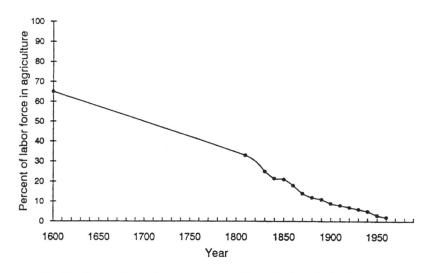

Fig. 41. Proportions of persons engaged in agriculture in the United Kingdom, 1600 to present (From Mitchell and Deane 1962.)

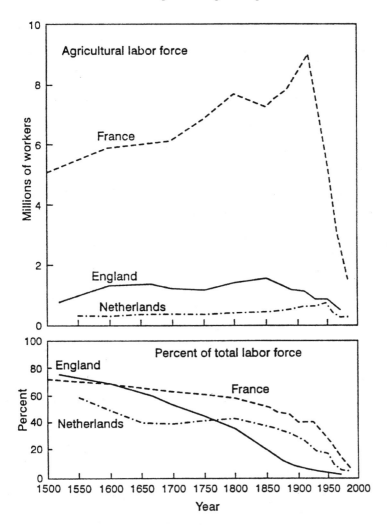

Fig. 42. Agricultural labor force in England, the Netherlands, and France. (From Sullivan 1995.)

feed a person has declined extraordinarily over the years; measured by "best commercial practice," it has fallen by a factor of perhaps 25 million compared with hunting and fishing and by almost as much in standard practice. This indicates an extraordinary increase in productivity.

Still another measure of agricultural technology is yields of particular crops per acre (see figs. 30*a* and 30*b* in chap. 2). It is relevant that

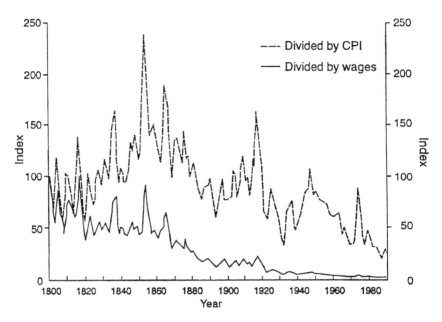

Fig. 43. Wheat prices indexed by wages and consumer price index

despite the vast experience in agriculture over thousands of years, the increase in recent decades has been particularly rapid. This shows the opposite of the diminishing gains over time that one might expect from a narrowly construed learning curve.

Technology in Metals Production

Analogous to the decline in the price of food, as measured by the amount of time required to produce it, is the decline in metal prices. The decline with respect to the price of labor in rich countries has been enormous, as seen in figure 45 for copper for the last five millennia. The price decline has been large even compared with the consumer price index over the past two centuries (fig. 46; Simon 1996). Another indication of an increase in supply is the observed increase in known reserves as a multiple of yearly consumption. These data are shown for a variety of metals in figure 47, and for oil in figure 48.

The increases in production of the metals over the centuries and millennia — which may be considered an index of increases in both supply and demand — also are relevant evidence. These, too, are shown in figure 47.

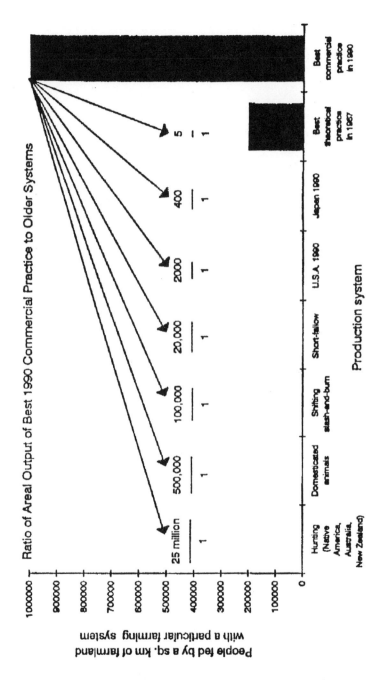

Fig. 44. Number of people fed by a square kilometer of farmland under various food production systems. (Adapted from Clark 1957; Clark and Haswell 1967.)

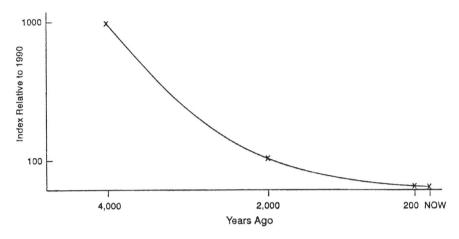

Fig. 45.   Price of copper relative to rich-country labor

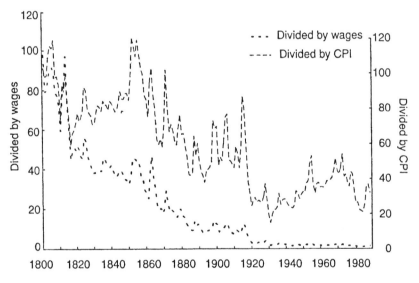

Fig. 46.   The scarcity of copper as measured by its prices relative to
wages and to the consumer price index. (From Simon 1996, 25.)

The supply of copper may be viewed in this context both as a final
good and as a component measure of the standard of living. It may also
be seen as an element in the progress of general productivity. As will be
discussed in more detail later, the causation from population to price
seems rather clear here. There is no other reasonable explanation for

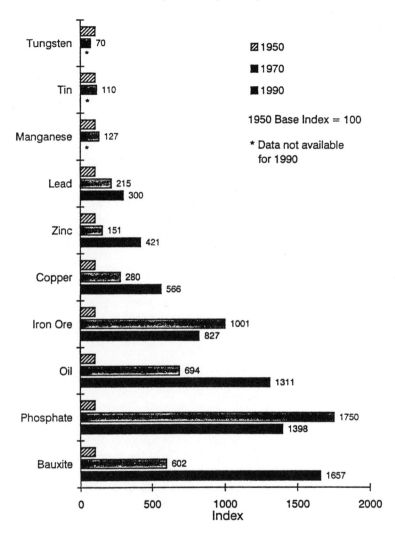

Fig. 47.   Known world reserves of selected natural resources, 1950, 1970, 1990. (From Simon, Weinrauch, and Moore 1994.)

the increase in supply of copper and other natural resources except increases in the demand for goods and in the supply of minds to invent new ways to produce goods and invent new substitutes.

Further discussion of natural resources and population may be found in the "Natural Resources and Population" section of this chapter (see also Simon 1996).

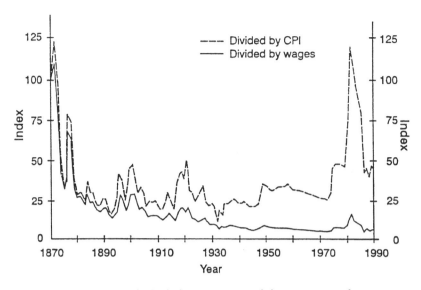

Fig. 48.   The price of oil relative to wages and the consumer price index in the United States

Transportation

Transportation is a good in itself as well as a component in producing the supply of food and other goods. And it is another product whose technology has improved greatly, as measured by speed and cost. Stylized measures of speed are shown in figures 49, 50*a*, and 50*b*. In just the past two centuries speed has risen from the three-mile-an-hour walking pace of a human,[3] or the somewhat faster pace of a horse or ship, to hundreds of miles per hour on land, thousands of miles per hour in the air, and even faster in space. Figures 51 and 52 provide data for interurban travel over the years in England and in the United States.

In a cross-national study, Glover and Simon (1975) show that road density is greater where population is more dense[4] (see fig. 53). And roads are a crucial element in the transmission of knowledge. A study relating population density to the provision of electricity finds an analogous result (Frederiksen 1981).

Other Advances in Technology

Other technological advances of the past century or less also point to increases in the rates of change so large as to deserve the label "break-

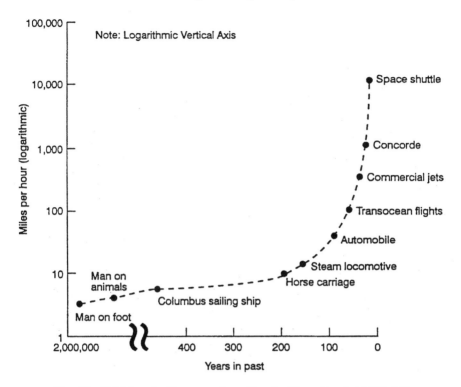

Fig. 49. Vehicle velocities over the millennia. (From Cambel 1993, 84.)

through." The advances include the speed of computing (from counting on fingers to computers), the intensity of lightning (from fires to lasers), the speed of communication of messages (starting with the telegraph, in comparison to the carrier pigeon), and the precision of measurement of time and other magnitudes (from sundials to nuclear clocks; Klein 1974). Until recently, there were no timekeeping aids at all to the daily cycle of the sun. After hundreds of thousands of years of excruciatingly slow progress, we now have highly precise devices for measuring time.

Printing may have been the earliest process to take off into rapid production, starting with Gutenberg in the fifteenth century. The abacus and mathematical algorithms may be another outstanding early example.

When graphed, many of the advances in technology have been so sudden that their values were zero before the twentieth century or even before the last few decades of the twentieth century; examples include various measures of genetic research and computer engineering. And many of the advances have been so sudden that logarithmic graphs are

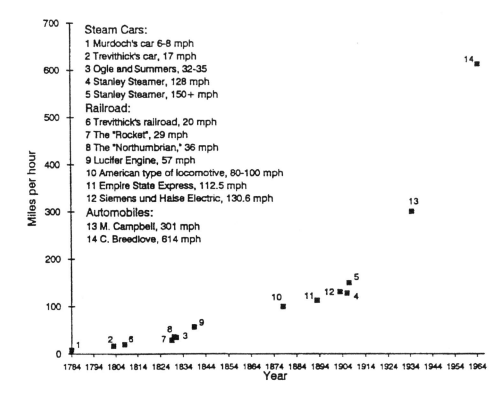

Fig. 50a.   Top speed of ground transport of humans, 1784–1967.

needed to plot their data. In many cases, linear plots look like a horizontal line, a kink, and a vertical line.

Concerning communication: Is there a single early instance of any task whose execution was sped up nearly so rapidly in anywhere near so short a time as printing sped up the production of words on paper? Indeed, there seem to be few tasks that could be done even 10 times as rapidly in the sixteenth century as 1,000 years earlier. Exceptions may include some water-powered tasks such as grinding; some arithmetic operations; and perhaps early factory operations such as pinmaking and clock construction.[5] But aside from the discovery of fire for heat and light, printing—followed by the steam engine, the telegraph, and perhaps vaccination and pasteurization—was the first invention whose benefits were revolutionary and discontinuous rather than incremental.

Intercontinental communications offer another spectacular case.

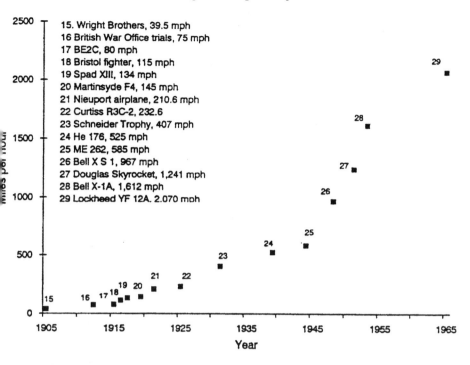

Fig. 50*b*.   Top speed of air transport of humans, 1905–65 (excluding space travel).

Up to the 1830s, a letter from Europe to India took five to eight months to round the Cape on a sailing ship. To receive an answer might take as long as two years. By the 1850s, the combination of train and steamer could bring a letter from London to Calcutta in thirty to forty-five days. By the 1870s, submarine cable had been laid and a message from Britain to India could be answered the same day. (Curtin 1984, 252)

Indeed, the message traveled back and forth at almost the speed of light.

Figures 29*a* and 29*b* in chapter 2 provided long-run data on increases in the stock of knowledge (as measured by the number of scientific journals and patents in the past five centuries) and in human capital (as measured by numbers of literate persons and of persons with given amounts of education). In both cases, the absolute numbers are more

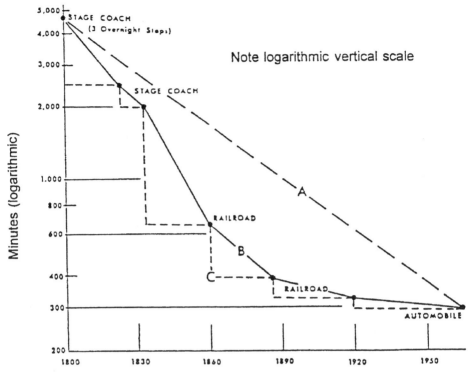

Fig. 51.   Travel time, New York to Boston, 1800-1965. (From Janelle 1968, 7.)

relevant than the proportions, although the proportions also are relevant here.

Some writers have suggested ancient Greece and Rome as counterexamples to the hypothesized connection between population and knowledge production. But the rates of discoveries of important new ideas were fastest at the peak ancient periods of population (see figs. 54 and 55).

Another long period whose data are relevant is the Dark Ages. Nowadays most commentators, including Pirenne, agree that after population declined, the standard of living fell and technological progress ceased despite the increase in agricultural land per agriculturalist and the consequent drop in the price of land; this retrogression might have been caused by the decline in total population, or by the lack of its growth, or by both.

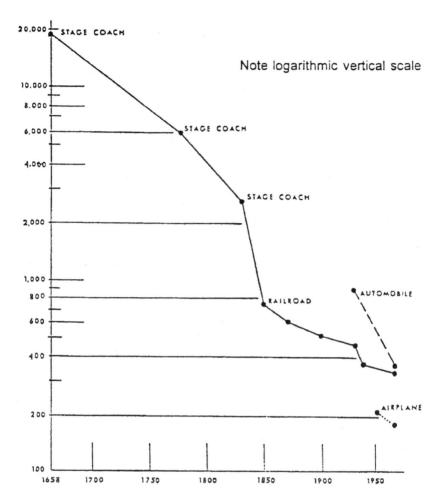

Fig. 52. Travel time, Edinburgh to London, 1658–1966. (From Janelle 1968, 6.)

Much the same seems to have been true of technological progress in the years after the Black Death. Slicher writes:

There is little new to report concerning farm implements in this period [1350–1450, which he referred to as a "depression"], nor, for that matter about farming literature. Agriculture had clearly lost the interest of the general public. These were difficult years for the peasants to endure. (1963, 144)

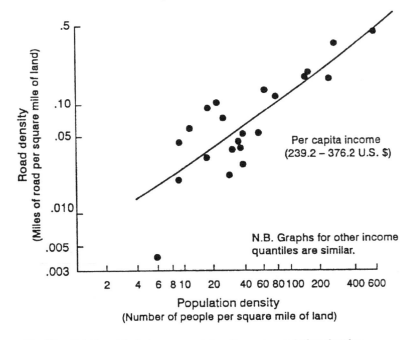

Fig. 53.   Relationship between road density and population density. (From Glover and Simon 1975.)

He adds that in the Netherlands,

> Reclamation and polder-making had come to a stop. . . . In some parts there was sand erosion. . . . In other places land was lost by inundation. Men no longer had the courage to fight the waters and win back their lost territory. (1963, 142)

In contrast, the rapid increases in population starting around 1000 and 1500 were accompanied by buoyant economic progress as well as the exuberant building of cathedrals.

Simon and Sullivan (1989) show that in England from 1500 to 1800 population and knowledge (as measured by patents) do not just grow together secularly; rather, there is a causal relationship between them when other variables are held constant.

Progress in Social Organization and Practices

Sudden progress after 1750 or 1800 may also be seen in social practices and organization. Figure 3 in chapter 1 shows that after remaining al-

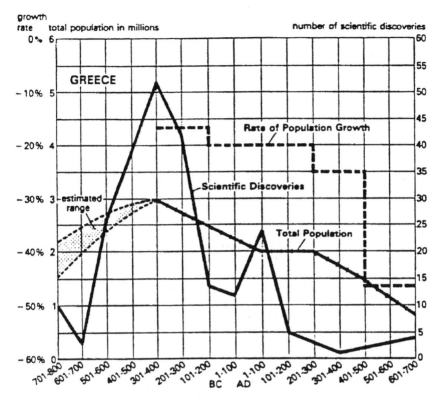

Fig. 54.   Population and scientific discoveries in ancient Greece.
(Adapted from Sorokin 1978, 148; Clark 1957; McEvedy and Jones
1978.)

most constant at very low levels throughout most of history, the urbanization rate suddenly began to shoot up worldwide, so that by the end of
the twenty-first century most of the world's population surely will live in
cities. And figures 15, 16, and 17 in chapter 1 show an astonishing rise in
literacy, from almost none at all to almost complete literacy in the developed countries. As of the close of the twentieth century, progress is
being made toward this state of literacy in the poorer countries, too.

Disconfirming Evidence in Cumulative Population?

One might consider the long-run cumulative population history as
disconfirming the basic proposition of this essay. The total number of

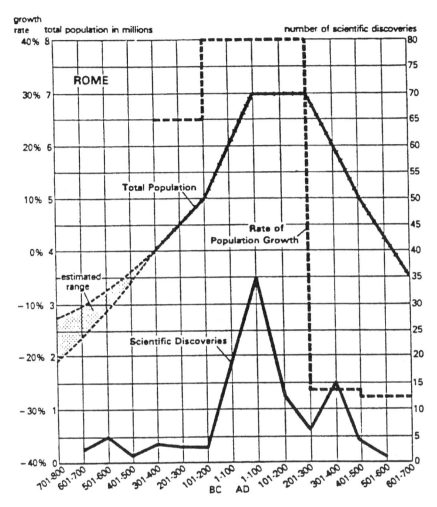

Fig. 55. Population and scientific discoveries in ancient Rome. (Adapted from Sorokin 1978, 148; Clark 1957; McEvedy and Jones 1978.)

human beings who ever lived before (say) 6,000 years ago was not small (see fig. 9 in chap. 1). A reasonable estimate is that of the 77 billion human beings born from 600,000 B.C.E. to 1962 C.E., 12 billion lived before 6000 B.C.E. (Desmond 1975).[6] These figures are to be compared with the less than six billion who may be alive now. Of course many of the people born in earlier years died at young ages. Even so, the number of years of human life lived on Earth in the long-ago past was not small relative to any recent period. This raises the question of whether these numbers are inconsistent with the total intellectual production in various periods and hence confute the thesis of this essay. I shall argue to the contrary.

Before explaining the aspects of this matter that seem to be inconsistent on the surface, let us notice that at least certain compilations of knowledge do seem to have been the result of a large number of earlier minds. These include the Hebrew Bible, other ancient religious writings, and the great dramas of the Greeks. Many moderns have been amazed that the relatively small total population of Israelites could have produced the glories of the wisdom books of the Bible. But there is clear evidence that the Bible drew upon earlier writings of earlier peoples, such as Babylonian accounts of the creation. It is quite reasonable to suppose that among peoples who were mainly illiterate there should have been a great deal of oral transmission of such sayings as "Don't give me your honey because I don't want your sting." "So teach us to number our days that we may get a heart of wisdom" (Psalms 90:12) is another saying that probably has been in currency for millennia.[7] The same line of thought might apply to the dramas of the Greeks. And the outcroppings of such collections of the past might well be expected in peoples who were long-distance traders such as the Greeks, or were on long-distance trading routes, as were the Jews of ancient Israel.

Indeed, one might also expect a greater amount of such oral transmission in those earlier times than now, because there was less new material coming into people's perceptions. The reasoning here is analogous to that of the observation that French and English writers in the eighteenth century were more likely to rely on the classics than are writers of the late twentieth century.

Now to consider the harder case of whether the numbers for the cumulative populations of the past are inconsistent with the total intellectual production in various periods. If so, the thesis of this essay might be refuted. The production of knowledge does not depend upon the number of human minds alone. If it did, total medical progress during the long period before (say) 6000 b.c.e., during which life expectancy increased only a few years, should have been as great as in (say) the last 50 years, during which life expectancy increased rapidly and hugely. But earlier progress was nowhere near that fast. Many humans who lived in early millennia apparently produced little new knowledge, as the slow progress in the healing arts attests. The absence of rapid population growth as a stimulus is not a reasonable explanation of this slow progress in medicine. The presence of sickness and the danger of death certainly have at all times been sufficiently powerful motivations to induce major efforts at innovation. So this evidence immediately requires that a theory be more complex than the total number of persons alive among whom the spark of invention and progress might somehow arise spontaneously.

The most reasonable additional explanatory variables are the existing stock of knowledge, the population size and density, and the availability of a written means of recording and storing knowledge.

In historic times production of new knowledge is known to have been influenced by the *stock of existing knowledge.* The more existing ideas that could be built on, the greater the propensity to create new ideas. This is demonstrated for the case of patents in England over many centuries by Simon and Sullivan (1989). There is every reason to believe that this pattern applies to prehistoric times, too, when there was a much smaller stock of knowledge to serve as the basis for new knowledge. This element will be discussed in more detail in the next section of this chapter.

Population *density* promotes the production and transmission of new ideas, according to the theory of Simon Kuznets and the study by Kelley (1972) of Higgs's data on American inventiveness (1971). The relative propensity for urban and rural people to make inventions, in three countries in various periods in the eighteenth and nineteenth centuries, is shown in table 6. Indices above unity indicate a higher urban propensity to invent, and such a propensity is shown throughout the table. The data for place of birth, together with the data on the place of residence, are more telling than are data for urban residence when shown in isolation, because they are not subject to the possibility of self-selection of urban residence on the part of inventors. The correlation

TABLE 6.   Relative Propensity for Urban and Rural People to Invent

	Place of Birth		Place of Innovation	
	Period	Concentration Index[a]	Period	Concentration Index[a]
United Kingdom	1700–1780	2.6	1760–1820	3.9
	1780–1820	3.3	1820–1880	2.3
	1820–1860	1.8	1880–1900	1.4
France	1800–1830	5.3	1800–1850	6.1
	1830–1880	3.6	1850–1900	3.6
Germany	1800–1840	5.5	1800–1850	7.1
	1840–1860	4.9	1850–1900	3.2

Source: Bairoch 1988, 325.
[a]Relation between relative population of urban places where the inventors were born or resided and the relative urban population.

between the measures using birthplace and residence lends credence to data on place of residence used in other studies, such as the following.

[T]he approximately 57 per cent of the population who resided in standard metropolitan areas (in 1945) or within twenty-five miles of the central city of such an area received (in 1947–48) approximately 90 per cent of the patents granted in sixteen selected patent classes covering chemistry, metal, machinery and engine products and processes. (Thompson 1962, 259)

Jane Jacobs (1969, chap. 1) argues with impressive anecdotes that even ideas that were mainly practiced in the countryside and have long been thought to have been developed there—for example, cottage-industry textile production and even agriculture (though there is much counterevidence for that proposition)—were really invented in cities and then diffused to the countryside. Density is an index of both the *supply of* new technology, through the number of trained minds to produce new ideas, and *demand,* including (1) the number of producers who will use the new techniques (e.g., the tablet writing that was used by merchants in Assyria to keep track of their transactions); and (2) consumers who will buy the products that are supplied with the new techniques. Slicher was quoted earlier saying that there was no new literature on farming in the years following the great plague because land was so abundant and population so scarce. Population density was mostly very low in prehistoric times, which helps explain the slow growth of knowledge during that long period when many people lived (See Simon 1992 for more discussion of supply and demand in the market for new technology).

Population density also speeds the production of new ideas by supplying more sources of information. Figures 56*a* and 56*b* show that larger places are more likely to have institutions of higher learning and of the arts, as well as more media of communications. Duncan (1956) notes that "libraries . . . generally meet desirable minimum professional standards only in cities as large as 50,000–75,000" (381). Surprisingly, however, Duncan found that per capita use of libraries and of museums (where they existed) was lower in larger cities than in smaller cities (351).

There also is evidence for the effect of *demand* for new inventions, in data on the relationship of city dwelling to the rate of invention. Khan and Sokoloff found, in patent data from 1790 to 1846, that there was a concentration of inventions in southern New England and New York, prime markets (discussed in Campbell 1996, 10).

In early times there was no mechanism for the recording and diffusion of new hypotheses and tests. There was no writing, let alone printing.

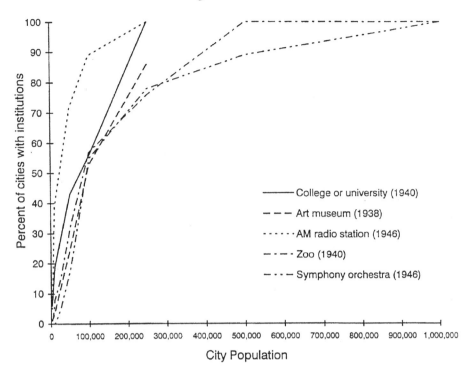

Fig. 56a. Presence of institutions and city size (linear population scale). (From Spengler and Duncan 1956, 381–82.)

The absence of widespread printing may have been a major constraint in China in the century or more after the first development of printing in Europe just before 1500; more about this in chapter 5.

The Accumulation of an Infrastructure of Knowledge and Skill

The fact that so many of the graphs of technical and institutional achievement turn upward so sharply within the 1900s and 1800s seems at first inconsistent with the great achievements over thousands of years in building awesome monuments and edifices and the enormous accumulations of knowledge about mathematics, metallurgy, mining, and other engineering (including the maneuvering of very heavy weights). An important part of the post-1750 achievements was those that required a wide complex of precision skills that act in a complementary fashion.

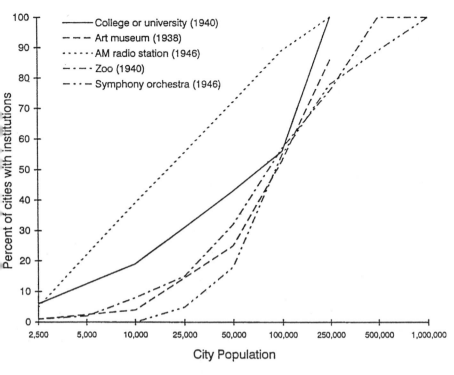

Fig. 56*b*. Presence of institutions and city size (arbitrarily innumerated population scale). (From Spengler and Duncan 1956, 381–82.)

This important idea has been adduced elsewhere in this essay in discussion of the development of the navigational chronometer and of the steam engine, following North (1981), Rosenberg (1976), David (1975), and Mokyr (1990a). But it bears amplification by quotation, because these authors know and tell this important story much better than I could.

[B]etween 1500 and 1750 . . . there was no scarcity of bold and novel technical ideas, [but] the constraints of workmanship and materials to turn them into reality became binding. . . . [T]he paddle-wheel boats, calculating machines, submarines, parachutes, fountain pens, steam-operated vehicles, power looms, and ball-bearings envisaged in this age — interesting as they are to the historian of ideas — had no economic impact because they could not be made practical. (Mokyr 1990a, 35)

Much apparatus was conceived long before there was any effective possibility of making it, and the tone of struggle and frustration that appears in the lives of the inventors of the sixteenth and seventeenth centuries may be largely explained by the degree to which their power to conceive had outstripped their power to give material substance to their dreams. (Usher 1988, 112)

Mechanics had to build their own parts, and often the gap between the visionary who saw what *might* be done and the craftsmen whose material and tools limited what *could* be done was too wide to be bridged. The most famous of these visionaries was of course Leonardo da Vinci, whose mechanical brilliance was on a par with his other talents. Leonardo left us with five thousand pages of unpublished notebooks, much of which dealt with machinery. Yet the Last Supper notwithstanding, Da Vinci's technical creativity produced few free lunches, and his technical insights were rarely realized in his lifetime. Neither, for that matter, did the equally prophetic technical dreams of Leonardo's precursor, Francesco di Giorgio (1439–1502). As we shall see, the Industrial Revolution became possible when mechanics and machine tools could translate the ideas and blueprints into accurate and reliable prototypes. Until then instruments and tools were handmade, expensive to make and repair, and limited in their uses. (Mokyr 1990a, 45)

The last quarter of the eighteenth century is marked by the beginning of a rapid development of methods of refining and working iron, which opened up new uses of iron and steel and soon led to the building of industrial machinery of iron. The new technique of machine building, with some modifications and extensions, also made it possible to produce large quantities of metal wares for general consumption. The highest development of the new technique appears in the system of interchangeable-part manufacture — the manufacture of individual parts within such limits of accuracy that the complete device can be assembled without any significant shaping and fitting. The development of new methods for the production of iron made these new achievements possible; the invention of the steam engine made them immediately essential. Smeaton's comment on the model of the engine is significant. He reported to the Society of Engineers that "neither the tools nor the workmen existed that could manufacture so complex a machine with sufficient precision." At that time Smeaton must inevitably have regarded himself as one of the foremost authorities on machine building. He was then engaged in the manufacture of atmospheric engines, mills, pumps, and other large work. He had developed the compass of the boring machine to produce cylinders for engines and compressed-air pumps for blowing iron furnaces. But he was obliged to tolerate errors in his cylinders, amounting to the thickness of the little finger in a cylinder 28 inches in diameter. Watt had an early cylinder with an error of 3/8 inch. The beginnings of the new development are thus most significantly marked by improvements in the boring machine by Wilkinson (about 1776), which enabled him to deliver adequate cylinders to Boulton and Watt. His achievement made the steam engine immediately practical, though the early engines left much to be desired in accuracy of workmanship despite steady improvement in methods. The great balance beam was thus long retained, because it was not possible to make surfaces accurate enough to enable the engine builder to attach the crosshead to the crank. It was left to Maudslay to make this simplification in the machine after his improvements in machine tools. Each new step forward in tool building thus resulted in practical increases in mechanical efficiency of the whole set of machines.

This rapid conquest of such a new field indicates clearly that the times were ripe for the change, for, in many instances, concepts as brilliant as those of Watt have failed of immediate development in the face of apparently less serious difficulties of application. It is thus especially important to define with some measurable accuracy the conditions that prepared the ground for these truly great achievements in metalworking. The final achievement was based upon improvements in the design of certain basic machine tools, the development of rolling mills, heavy forge work, and the casting of malleable iron in wet green sand. Though these were originally separate accomplishments, the possibility of a new synthesis was perceived towards the close of the eighteenth century. When fully developed, this synthesis brought about more far-reaching economic changes than any previous group of technological innovations. (Usher 1988, 358–60)

Usher wrote of the turbine:

The complete machine involves mechanical features of a high order, not readily appreciated by the layman. The rotor is, of course, enclosed in a casing, which must be closely adjusted to prevent leaking of steam. The accuracy of workmanship required would have been unattainable prior to 1840. Owing to the difficulty of making the center of mass coincide exactly with the center of revolution, some allowance must be made for play on the bearings and specially designed bearings were essential. The speeds attained required grades of steel that could not have been produced with certainty much before the latter part of the nineteenth century. Reducing gears were required of better workmanship than any previously produced. The realization of a principle conceived in the seventeenth century thus involved most of the primary technological achievements of the entire intervening [*sic*] period. (Usher 1988, 394)

Here is another example.

Only after John Wilkinson's boring mill (in 1776) eliminated gaps between pistons and cylinders (which had previously been stuffed with rags) and William Murdock's sun and planet gearing system (in 1781) provided a means of converting vertical motion into rotary force did the steam engine become a generally useful source of power.[8] (Young 1993, 446)

The story of the development of the mechanical clock in the seventeenth and eighteenth centuries, eventuating in a marine chronometer accurate enough to serve in the measurement of longitude for navigation, is illuminating (Landes 1983; Sobel 1995). John Harrison, the man who finally turned the trick in 1726, was a genius as an artisan; nevertheless, it is unlikely that he could have succeeded a century earlier, because the necessary techniques and materials and tools were not available. And Usher tells us that "the achievements of Bradley's clock of 1758 were essentially new; they would have been unattainable as late as 1700, and not possible to good workmen for some time after the important work of Graham in 1715" (1988, 315).

In some cases the modern achievements also required the ability to bring to bear materials collected from a large geographical span. A pyramid or cathedral can be built largely with a few kinds of local materials, or with material from only one or two remote locations, and the construction requires relatively few precise machines and skills. But until the nineteenth century (or perhaps the eighteenth century) the machinery did not exist to mass-produce (say) rifles with interchangeable parts. And even if one had complete instructions of all kinds, one probably could not have produced as simple a device as an alarm-clock radio with a snooze alarm before a few decades ago. Also, the explosion of new medical advances in the latter part of the twentieth century illustrates the interdependence of advances in a variety of technologies.[9]

Here we must distinguish, along with thoughtful historians of science, between science and applied technology, perhaps distinguishing both from technical skills. A scientific discovery can occur almost in isolation and in the absence of other skills. Think of Newton and gravitation and the work of the European probabilists, including Pascal and Bernoulli. But the steam engine could not be built before the existence of the necessary metalworking technology. Therefore, the appropriate production function for the technology in a given industry may well depend upon the states of technology in other industries.[10] And with the passage of time the number of relevant existing technologies increases, which increases the number of terms in equation (9a) and pushes the function up even faster, explaining the very rapid acceleration in recent times. This is very much a case of increasing returns, at a rapidly increasing rate, though a more general function is usually comprehended by the term *increasing returns*. The term *coalescing* describes the process under discussion.

The accumulation of science and general knowledge can take place without the results appearing in practical applications for a long time. For example, knowledge accumulated for eons about how to travel through the air — insights into jumping, swinging on vines, hot air balloons, and the like — before the first airplane took off.

The process of coalescing can be seen in the progress of life expectancy. The transition to low mortality required (at a minimum) improved nutrition, better sanitation, and new medical practices such as vaccination. Each of these was the result of earlier gains in knowledge that had no immediate effect upon health, as well as increases in numbers that led to better transport and hence better famine relief; greater density in cities that (though they initially were less healthy) resulted in such discoveries[11] as the mechanism of transmission of cholera.

Discontinuity in the Analysis

The discontinuity of the SMP process, evidence for which was offered in chapter 1, requires discussion because in economics continuous processes are the norm. Not all economic phenomena need be considered continuous, however. There is some analogy here to a bingo game. This game is in state zero until the event of the completion of a row occurs, at which point someone hollers, "Bingo," and the game turns to state one.

There are many models of such discontinuities in the natural sciences. They include the following: (1) the sudden fall of a temporarily stationary raindrop on a windowpane; (2) a baby starting to climb steps and beginning to talk; (3) ice becoming hard enough for a person to walk on (the discontinuity being not in the ice formation but in what becomes possible for humans); (4) the proverbial straw that breaks the camel's back.

Even sharper discontinuities than portrayed here have been experienced in smaller microcosms. Consider, for example, the discontinuous peopling and development of the New World, following slow accumulation of such technology as an accurate chronometer and improvements in sailing ships, as well as the increasing population of Europe that increased the demand for agricultural land.

Economists tend to shy away from discontinuities for many good reasons. But one bad reason often operates, too: the mathematical difficulty that discontinuity causes, especially for the use of the calculus; the latter excuse should not be allowed to be operative here.[12]

Natural Resources and Population

Natural resources have been a major topic since the first recorded discussions of population growth. North began his *Structure and Change in Economic History* by remarking on "the basic tension that has been and remains the center of economic history—that between population and resources" (1981, 13). "[D]iminishing returns to the stock of natural resources has been the most critical economic dilemma of mankind" (6). Because of that tension, the issue must be raised here in order to dispose of it as an intellectual obstacle to the thrust of this essay. That is, the constraint of natural resources must be considered before one can accept a theory of past human progress despite the perceived limits of natural resources.[13] This section presents a short precis of the topic. Culled from my other writings, it gives the basic theory and data.

Astonishingly, the importance of land and other natural resources diminishes with every passing decade. Such was the great discovery of Theodore Schultz about land in 1951 and of Harold Barnett and Chandler Morse in 1963 (see also Hayek 1960, chap. 23) about agricultural and mined resources; extensive data on the declining prices of natural resources, and increasing known reserves of the mined resources, even as their quantities of production increased greatly, were shown earlier (see the "Technology in Metals Production" section in this chapter and figures therein). The forecasts of those writers, based on the historical record and theoretical analyses, have been borne out perfectly by events since then as food and all metals—indeed, all natural resources—have continued to get cheaper rather than more expensive (see figs. 44 and 45 as examples). Indeed, as Simon Kuznets was aware early on, natural resources have not been decisive in the development process. "[T]he supply of natural resources is a secondary factor in economic growth," and "natural-resource potential is a function of the changing stock of technological knowledge" (1965, 31). As North notes, "[I]n the modern era . . . science and technology have been wedded so that the overcoming of diminishing returns has been a reality (1981). The idea that a large amount of (say) farmland or copper deposits can make a country rich — a view held to their great detriment by such peoples as the Ukrainians following the breakup of the Soviet Union — is only a "commonsense" variant of this sad misconception.

The prescience of Schultz, and of Barnett, is illuminated by the failures of the conventional forecasts of resource scarcity using simple extrapolations of recent trends in prices and consumption. The most famous such prediction was that of Jevons in 1881 — that a shortage of coal would halt the expansion of Britain's industry by 1900. Jevons's prediction was followed by an amended forecast by Flux in 1904. Both forecasts are shown in figure 57. And figure 58 shows a more recent prediction, for mercury prices, by the eminent geologist Earl Cook, made amid the mid-1970s price run-up of all raw materials. Figure 59 then shows what happened after Cook's forecast was made.

Natural resources are the most dramatic examples of the fundamental process that has been at work in the long course of economic progress: Increasing population and/or rising income raises the demand for a commodity, which usually induces a higher price for awhile. The higher price represents an opportunity for businesses to make a profit and for inventors and institutions to realize their desires to make creative social contributions. Most prospective discoverers fail to find solutions to the problem, and they pay the cost themselves. Eventually, however, one or more seekers succeed in finding solutions. And the outcome — a most unexpected though very important phenomenon — is that the solution usually leaves humanity better off than before the problem arose. That is, the process ends up with cheaper resources than before the problem signaled by a rise in price first occurred.

The story of this process at work in the case of the supply of energy since about the fifteenth century in England — from wood to coal to oil to nuclear power — is told at greater length in Simon 1996, as is the story of copper during the 4,000 years since Hammurabi. The increase in the availability of the services that we seek from natural resources becomes even more dramatic when we observe not only the substitution among various energy sources and the decline in price of energy but also the decline in the amount of energy needed to produce our goods — from the

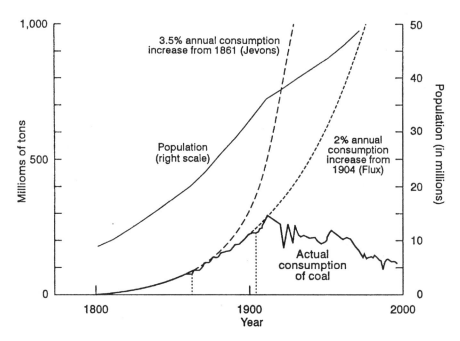

Fig. 57.   Forecasts versus actual consumption of coal in Great Britain,
1800–2000. (Adapted from Kates and Burton 1986, 397; Robinson 1992,
16; Mitchell 1978, A1, p. 8.)

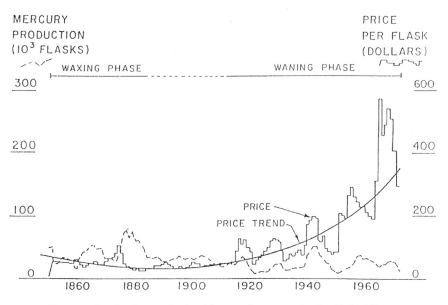

Fig. 58.   Production and price history of mercury in the United States

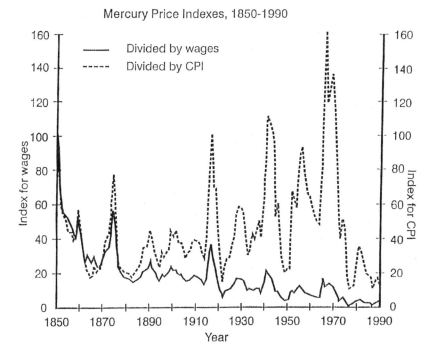

Fig. 59. Mercury price indexes, 1850–1990

1 percent efficiency of the early steam engines to the roughly 60 percent efficiency now and the tiny amount of energy needed to cook food in microwave ovens. The same story plays out in the substitution of space satellites and wireless telephonic communications for the huge amounts of copper used for copper telephone wires.[14]

A formal model of this process using the example of farmland may be found in Simon and Steinmann 1981; or in Simon 1992, (chap. 5). We simulated the model with meaningful parameters and analyzed how the course of food prices and land availability would change over centuries. We also analyzed the steady-state properties of the system to show how it is consistent with long-run growth in the standard of living as human numbers increase.

What Caused the Fall in Mortality?

We must be interested in the causes of the decrease in mortality as well as its course, because longer life promotes progress. It is usually assumed, conversely, that progress also produces better health and reduced mortality, and health certainly is valuable both as an intrinsic good and because of its positive effect upon progress. But if better health and consequent increased life expectancy are not endogenous to the system, that would complicate the analysis.

There has been a grand argument about the causes of the decline in mortality in the nineteenth and twentieth centuries. Most recently, Richard Easterlin (1995) has suggested that the rapid increase in life expectancy in the twentieth century (and it is important to note that the subject here is only the twentieth century) was independent of other improvements in consumption. "Neither facts nor theory support the view that the Mortality Revolution is due to the Industrial Revolution and the era of rapid economic growth that ensued. Rather, both revolutions mark the onset of accelerated and sustained technological change in their respective areas" (393).

Easterlin's assessment induces the following too-extended response about epidemic disease and its conquest. The subject is important to the argument of this essay for two reasons: (1) Epidemics affect the rate of growth of population, the crucial variable here. (2) The extent of the endogeneity, as a function of wealth and knowledge as well as population density, is important in the argument.

How one thinks about a problem affects one's aims — whether, for example, one seeks a causal explanation, or the basis for a forecast, or a model that would help one control a system's outcome (see Simon and Burstein 1985 for discussion of these various modes). In the case at hand, the aim is closest to the last of the three, to understand which counterfactual events, if they had occurred, would have led to which changes in outcomes. More specifically, the aim of the present section is to ask whether additions or subtractions of particular knowledge, and additions or subtractions of wealth levels, would have caused major changes in the speed of decline in mortality in the various centuries and countries. I do not seek to "explain" the decline in mortality in the sense that a regression model might do so.[15]

Easterlin bases his interpretation upon Preston's analysis (1975, 1980). "Preston (1975) found, contrary to the McKeown thesis, that economic growth played a very small role in the improvement of life expectancy, although his focus was on a somewhat later period, the 1930s to the 1960s (Easterlin 1995, 394). That is, Easterlin suggests that the cause of that decline in mortality is some unspecified force of technology that he likens to the "residual" in the economic-growth analyses of Abramovitz (1956) and Solow (1957). I do not think that this is a sound reading of either the facts or Preston.

Schofield and Reher also read in Preston's data that the twentieth-century mortality decline in poor countries was due to "the efficiency of public health technology" and that this operated "despite few improvements in the standard of living" (1991, 8–9). But they do not explicitly accompany Easterlin with respect to the creation of new knowledge in the twentieth century.

The labeling of the driving forces can induce important confusion. Vaccination certainly deserves the label "technology" in this context. But does sanitation deserve the label? Should sanitation's effect in the twentieth century be ascribed to wealth instead of to technology? I answer "yes" to this latter question, whereas Easterlin, if I understand him correctly, answers "no." My reason for answering affirmatively is that the knowledge that—together with wealth—produced improvements in twentieth-century sanitation (both public and private) was the continuation of a long process of improvements in knowledge of epidemic diseases since at least Old Testament days (see the following; and Winslow [1943] 1980, esp. chap. 6), a process of learning that combined both empirical knowledge and a gradually refined germ theory of disease. Most of the knowledge that was needed to impel the sanitation improvements in poor as well as rich countries in the twentieth century was known at the turn of the century or before. It was wealth (including injections of wealth by colonial nations) that mobilized this knowledge in the poor countries. Hence labeling is at the heart of this essay.

Though Schofield and Reher (1991) do not necessarily share Easterlin's view in general, they do consider public health and wealth creation as separate elements and opposing explanations of mortality decline. They submerge income in a more general factor they call "standard of living," as when they write that "income, nutrition, and other indicators of the standard of living cannot have been responsible for more than 25 percent of the rise in life expectancy at birth in a number of national populations during much of the twentieth century" (8). They quote Preston with approval that in the twentieth century "the efficiency of public-health technology becomes the most important, albeit residual, explanation for declining mortality . . . despite few improvements in the standard of living" (9). They view the causes of improved public health activities as "Spurred on the one hand by the appalling squalor of urban industrial life and on the other by a vocal and influential reform movement" (15), and they do not say that with higher income, societies buy more cleanliness in general and increased public health activities in particular.

In contrast, this essay argues that cleanliness is a good for which the demand increases because of increased income and that the supply increases for the same reason. Public health measures are directly caused by income, though changes in taste and public opinion may also be important. Such non-wealth-related forces as climate, disease evolution, and ecological shifts may also have caused some decline in mortality. But higher income — in conjunction with increased knowledge, which itself is largely the result of higher income (and more public health activities in the past) — is the main driving force in the mortality decline.

The Causes of the Decline in Epidemic Disease Mortality in Earlier Centuries

Let us consider the first triumphs over epidemic disease; we will return to the twentieth century later. According to Rosen ([1958] 1993, 38) the two diseases that "take pride of place in the history of medieval public health . . . are leprosy and bubonic plague." The weird and ineffica-cious accompaniments of earlier campaigns against epidemics (such as the bizarre-looking clothing worn by health workers), can convey the impression that all efforts were worthless and merely superstitious. This is not true.

Leprosy. The story of leprosy starts with the isolation procedures described in the Old Testament. These were sensible, given that trans-mission is caused by close bodily contact with an infected person over a long period of time. These biblical procedures were cited in medieval times as the basis for treatment (Winslow [1943] 1980, 78–80). When leprosy became a major problem in Europe in the sixth and seventh centuries after it reached that continent from the East, the church took the lead in restricting the lepers' contact with others and in creating leprosaria of which there were 19,000 in Europe by the beginning of the thirteenth century (Rosen [1958] 1993, 38–40). The economic where-withal to create and maintain the leprosaria depended upon the wealth of the community, in accord with the argument of this essay.

Another probable economic element in the decline of leprosy:[16] McNeill (1977, 157–59) makes the point that increased productivity and wealth in Europe brought an increase in the amount of clothing people wore. This decreased the amount of skin contact for the purpose of keeping people warm, especially when sleeping, and this tended to re-duce leprosy. However, it also had the opposite effect of increasing the lodging places for fleas, bedbugs, and lice that transmitted typhus and other diseases. So economics matters here.

Bubonic Plague. The story of the decline of bubonic plague — the other great triumph of medieval medicine, according to Rosen — is much the same. It stemmed from the combination of (1) increasing experience and knowledge; and (2) the use of resources, often mandated by government, to prevent contagion.

The experience gained by isolating lepers certainly influenced the measures taken against the Black Death. Since the disease was generally considered communicable, it was combatted on the same principles as leprosy. The chief defense was avoidance of infection; as a result, the principle of isolation underwent a rapid and general development. Patients had to be reported to the authorities. They were then examined and isolated in their houses for the duration of the illness. Every house containing a plague victim was placed under a ban. All who had come into contact with the patient were compelled to remain in isolation. Food and other necessities were provided by the municipal authorities through special messengers. The dead were passed through the windows and removed from the city in carts. Burial outside the city was likewise intended to prevent extension of the epidemic. When a plague patient died, the rooms were aired and fumigated, and the effects of the deceased were burned. (Rosen [1958] 1993, 43)

Though Rosen accords some efficacy to the quarantine as a way to prevent plague, and to hospitals and nursing care as ways to reduce mortality from it, there certainly were, as with leprosy, other possible causes of the disease's sharp decline. These elements include the following: (1) a decline in the number of black rats that carry the fleas that transmit plague, because the disease kills the rats, too; (2) faster and more frequent communication among the various parts of the world, which tends to reduce the lethality of plague and other diseases and renders them childhood diseases that do not kill (McNeill 1977, 111, 197–98); and (3) climate.

Interestingly, though the main vector in the Black Death and other major epidemics of plague probably was the rat with the flea, the long-discredited theory of transmission from person to person may not be entirely invalid. It is now known that the pneumonic form of the plague passes by means of coughing and spitting (McNeill 1977, 110). The accumulation of medical knowledge of epidemic diseases has been more gradual than was hitherto imagined.

During the late Middle Ages, the cities, particularly through the guilds, took an active part in founding hospitals and other establishments for medical care and social assistance. Proud of their community, wealthy citizens sought to outdo one another in advancing and adorning their beloved city. As early as the twelfth century, merchants were devoting a good share of their profits to benefit their fellow citizens. Hospitals, refuges, and homes were established for all sorts and conditions of men, women and children. The guilds developed funds for the relief of their sick and disabled members. Wealthy guilds built their own hospitals; others paid regular fees to a cloister hospital, which assumed responsibility for the accommodation and care of their sick members. (Rosen [1958] 1993, 52)

Eighteenth- and Nineteenth-Century Progress

Though much is in dispute about the worldwide transition in mortality patterns from before the eighteenth century to the end of the twentieth, and also about the causes of the mortality revolution in Europe, there is agreement (even among those who deemphasize the role of nutrition, e.g., Livi-Bacci 1991, chap. 1) that "the recurring catastrophes of mass starvation in times of peace were largely eliminated from most of Europe during the eighteenth century" (Flinn 1981, 97). The last great crisis in France was in 1729 (Vallin 1991, 42), and "the last great 'European' subsistence crisis" occurred in 1817 (Flinn 1981, 94), though the peak mortality rate in Finland—an astounding 78 per thousand—occurred as late as 1868 (Vallin 1991, 42). And while some observe that in Europe prior to the twentieth century "mortality appears to be a phenomenon by and large autonomous of the Malthusian system which links population and resources" (Livi-Bacci 1991, 120), no one disagrees that economic development was beginning to take place rapidly and that food prices became less variable, in part due to improved transportation (part of economic development) and perhaps in considerable part due to better weather. And while there is dispute about the possible effects of spontaneous diminutions in disease virulences, no one disagrees that some connection existed between the drop in mortality and the economic development that included (see Flinn 1981, 96–98): (1) new crops from the Americas, whose exploration and settlement were themselves the results of economic development; (2) improved transportation; and (3) "the evolution of more sophisticated social administration." The dispute concerning the effects of European economic development is only about the extent of the connection as well as its directness (e.g., whether wandering beggars, due to deficient government action, were important causes of increased mortality during subsistence crises). It seems fair, then, to assert that data from that period are consonant with the main point of this essay: The standard of living matters with respect to mortality, and economic development leads to higher life expectancy.

Moving on in time, and getting more specific about causes of mortality, Winslow ([1943] 1980) describes the eighteenth- and nineteenth-century progress in the "conquest of epidemic disease" as due to cleaning up filth both for aesthetics and to kill germs believed to be infectuous. He headnotes a chapter with this comment by John Simon, whom Winslow considers the greatest public health figure of the nineteenth century: "It has been among the oldest and most universal of medical experiences that populations, living amid Filth, and within direct reach of its polluting influence, succumb to various diseases which under opposite conditions are comparatively or absolutely unknown" (236).

Winslow sums up the great nineteenth-century miracle as follows.

When Chadwick and his followers cleaned up the masses of decomposing matter in which our forefathers lived (and died), the prevalence of typhus and typhoid and cholera was strikingly reduced. (vii)

To set the scene, Winslow quotes from a survey of Inverness, worth reproducing here.

At Inverness, the local observer reports, "There are very few houses in town which can boast of either water-closet or privy, and only two or three public privies in the better part of the place exist for the great bulk of the inhabitants." At Gateshead, "The want of convenient offices in the neighborhood is attended with many very unpleasant circumstances, as it induces the lazy inmates to make use of chamber utensils, which are suffered to remain in the most offensive state for several days, and are then emptied out of the windows." A surveyor reported on two houses in London, "I found the whole area of the cellars of both houses were full of night-soil, to the depth of three feet, which had been permitted for years to accumulate from the overflow of the cesspools; upon being moved, the stench was intolerable, and no doubt the neighborhood must have been more or less infected by it." In Manchester, "many of the streets in which cases of fever are common are so deep in mire, or so full of hollows and heaps of refuse that the vehicle used for conveying the patients to the House of Recovery often cannot be driven along them, and the patients are obliged to be carried to it from considerable distances." In Glasgow, the observer says, "We entered a dirty low passage like a house door, which led from the street through the first house to a square court immediately behind, which court, with the exception of a narrow path around it leading to another long passage through a second house, was occupied entirely as a dung receptacle of the most disgusting kind. Beyond this court the second passage led to a second square court, occupied in the same way by its dunghill; and from this court there was yet a third passage leading to a third court and third dungheap. There were no privies or drains there, and the dungheaps received all filth which the swarm of wretched inhabitants could give; and we learned that a considerable part of the rent of the houses was paid by the produce of the dungheaps." At Greenock, a dunghill in one street is described as containing "a hundred cubic yards of impure filth, collected from all parts of the town. It is never removed; it is the stock-in-trade of a person who deals in dung; he retails it by cart-fuls. To please his customers, he always keeps a nucleus, as the older the filth is the higher is the price. The proprietor has an extensive privy attached to the concern. This collection is fronting the public street; it is enclosed in front by a wall; the height of the wall is about 12 feet, and the dung overtops it; the malarious moisture oozes through the wall, and runs over the pavement. The effluvia all round about this place is horrible. There is a land of houses adjoining, four stories in height, and in the summer each house swarms with myriads of flies; every article of food and drink must be covered, otherwise, if left exposed for a minute, the flies immediately attack it, and it is rendered unfit for use, from the strong taste of the dunghill left by the flies. (Winslow [1943] 1980, 244, 245)

Wealth certainly was absent in these conditions, even though Great Britain was a very rich country. And these conditions were "faithfully duplicated in Stephen Smith's survey of New York City in 1865 . . . conditions which had their counterpart in every country." (Winslow [1943] 1980, 244)

Zinsser described such unhygienic conditions.

Cities and villages stank to heaven. The streets were the receptacles of refuse, human and otherwise. The triangular intervals which one sees between adjacent mediaeval houses in streets still inhabited are apertures through which waste, *pots de chambre,* and so forth, could be conveniently disposed of from the upper stories. The opulent used the *chaises precées* as the last word in fastidiousness. Baths were therapeutic procedures not to be recklessly prescribed after October. The first bathtubs did not reach America — we believe — until about 1840. And public bath houses lacking sanitary laundry arrangements were as likely to spread disease as to arrest it. Schools, prisons, and public meeting places of all kinds were utterly without provisions which might have limited the transmission of infection. (Zinsser [1935] 1960, 217)

The following observation suggests that specific scientific knowledge of disease etiology was not crucial.

As Chadwick says, at one point in the Survey, "The medical controversy as to the causes of fever; as to whether it is caused by filth and vitiated atmosphere, or whether the state of the atmosphere is a predisposing cause to the reception of the fever, or the means of propagating that disease, which has really some other superior, independent, or specific cause, does not appear to be one that for practical purposes need be considered, except that its effect is prejudicial in diverting attention from the practical means of prevention." (Winslow [1943] 1980, 249)

Please notice that there is no dispute here about the role of "public health" or government. There is wide agreement that in the case of leprosy it was a public health activity that removed lepers from the community and that established and enforced quarantine rules in the bubonic plague years.

The European statistical trends in mortality starting about 1750 are still a murky and tangled story. However, the editors of the proceedings of a conference on the subject (Bengtsson, Fridlizius, and Ohlsson 1984) that included many of the best writers on the subject could find some consensus on long-run factors.

1. "[M]any of the authors do not regard the first phase of the mortality revolution as a unique phenomenon connected with the so-called industrial revolution. Instead they tend to look upon the decline as a phenomenon which had occurred earlier in history" (12).
2. The conference "certainly strengthens the doubts raised against the classical Malthusian model of explanation" simply in terms of wages and the secular food supply (12). Over time the Malthusian pattern became weaker in Sweden, and "the remains of the Malthusian pattern were primarily left in the winter" (14).
3. "[A]n immunological explanation appears to find an increasing number of supporters" (12).

To this summary may be added other observations:

4. Nutrition mattered. In France "A more varied diet [in the nineteenth century] helped to improve the health of a larger part of the population (Goubert 1984, 153). Increasingly the average level of food production exceeded minimum needs (see figs. 60 and 61). That is, that nutrition matters is evidenced by the decline in spike mortality. Yet maldistribution among the income classes and throughout the year still claimed many victims, often in conjunction with disease.
5. Improvement in sanitation was very important in France (and presumably elsewhere). And economic development was crucial in the sanitation movement. "[T]he private wealth of French people grew twofold from 1851 to 1911. . . . Therefore, public and private hygiene could be raised to a higher level, supported by widespread public opinion" (Goubert 1984, 153).
6. The sanitation movement did not hinge on new medical knowledge. "The struggle for a better supply of clean water and basic cleanliness [in France] preceded then by far, the microbic revolution" (Goubert 1984, 158).

Certainly much of the nineteenth-century cleanup of England and the rest of Europe, as with the Hudson River at the turn of the twentieth century, may be ascribed to the general belief that dirty water and filthy living conditions are unhealthy. This belief was abetted by aesthetic impulses that wealth enabled the European and New York communities to carry out, in the cases mentioned.

Polluted water had long been thought to be a carrier of disease, Rosen tells us. Acting on the theory that "a clean city is a healthy city," housing was improved, the physical environment was cleaned up, efforts were made to provide unadulterated food and clean water, in short, action was taken to provide decent living conditions. The English experience with typhus fever is an excellent case in point. Until 1870 there was very little variation in the death rate from "fever" in London. For the decade 1861 to 1870 the rate was 904 per million, but in the succeeding decade (1871 to 1880) it declined to 374. During this period, typhus fever was officially separated from other "fevers," and in the next two decades its decline was nothing short of spectacular. *In 1906, three years before Nicolle's discovery that the body louse transmitted typhus, the annual*

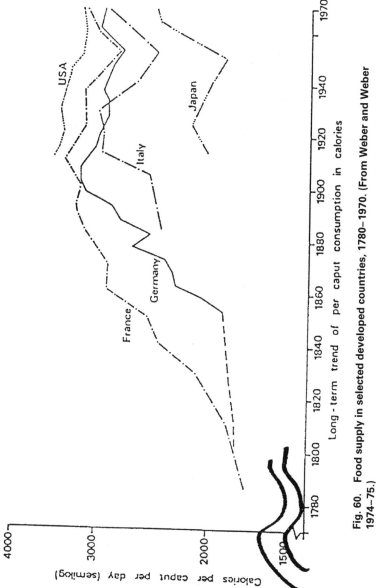

Fig. 60. Food supply in selected developed countries, 1780–1970. (From Weber and Weber 1974–75.)

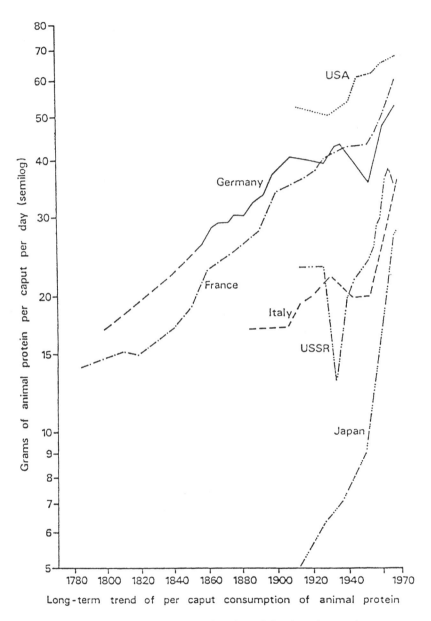

Fig. 61.   Supply of animal protein in selected developed countries,
1780–1970. (Adapted from Weber and Weber 1974–75; Grigg 1993, 34.)

report of the London County Council stated that there were no more deaths from the disease that year. Slum clearance, regulation of lodging houses, increased use of cotton clothing, especially underwear, and consequent improvement in personal cleanliness played their part in reducing the prevalence of typhus fever.

The course of typhoid fever during this period was almost as dramatic as the experience with typhus. Its decline in England and Wales is clearly shown in table 7 by the death rates from 1871 to 1925.

The trend in the United States was equally phenomenal, so that by 1947 the death rate was 0.2 per 100,000 persons for both typhoid and paratyphoid fevers. The initial decline in typhoid fever coincided with the introduction of proper sewerage systems and even more of protected water supplies. Later, further improvements in sanitary engineering, specifically protection of water through purification and of milk through pasteurization, fly control, detection of well carriers, isolation of patients and bacteriological diagnosis continued and intensified the earlier trend. Vaccination against typhoid was significant in specific groups, such as armies. In the case of typhoid fever, the influence of the bacteriological era in extending the work of the sanitary reformers is clearly apparent. (Rosen [1958] 1993, 315, 316; italics added)

Amory comments as follows.

The "great sanitary awakening" of the middle nineteenth century was based on the assumption that disease was generated by decomposing filth. Crude as this conception was, it had in it enough truth to work; for dirt, if not the mother, is the nurse of disease. . . .

From 1850 to 1890, the empirically-justified filth theory of disease was gradually transformed into a more complete formula. Snow and Budd, in England, proved the importance of water supply and direct contact by some of the most competent investigations in the history of epidemiology. (Qtd. in Winslow [1943] 1980, vii)

TABLE 7. Average Annual Death Rate from Typhoid Fever in England and Wales (per million persons)

1871–80	1881–90	1891–1900	1901–10	1911–20	1921–25
332	198	174	91	35	25

The Experience of the British Military in India

The experience of the British military in India is important evidence, because it shows that those who have the appurtenances of wealth can achieve a mortality reduction that is not achieved by those in the same geographical area who inevitably have access to the same knowledge but are not sufficiently wealthy. Figure 62 shows the decline in morbidity among British soldiers in the nineteenth century in India, a decline that was not experienced by the civilian population of India. Figure 62 also shows a marked decline among Indian soldiers, eventually reaching the same level as among the British soldiers, which was about the same level as for soldiers in Europe. Hence, the difference between the military experience and the civilian experience throughout India was not due to innate or cultural differences related to race.

Figure 63, which shows an upward trend in public health expenditures, adds support to the proposition that the activities and goods that money can buy were influential in the morbidity decline.

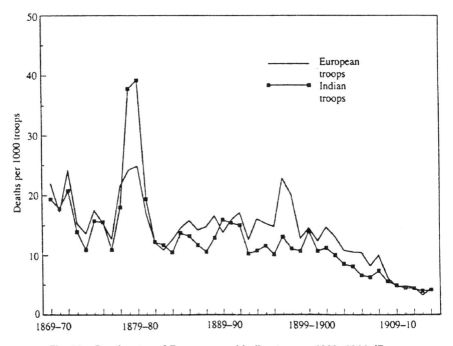

Fig. 62.   Death rates of European and Indian troops, 1869–1914. (From Harrison 1994.)

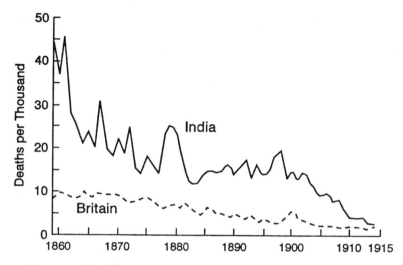

Fig. 63*a*.   British army mortality per thousand in Britain and India,
1859–1914. (From Curtin 1989, 89.)

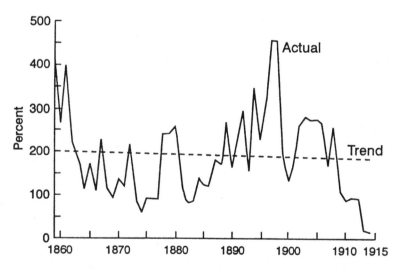

Fig. 63*b*.   Relocation costs in mortality for British troops serving in
India, 1859–1914. (From Curtin 1989, 89.)

Given that the trend observed for the British military in nineteenth-century India has appeared in quite similar form among the civilian populations of the poorer countries during the twentieth century, would it not make sense to assume that the process has similar causes in both cases, without needing to invoke new causes. And it is amply clear that the continued high mortality in India from waterborne diseases (though falling) right up to the end of the twentieth century is not explained by the absence of knowledge among decision makers but rather by insufficient wealth (and associated political will) to take the necessary public health measures.

Before proceeding, let us summarize what the British Army data tell us: As of the early part of the nineteenth century, even well-fed men in the prime of life died at horrifyingly high rates from infectious diseases in the tropics and even in Europe. There was then an amazingly large decline in the mortality of the soldiers (Curtin [1989] mentions his surprise at the extent of the drop, and I am surprised, too). The data refer to young men, because they would be least likely to die in the absence of infectious diseases. The improvement in health was largely due to public health measures to improve the drinking water and to control mosquitoes; good nutrition is presupposed because the army fed the soldiers plentifully.

The improved medical knowledge during the nineteenth century certainly contributed considerably, though no one seems to have computed what the mortality in and out of the army would have been if the state of knowledge had remained at its level of 1800. Given that the new knowledge arose in the rich countries, and the public health measures were enacted by colonial regimes, one can say that the improvement in mortality was the result of increased wealth acting through knowledge and the public health activities.

The improvement in health due to better sanitation even spread to the civilian populations of small islands where the improvements from which the civilians benefited were necessary for soldiers' health. But India (and also Algeria, in the case of the French) was too vast a country for the cantonments to affect the civilian population appreciably.

The military experience implies that at the turn of the twentieth century the necessary knowledge existed to accomplish most of the progress toward the conquest of premature death that has occurred in the poor countries since then. Therefore, the apparent discontinuity in the rates of improvement in the twentieth century, when viewed in relationship with wealth changes, would seem to be largely the result of a decline in the cost of public health measures (including such elements as decline in the cost of transportation of health workers to give vaccinations), globalization of knowledge due to improved communication, and changes in government attitudes toward public health (especially in China). The fact that so many health problems remain as of the turn of the millennium — for example, the continuing presence in India of dysentery and other gastrointestinal diseases two and a half centuries after John Pringle had learned in 1752 that dysentery was associated with bad sanitation (Curtin 1989, 51) — attests to the fact that it is not the absence of knowledge that shortens life from infectious diseases in poor countries.

Winslow ends his book by saying that "a series of clear thinkers and brilliant investigators — from Fracastorious [mid–sixteenth century] to Chapin [major work 1910] — has forever banished from the earth the major plagues and pestilences of the Past." He refers to a body of knowledge asserting that, from his standpoint in 1943 (and, I hazard, from our standpoint in the late 1990s), "the broad principles of the epidemiology of 1910 remain unchallenged." Indeed, some propositions that recently have been presented as new — for example, that hand contact spreads the secretions of the nose and throat associated with flu and the common cold — were stated very clearly by Chapin in 1910 and probably well before that as well.

It is often difficult to nail down the causal connections among income, environment, and health. For example, data for Glasgow show that "in 1911 the standardized death rate in one-room dwellings was 20.1, in two room 16.8, in three-room 12.6, and in four or more 10.3" (Burnett 1991, 171). We cannot know whether the housing density (induced by low income) directly caused the deaths, or simply the low income that brought people to cramped quarters. But for present purposes it does not matter; the data suggest that low income caused the deaths either directly or indirectly. An additional strand in the same complex argument: "housing reform began as a by-product of the 'sanitary idea' which the cholera outbreak of 1831 had inspired" (173). Wealth makes housing reform possible.

The complexity of the issue may be typified by the case of cholera and John Snow. Why did that event happen in a rich country and not a poor one? Why did it happen then and not hundreds of years earlier? Did the subsequent mortality decline result from technology or from wealth? And why does cholera continue to plague poor countries? I think we need a path analysis for this. But if wealth is the prior causal factor here, I think it should get the credit.

The Twentieth Century

Winslow's conclusion adds weight against the proposition that recent technology accounts for the decline in mortality in poor countries since around the 1930s (Easterlin's hypothesis).[17] The knowledge existed, but it was not enough. It was the powers conferred by wealth, education, modern communications, and facilitating political institutions that translated that knowledge into the mortality decline in Europe.

One should not be any more surprised or bemused at today's poor countries taking advantage of health advances seemingly ahead of their wealth statuses than one should be at the appearance of advanced technology such as transistor radios in the poorest of countries.

These scraps of data suggest a connection of economic condition to disease and death incidence in the twentieth century.

An analysis of the incidence of tuberculosis in the various districts of the city of Paris, in France, revealed that in 1923–1926 the average death-rate was 130 in the well-to-do 16th district while it was 340 in the 20th, a working class district. The variations within this one city were even more striking in 1926, when the 8th district had a death-rate of 75 and the 13th one of 306. This was a ratio of one to four, or about the same as existed in the incidence of tuberculosis among whites and negroes in the United States. In 1924 a group of 17 blocks in Paris with 4,290 houses and a population of 185,000 had a death-rate of 480. In other words, the mortality was higher there in 1924 than it was in Massachusetts in 1857.

American statistics of Rollo H. Britten published in 1934 illustrate very graphically the role of economic determination in disease. The mortality from pulmonary tuberculosis per 100,000 for the age groups from 25 to 44 years in 10 states was:

Professionals	28.6
Clerks	67.6
Skilled workers	69.0
Unskilled workers	193.5

This applies not only to tuberculosis but to other diseases also, although the differences are not so outstanding. According to the same study, the percentage of deaths due to pneumonia was:

Professionals	5.8
Clerks	6.5
Skilled workers	7.2
Unskilled workers	9.4

Even such a highly infectious disease affects the various socio-economic groups differently. In one of the Indian epidemics the deaths per 1,000,000 population were:

Low caste Hindus	53.7	Jews	5.2
Brahmins	20.7	Parsees	4.6
Mohammedans	13.7	Europeans	0.8
Eurasians	6.1		

(Sigerist 1942, 56, 58, 59)

Evidence for the view that the experience of poor countries in the twentieth century is not different in kind than the nineteenth-century experience of the advanced countries is shown earlier in figure 62. The combination of advanced-country nineteenth-century knowledge, several decades of military discipline, and British expenditures for public health produced levels of mortality for Indian as well as British troops in India of the same order as the mortality of British soldiers in Britain. The history of poor countries in the twentieth century is this graph writ large.

The effect of wealth is clear in the case of the toll taken by malaria on British soldiers in India early in the twentieth century. "[T]he Indian army refused until 1912 to issue mosquito nets to all soldiers — on grounds of expense — although individual regiments sometimes found funds to do so" (Curtin 1989, 14). And the main elements in the successful fight against malaria — quinine and mosquito control — could be more afforded by the British than by Indians. But in his wonderfully informative story of the mortality of European soldiers in the tropics, Curtin seldom, if ever, labels wealth as the central force for life and poverty as the central force for death.

But one should not overstate the extent of the variance that economic factors explain, either before or during the twentieth century. Kunitz and Engerman (1992) remind us that "the secular trends in per capita income do not invariably predict the secular trend in mortality"; they even find this "on the face of it surprising" (29). They cite such facts as that British officers died at a higher rate than other ranks in India from 1899 to 1913 and that in many places Jewish infants had lower mortality rates than did other nationalities, even holding various factors constant. They are of course correct that "Since mortality has always been influenced by so many factors, including income, it would not be expected that any simple one-to-one relation within a limited time span could be found." But they would seem to underassess the effect of income because they view public health as unrelated to income and therefore see "a trade-off between the effects of individual income and social measures, such as public health" (44). For example, they cite British investments as reducing famine in India. However, as argued earlier, British government action in India followed from British national wealth.

To return now to Preston's (1975) work on the twentieth century: He begins with the observation that "it is clear that, in high-mortality populations, infectious and parasitic diseases bear almost exclusive responsibility for shortening life below the modern Western standards" (293). Rather surprisingly, decline in mortality from influenza/pneumonia/bronchitis accounted for the largest fraction of the mortality decline from 1940 to 1970, almost four times as much as the next-greatest cause, diarrheal diseases. For the latter, "the principal method of control has been improvements in water supply and sewerage that, *because of their expense,* are closely associated with economic development" (313; italics added). And with respect to the most important element (respiratory diseases), "No effective preventive measures have been deployed against these diseases." Hence, Preston concludes, in agreement with the argument here, that "It is likely that social and economic development—especially as reflected in water systems, nutrition, housing, and personal sanitary knowledge—have operated largely through these diseases" (313). This seems to fully support the view that even for the twentieth century, "the Mortality Revolution is due to the Industrial Revolution and the era of rapid economic growth that ensued."[18]

Preston's ingenious analysis of the cross-country data on mortality, income distribution, and mean income for 1940 and 1970 led him to the conclusions that "relations between mortality and income at the national income level are . . . dominated by relations between mortality and income at the individual level" and that they "are not strongly influenced by the prevailing level of average income in the nation to which they reside" (1980, 292–93). But this does not imply that a change in the mean income level of a country at the national level—through, for example, the discovery and development of an oil field or the injection of a public health program paid for by an international organization—would not affect the mortality prospect of any or all individuals within the country, because individual incomes may well be influenced by the national-level change.

An analogy may help here: People below the U.S. poverty line mostly own autos. May one not attribute that ownership to high societal per capita wealth? If so, should one not attribute some recent increases in life expectancy in poor countries to high per capita wealth in the world as a whole?

Still another analogy from our own times may enable us to exploit our firsthand contemporary knowledge so as to understand the past. People have long known that exercise improves health and reduces mortality. But the propensity to exercise is related to both average and individual wealth; one seldom sees joggers in poor countries, and surveys indicate that in rich countries poor people engage less in sport exercise than does the middle class. These observations are also consistent with the increase in excellent sporting performances in countries, as measured by the Olympics performances, as they get richer.

Yes, the medical profession now has much more solid evidence about the effects of exercise than it had in the past, and biologists can much better explain the workings of the mechanisms by which exercise improves health. But does it not seem likely that even without that recent scientific knowledge about exercise, as wealth increased, people would spend more of their time in sporting and nonsporting exercise, and gymnasiums and health clubs would begin to proliferate, with improved average health as a result? The sanitation movement and the consequent decline in mortality may bear much the same relationship to medical knowledge as does the exercise movement.

The point of this discussion is that nutrition (and the standard of living, in general) may be receiving less credit than it deserves in explanation of mortality declines in the nineteenth and twentieth centuries.

Concluding Comments

The most important facts relevant to the argument of this essay are the following: (1) The long secular drop in mortality in Europe began at the same time as did the long secular increase in the standard of living — about 1750 or 1800. (2) The poor countries of the world experienced sharp falls in mortality long after the rich countries and as they began to experience economic development in the twentieth century. Though the patterns differ from country to country and period to period, and though such elements as disease, food intake, and climate cannot yet be disentangled, for both phenomena 1 and 2 there is much evidence to connect mortality to income causally and little or no evidence showing that a causal connection is merely an artifact.

The argument here does not address the relative importance of nutritional and public health elements, which have been the subject of hot controversy (e.g., compare Floud et al. 1990; and Livi-Bacci 1991).

Subsuming both these elements, the concept of wealth used here finesses that controversy.

The difference between Easterlin's view and the more traditional view (including that offered here) is that he implies that much less cleanup would have been done without the specific knowledge obtained in the 1880s and thereafter. By contrast, the traditional view implies that the cleanup would have continued even in the absence of this knowledge, though perhaps not so effectively or extensively.

The health gains resulting from cleanups for aesthetic purposes may also be attributed to increased income, because aesthetic improvement is a luxury good that an individual or a group purchases after it has addressed its primary material needs of food and shelter.

> Much disease in northwest Europe . . . is transmitted by houseflies. Beginning in the eighteenth century, the environmentalist movement demanded better drainage, better ventilation, and the abolition of obvious filth from the cities. These measures were mainly aesthetic in intent . . . but the by-product was fewer insects . . . and . . . less infectious disease. (Curtin 1989, 41)

The role of new knowledge would seem to be called into question by the extraordinary differences in timing of mortality decline among nations. If wealth were not crucial, why did India, China, and the rest of the world's poor countries lag behind Europe so badly? Surely the knowledge was shared by many educated and medical persons in those countries.

Schofield and Reher (1991) mention that "acceptance of new [medical] ideas at a local level often took a considerable amount of time and education" (15). They were referring to Europe in the nineteenth century, especially, but the same concept helps explain why only in the middle of the twentieth century did poor countries force down mortality with the means that the advanced countries successfully used earlier. Higher income buys both public health activities and the means to communicate these ideas.

Would simply raising income in poor countries have reduced mortality in the twentieth century? Likely so. To help discriminate between (1) the hypothesis of wealth; and (2) some other wind of change or some wave of immunity to diseases, we have examples such as Australia and North America and even Japan, where poverty was being alleviated relatively early and mortality fell early (later in Japan than in Europe but much earlier than in China and India). It fits this line of thought that there was continued high mortality in Eastern Europe, where income lagged.

It is often helpful to ask what evidence might invalidate one's own conclusion and support another that runs counter to that which one has reached. In this case, if one could show that a single sharply defined new piece of knowledge had been discovered that reduces the incidence of a lethal infectious disease, that was then quickly picked up and transmitted to people in poor countries throughout the world and was adopted with the same speed in countries at different economic levels, that would invalidate the McKeown thesis and the more general thesis (nutritional status plus public health) espoused here. But there does not seem to be any such example.

Problematic for the current thesis of the importance of the standard of living, however, is the rapid mortality decline in China starting in 1950, when China was still very poor. The crucial element seems to have been a new social invention, the "barefoot doctors," who were paramedics operating at the village level throughout the country. These barefoot doctors raised life expectancy further and faster than in India. Moreover, they were a product of the larger totalitarian Communist system, which cannot be said to be endogenous within the overall system proposed here. This observation must be seen as either a chance outlier or a contradictory observation or both.

Another countercase is that of the Indian state of Kerala. As of 1997 it has very low average income (no higher than average for India) and a lower economic growth rate than the rest of India. Yet, as Table 4 shows, Kerala's life expectancy is higher than China's and vastly higher than the average in India as a whole; its infant mortality is much lower than that of all India or even China and approaches that of developed countries; it also has low fertility and high literacy. All this has come about under state governments that have sometimes been controlled by Communists and always heavily influenced by socialist unions.

What can one say about the case of Kerala and China? If every case fitted a pattern perfectly, the study of economics would not be difficult, and economists would be out of a job.

Still another sort of case that does not immediately fit the pattern set forth here is the demographic history of England as written by Wrigley and Schofield (1981). One discordant element is that mortality apparently was exceptionally low (perhaps unbelievably so) from perhaps 1550 to 1650, reaching a life expectancy of 40 in one period (see their fig. 7.6, 231); there has been no solid explanation of this phenomenon, except perhaps a very good climate plus an unusually low incidence of epidemics. A second discordant element is that increased fertility, and not decreased mortality, seems to have been the crucial element in England's rapid population growth, unlike in other European nations (247). However, this case does not tend to refute the thrust of this essay.

Incidentally, one may certainly consider an improvement in material human welfare the improvement in food supply in Europe as seen in figures 60 and 61. There probably were periods prior to 1750 when the majority of Europeans were generally well fed. But it was only after that date that eating plentifully became a continuous fact of life for the large majority of those countries' populations.

CHAPTER 4

Very-Long-Run, Slow-Changing Processes

This chapter discusses the disaggregated sinews of the theoretical process outlined in chapter 3. This material provides evidence for the propositions that (1) the rate of progress is a function of human numbers; and (2) in the very long run, all political, social, and economic dimensions are a function of population size and density and constitute endogenous intermediate variables rather than independent causal variables.

The elements on which this chapter will touch include the development of markets, political and social and economic organization, law, disease, and evolved cultural patterns. Here the time horizon is so long that the phenomena undergoing change usually are not even mentioned in the context of population economics. As North wrote, "The major source of changes in an economy over time is structural change in the parameters held constant by the economist — technology, population, property rights, and government control over resources" (1981, 57).

The latter two items in North's list are central in this chapter. These phenomena have been studied little, so the amount of data is small. But the paucity of data does not diminish the importance of these phenomena.

The Development of Markets

The size of a market depends upon both the *number of people who are potential participants* and the *levels of their income*. The multiplicand of population size and income per person — aggregate income — is perhaps the most basic measure of the size of major consumer markets. The sizes of the markets for particular goods will of course be affected by the *distribution* of income among persons, but that matter can be left aside here. There is a presumption, then, that more people imply more and bigger markets.

The most compelling demonstration of the effect of population size upon the presence of markets is data on the distributions of stores of various types in communities of various sizes (fig. 24 in chap. 2). The bigger the municipality, the more types of stores may be found. The effect of community size on the number of competitors in the same markets is equally obvious; one need merely compare the number of movie theaters, gasoline stations, or plumbers in the telephone books of cities of different sizes.

Increased population density also leads to better-organized markets. Hicks (1969) and North (1981) have shown the connection throughout history between these variables at the local and regional levels. As noted earlier, this phenomenon was seen vividly after the depopulation of the Black Death. Despite higher wages and increased land available to cultivators, overall economic conditions apparently were less favorable. There was a general economic depression as a result of the disappearance of markets, itself the result of a lack of people and products to support markets.

Connected with the development of transactions throughout early history was the development of commercial practices and of money. A community composed of only two families, or even a small self-enclosed tribe, has little need for money. But when an economy grows in population size and income, money becomes essential. So this crucial element of progress, fungible money, is an outcome of population growth, by way of economic development.

A review of microeconomic theory with the (absolute) change in population and market growth in mind immediately suggests many avenues through which competition improves with population growth—especially the effects of having more rather than fewer producers and sellers. Conventionally, economic theory compares only "monopoly" versus "perfect competition"—the latter implying an infinite number of producers. This contrasting pair of conceptual circumstances is often useful for policy purposes, but the comparison affords little insight into the process of economic expansion as population size (or income) increases. For present purposes it is better to compare markets with just one firm to those with two to three, rather than to markets with many firms.

In general, a larger number of competitors leads to a more responsive and more rapidly changing marketplace. These are some of the phenomena about which we have some knowledge when the market expands from, say, one to two sellers:

1. *Speed of price change* (Rotemberg and Saloner 1987; Simon and Rice 1983–84). Price is more sensitive to change in the economic environment when there are more sellers. And greater price sensitivity makes for a more responsive economy.
2. *Type of competitive tool used.* The incidences of price-cutting

and advertising may differ when the number of sellers changes (Simon 1967).

3. *Amount of effort.* The X-efficiency literature, beginning with Harvey Leibenstein, discusses a variety of cases wherein competition brought about a greater intensity of effort (see Simon 1987a).

Cities and Markets

Cities, along with infrastructure, apparently were a crucial precondition of the industrial revolution in England, Holland, and elsewhere. The existence of cities requires relatively dense populations in surrounding areas. Indeed, cities and markets are closely related phenomena. Pirenne's magisterial analysis of city development ([1925] 1969) depends heavily on population size and the (absolute) change in population. Larger absolute numbers of people were the basis for increased trade and consequent growth in cities (see fig. 3 in chap. 1), which in turn strongly influenced the creation of an exchange economy in place of the subsistence economy of the manor.

According to Pirenne, the growth in population that caused cities to grow also reduced serfdom by offering serfs legal haven in the city, as memorialized in the saying "City air makes free," mentioned in chapter 2 in connection with Hume's analysis of the development of the arts and sciences. The alternative of moving to the city to work must also have reduced the power of landlords over tenant farmers. In turn, this must have improved rent terms from the tenant's point of view. Together with the freedom of town life, these transformations must have contributed to an increase in personal liberty and worked to end feudalism, though the causes of the end of serfdom are a subject of much controversy (see Domar 1970; and brief further discussion that follows).

Disease

The evolution of the disease environment is another of the crucial evolutionary processes that population variables have influenced—directly through density and indirectly via wealth. The importance of disease in influencing the pattern and rate of progress is seen dramatically in the absence of major European colonization in sub-Saharan Africa until the nineteenth century, even though Africa was much closer to Europe than was South America. Bairoch tells us that, for a European who settled in the small coastal enclaves that served the slave trade until its abolition starting at the beginning of the nineteenth century, "life-expectancy was only three to four years" due to "climatic conditions and above all epidemics" (1988, 391). And Curtin mentions a yearly mortality rate as high as 40 percent in Sierra Leone (1989, 18). It is not surprising, then, that Europeans did not colonize Africa in substantial numbers in those earlier centuries, not beginning to do so seriously until 1880–90 (Bairoch 1988, 412), even though there were European settlements in seaports much earlier. Then drainage, quinine, and other innovations began to reduce malaria mortality (Curtin 1989, 62–67), thus facilitating the conquest and colonization processes.

The Effect of Population Density on Disease

Density of population affects the virulence of disease; sometimes it makes disease spread faster by bringing people and vectors to each other, as in the case of epidemics. At other times density suppresses disease, as in the case of malaria; by causing the land to be cropped closely, increasing population density reduces the virulence of malaria, perhaps the greatest killer of all; an important example was south China, which was only colonized after this process had made it habitable. A further complication is that increased virulence leads to immunities that check the spread of diseases. McNeill (1977) described how the evolution of the disease environment has been greatly influenced in complex ways by population density and therefore by the (absolute) change in population.

For most of the great diseases, the growth of population in earlier centuries represented a one-time "investment" of our species into developing resistance to mass killers; once our ancestors had suffered this experience, later generations could live their lives with less threat from these diseases. Increasing communications between the various parts of the world, the result of both denser population and increasing wealth (together with better transportation), also speeded the development of immunity.[1]

A body of knowledge about the prevention and cure of diseases also has evolved, much of it by means of prescientific trial and error; an example of the latter is the practice of quarantine. More recently, health knowledge has begun to evolve from systematic scientific work; smallpox vaccination offers an example. Such advances in medical practice can be attributed to the combination of a scientific attitude and a greater base of scientific medical knowledge, both of which were enhanced by the industrial revolution. The advances occurred in countries experiencing the industrial revolution but not in countries such as India and China that remained outside the ambit of the industrial revolution. This greater capacity to deal actively with the disease environment may be seen as a consequence of population growth.

The Effects of Population through the Growth in Income and Wealth

The causes of the fall in the death rate during the industrial revolution are somewhat unclear, as noted in chapter 3. Some part of the mortality drop may have been unconnected with economic progress; the climate may have improved and yielded better crops, the rat population may have spontaneously altered its species composition in such fashion that the rigors of plague diminished, and the disease environment may otherwise have become less dangerous. Another part of the improvement may stem from economic progress in only very indirect fashion, if at all, notably through shorter periods of breast-feeding and hence less inhibition of pregnancy. But economic progress was surely responsible for much of the improved life expectancy.

The roles of income and of new scientific knowledge in reducing mortality in poor countries in the twentieth century are a matter of some controversy. The matter is discussed in the section "What Caused the Fall in Mortality?" in chapter 3. That issue is outside the scope of the following discussion, however.

Income and wealth have affected mortality through two main channels, better nutrition and improved sanitation. We shall discuss them separately.

The Effect of Better Nutrition. Economic progress, which is the result as well as the cause of population growth, helped people live longer by providing better diets. McKeown (McKeown and Brown 1955: McKeown 1983) has argued forcefully that "the slow growth of the human population before the eighteenth century was due mainly to lack of food, and the rapid increase from that time resulted largely from improved nutrition" (1983, 29). Fogel's work agrees (1989; see the following).

The importance of nutrition has proven surprisingly difficult to establish conclusively, however, and some scholars have recently wondered whether sufficiency of nutrition was at all important (see Easterlin and related discussion in chap. 3), some citing the puzzling fact that in the late middle ages nobles apparently did not live much longer than commoners (see, e.g., Livi-Bacci 1992; and other discussions in the same volume; but also the positive relationship between social class and life expectancy shown in fig. 64, which contradicts Livi-Bacci's assertion). Yet it is an obvious fact that where sustenance is very difficult to

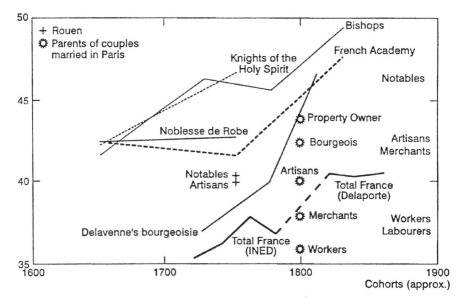

Fig. 64. **Life expectancy at age 20; various groups in France (Source: Houdaille 19??)**

achieve, as it is, among the Eskimos and among desert nomad tribes, population grows slowly or not at all. This would seem to be sufficient proof of a relationship between availability of food and how long people live, in connection with the number of children that they bring into the world or allow to live (a number that the available evidence suggests is small, on average, among such groups as the Eskimos and nomads.) And his work on the history of people's heights, as well as other biometric work, led Fogel to conclude about "The modern secular decline in mortality in Western Europe [which] did not begin until the 1780's" that "reductions in chronic malnutrition . . . may have accounted for most of the initial improvement" that occurred before 1830 and 1840 in Britain and France respectively (1989, 1, 2).

Important concomitant evidence is found in the amazing decrease in the age of menarche in Europe from above 16 years to little more than 13 years during the period from the latter half of the nineteenth century to the middle of the twentieth century (fig. 65). The soundness of this indicator of health is corroborated by the fact that the age of menarche is found to be 16.5 (Howell 1976, 144) or "late, at about fifteen years" (Truswell and Hansen, 1976, 180) among the Dobe !Kung bushmen

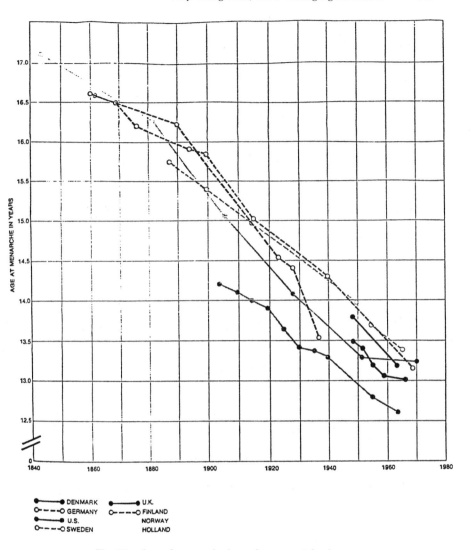

Fig. 65.   Age of menarche in various countries by year

pygmies; these people are "undernourished," "a clear case of semi-starvation," and in a "still poor . . . nutritional state" (Truswell and Hansen 1976, 189, including quotes by co-workers), which may be responsible (at least in part) for their very short stature.[2] The data for food intake in Europe starting in the eighteenth century (see fig. 61) together with the data on heights in Europe over the same period (see fig. 66)

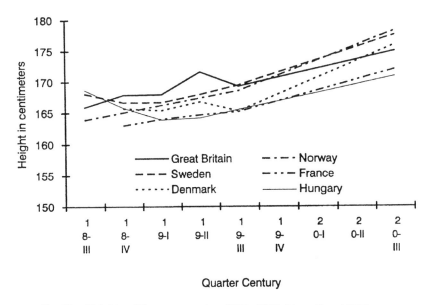

Quarter Century

Fig. 66.   Heights of European males, 1775–1975. (From Fogel 1992, table 9.)

strongly suggest a nutrition-and-health explanation of the trend in menarche in Europe.[3] And the data for nutrition in Japan are dramatic; in just the past half-century the height of Japanese males went from an average of perhaps 4 feet 7 inches to 5 feet 5 inches, as nutrition improved greatly (see fig. 67).

Figure 68 shows the relationship of average national income to quantity of food eaten recapitulated in a 1950s cross section, and figure 69 shows a similar analysis for the proportion of the diet that starchy staples occupy.

The Effects of Wealth through Sanitation Systems and Other Infrastructure

Economic progress also helped people live longer by developing the physical infrastructure of society, especially provision of purer communal drinking water. Such improvements may not have been intended mainly to improve health and reduce death, but nevertheless they led to great improvement. Figures 62, 63a, and 63b show the decline in mortality of Empire troops in India (both British and native) with the improvement of

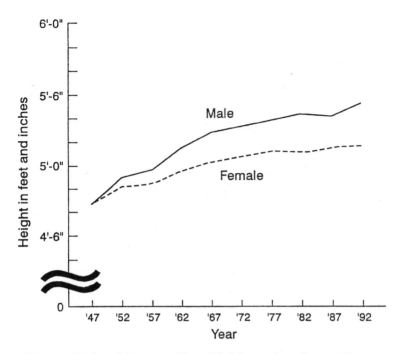

Fig. 67. Heights of Japanese. (From *Washington Post,* **January 23 1993, A14.)**

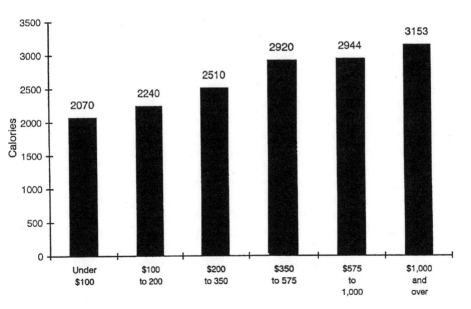

Fig. 68. Per capita calorie consumption by mean income, 1950s (40 countries). (From Kuznets 1966.)

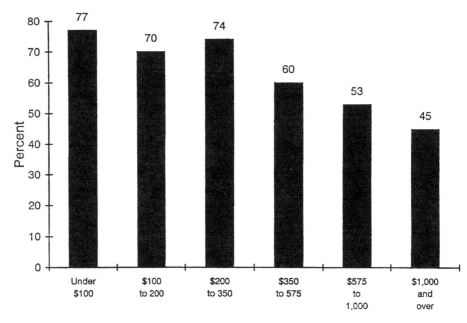

Fig. 69. Percentage of starchy staples in total calories by mean income, 1950s (40 countries). (From Kuznets 1966.)

attention to sanitation[4] and Figure 70 shows the increase in expenditure of funds for better sanitation.

Building infrastructure requires that farming be sufficiently efficient so that society can afford to employ people on such community projects. Also required is that the population be sufficiently large and dense that such projects are economical. The same is true for roads and other communication systems that contributed to the spread of health technology (see earlier discussion of road density and population density in the "Transportation" section of chap. 3).

Summary Judgment. Perhaps the most reasonable overall assessment concerning mortality is that while population and income may not have been the only important factors, both certainly affected mortality. And whereas better food supply was a major factor in Europe before the nineteenth and twentieth centuries, better sanitation was a major factor in the richer countries starting in the nineteenth century (and perhaps also in Europe in the eighteenth century). And starting in the twentieth century, sanitation also became an important factor in the less-developed countries.[5]

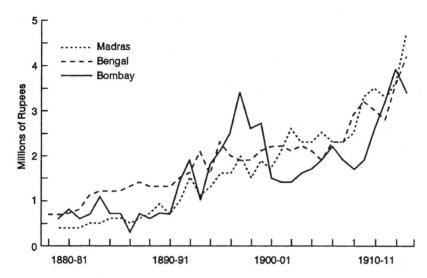

Fig. 70.   Allotments to sanitation: Mofussil municipalities. (From Harrison 1994.)

In some places (especially in cities such as London), greater population density must have had short-term negative effects upon health by temporarily lowering the standard of living; in other words, greater density might have imposed a Malthusian "positive check." The city death rate was much higher than the rural death rate until the twentieth century in Great Britain. But in the longer run, the overall result of population growth on the incidence of disease clearly has been positive.

At present, wealthier people live longer than poorer people, for all the reasons discussed earlier. And wealthier countries have longer average life expectancies than do poorer countries; indeed, life expectancies in the poorest countries just a few decades ago were no greater than in poor (or even "rich") countries 200 years ago. These facts would seem to confirm the causal connection between the increase beyond subsistence in the standard of living of the multitudes and the increase in life expectancy, both of which have been part of Sudden Modern Progress.

Social and Political Organization[6]

Basic institutions tend to change particularly slowly. Yet there is solid evidence that the structure and actions of government can, to a considerable extent, be considered a function of population and the standard of living, as well as of other forces within our system, including the state of knowledge. Indeed, though I am unaware of work that pins down the effect statistically, the influence of population size and population density upon social and political organization and its role in economic development are given ever-greater importance by historians such as Jones (1981), McNeill (1963), and North (1981).[7]

Population density and size apparently affect the mode of organization and the size of the government sector. Stevenson (1968) argues that increasing density leads to better-articulated organization of society; this seems plausible, though the phenomenon is difficult to quantify. He does, however, provide persuasive evidence from the study of African societies. And Murrell (1985) and Mueller have related the population sizes of countries to the relative sizes of the government sector, across a sample of countries. Kelley (1976) has also provided relevant evidence.

As noted earlier in the discussion of city development, the relationship of population growth to the abolition of feudalism and slavery is controversial; it obviously needs further investigation (see Domar 1970).[8] Work by Kahan on Russia in the eighteenth century, and by Lal (1990) on India over four millennia, bears upon this issue. Lal's work goes beyond the specific issue of legal bonds to consider the more general matter of the cultural arrangements of the Hindu caste system.

The provision of local government services depends heavily upon the size of the community. In communities of various sizes in the United States as of the end of the 1930s,[9] the probability of having a college, an art museum, or AM radio depended heavily on the population, as seen in figures 56a and 56b (see chap. 3). In the samples in question, the mean educational levels of native white males were almost identical across community size, ranging from 11.0 to 11.1 in the largest and smallest places, with 11.2 in the middle. Therefore, income is not the determining variable.

Property Rights and "a Theory of the State"

North argues that "a theory of the state" is necessary to understand economic growth. "[S]tudy of the state [is] central to economic history; models of the state should be an explicit part of any analysis of secular changes" (1981, 20), so it obviously behooves me to offer a "theory." Indeed, this essay's treatment of political institutions is likely to be a key factor in how certain readers view it.

North provides a "neoclassical" theory. And he goes on to say that "One cannot develop a useful analysis of the state divorced from property rights" (1981, 21); "A theory of the state is essential because it is the state that specifies the property rights structure" (17); and "A theory of property rights is necessary to account for the forms of economic organization that human beings devise to reduce transactions costs and organize exchange" (17–18).

Property rights are indeed at the heart of the state apparatus that North has in mind. Along the same lines, Hayek (1989) argues that property rights and the family are the two most important institutions in determining a nation's economic progress.

Much of North's discussion of the subject is quite congenial here. But he focuses on the role of the state rather than the causes of its nature and change from circumstance to circumstance. In particular, he hardly mentions the size and density of the population in explaining the evolution of property rights and the state. Outside of this theory of the state, he discusses the evolution of property rights from those characteristic of hunting-and-gathering situations to the property rights characteristic of settled agriculture (1981, 79–82). But he certainly and properly attaches great importance to this as an endogenous variable.

> The First Economic Revolution was not a revolution because it shifted man's major economic activity from hunting and gathering to settled agriculture. It was a revolution because the transition created for mankind an incentive change of fundamental proportions. The incentive change stems from the different property rights under the two systems. (1981, 89)

And because the shift from hunting and gathering to settled agriculture was a result of population growth, as we all agree, this process illustrates the development of property rights and "the state" as a function of demographic change.

There is an even more potent example of the development of property rights in response to demographic change; it has the advantage that it need not be conjectural—as is the change that North discusses— because there is plenty of solid evidence. The two enclosure movements in England, transiting from commons to individual landholdings, constitute a well-documented case of property rights evolving in response to population growth and associated demand for food.

The first such movement can be traced back to the Commons Act of 1235.

> It appears that in the early Saxon period, areas of open waste were much more extensive than they were to become in the medieval period, and the rights to their use were more loosely defined and

often exercised by much wider groups. . . . Limitation and closer definition of rights to common waste occurred during the population increase of the early medieval period: ". . . much of the wastes were ploughed up in the 12th and 13th centuries, as arable prices, and the need for food for consumption, increased. . . . [c]ommons survived best where population densities were low and where much land was unsuitable for arable agriculture." (Williamson 1987, 499)

The second enclosure movement occurred largely in the eighteenth century and early nineteenth century during the Napoleonic wars. Court tells the story succinctly, emphasizing the role of population increase and density.

[E]nclosure did permit a specialization of the land in the direction rendered most profitable by the existing state of demand. There had been much enclosure of open field for sheep pasture and wool in the sixteenth and early seventeenth century, and there was much for cattle and dairy purposes in the early eighteenth century. In that century, resources in capital grew. With many agriculturists, their savings must have grown almost automatically with their incomes. The contemporary increase of population in country districts turned on to the labour market a multitude of men and women without land of their own, often without alternative employment. The enclosed farm in the late eighteenth century was consequently becoming a formidable competitor for the use of the land, as better able to extract the maximum product for commercial purposes. The open-field farmer did not disregard the market, but he remained nearer than the capitalist tenant-farmer to the subsistence farming of his forebears.

The rising price of wheat after 1760 and the demand for meat in the towns both encouraged a type of business-like farming on enclosed land which was increasingly common and increasingly profitable. Moreover, the encloser could quote strong arguments of public advantage for what he was doing. That Great Britain depended on her fields to feed a rapidly multiplying people was something that few understood. But everyone could appreciate the pressure of that unseen demand reflected in high prices and the contention that open-field practice stood in the way of a higher yield of corn and more and better-fed cattle. The argument of demand was reinforced by war. Of the fifty years after 1760, more than a half were for Britain years of war. During the war with the American colonies and France (1776–82) command of the seas was temporarily lost to the French and self-sufficiency became indispensable. In the war against Revolutionary and Napoleonic France (1793–1815), British command of the sea became absolute after the battle of Trafalgar in 1805, but the pressure of population upon home food supplies was acute. In years of poor harvest, in 1800 and 1801, and again in 1810, 1812 and 1813, wheat prices at well over 100*s*. a quarter were little short of famine prices. It is not surprising that the two periods of war were also periods of rapid enclosure. The atmosphere which they created favoured quick action and was adverse to the cool consideration of agricultural and rural policy.

In centuries past, open-field holdings had been exchanged or enclosed from time to time by agreement among the parties concerned. The agreement might or might not be formally registered by the court baron or the local vestry. As many parties were sometimes concerned, agreements were slow to arrive at. A minority or one man might hold them up. Hence the practice which sprang up in the seventeenth century of ratifying such agreements in the Courts of Chancery or Exchequer, often after a collusive action, so as to obtain a decree which would bind the minority. What now happened, from about 1760 onwards, was that the older processes of private agreement and Chancery decree were abandoned in favour of the private act of Parliament, by men who were too deeply impressed by arguments of private profit or national need to be willing to wait. The private act was at first used to give legislative effect to an agreement already reached. Later, the practice was to appoint, as soon as the act was passed, officials known as enclosure commissioners to visit and survey the parish and re-allot the land in an award which became legally binding upon all the parties concerned. (Court 1954, 35, 36)

Williamson observes that "The high prices of arable land during the Napoleonic Wars were a particular stimulus to enclosure" (Williamson 1987, 500). He makes the illuminating side comment that "areas in which large commons survived tended to have a reputation for lawlessness" (500), which reflects on the development not just of property rights but also of law in general and its enforcement.

Evolution of the Law Generally

The story of the commons and property rights is also illuminating because it shows how the formal law itself is endogenous, responding to the process initiated by population growth and increased demand for food. These two elements tend to evolve gradually rather than being altered by political upheaval or legislation. Hayek suggests that these institutions, as well as the rest of the rich tapestry of cultural patterns, develop by a process of cultural selection wherein communities that grow in numbers are more likely to have their institutions be dominant in the wider world than are groups that do not increase in population. Much of this evolutionary process has taken place over thousands of years. But the effects were important for economic development; for example, the system of Anglo-Saxon common law and its protection for property surely aided the course of the industrial revolution in England and in its offshoots in North America and Oceania.

Though rules are often slow to change, there is much evidence that the structure of law in a given place is responsive to population growth and other changes in conditions. And in some circumstances the law can change very rapidly; consider, for example, the transitions to and from the Communist system in Russia. Law also can change speedily within a microcosm such as mining camps, which turned into boomtowns in the United States. The system *in practice* in the transition from rough mining camp to settled community can evolve rapidly under the pressure of population growth and increase in income, though the new law's forms may well come to resemble the communities the pioneers left. This maturation of legal institutions starting from rough-and-ready justice was described well by Pound (1921).

It is also relevant that the structures of law now existing in the developed countries have much more in common with each other — especially stability and the rule of law — than with the structures of law found in poorer countries; the state of economic development is the key determinant. And, of course, the development of the developed countries was in turn heavily dependent upon the preexisting structures of law; the Latin-American versus the Anglo-Saxon types of law and political structures provide an important illustration. But the Anglo-Saxon common-law system may be less uniquely favorable for economic development than some of its admirers are inclined to think. France, Germany, Holland, Italy, and Japan have developed rapidly with legal structures quite different than the Anglo-Saxon form.

The effect of population density and size upon the refinement and the changes in direction that occur in the law has been hinted at by my own and others' preliminary studies in the United States relating the size of state to the extent to which decisions are cited. This theme needs to be pursued more closely.

If more people cause there to be more ideas and knowledge, more growth of markets and cities, and hence higher productivity and income, why did the modernization revolution not begin in India and China? This topic is discussed at length at the end of chapter 5, which argues that the answer is neither crucial for this essay nor attainable in a scientific fashion. But for now we may note that China was indeed the technological leader until perhaps 1400 and apparently by a wide margin. And a technical point should also be noted: Population size in terms of numbers within national boundaries was less meaningful in earlier centuries when national integration was much looser than now; the relevant variable is population density rather than population size, and if borders had been drawn in such fashion that China and India each had comprised 10 states instead of one, the situation might not have been fundamentally different in the distant past. At present, differences in education may explain much of the phenomenon under discussion, but education does not explain the huge difference between the West and the East over the five centuries or so up to, say, 1850.

As noted previously, a particularly illuminating question is why the sparsely populated continents have *never* been the founts of advanced knowledge and progress; population size and density certainly seem a persuasive explanation.

As to *why* societies have more or fewer social rigidities, and *why* Europe should have been so much more open than India and China, historians answer with conjectures about religion, instability, and a variety of other special conditions. Population growth also may cause a rigid structure to break up. This is Boserup's thesis (1965) applied to simple, small societies, and Lal (1990) has made this case effectively for the history of India's economic development over thousands of years. Lal suggests that it was only the rapid population growth starting around 1921 that cracked the "cake of custom" and the Hinda caste system and caused the mobility that allowed India to begin modern development.

A fuller analysis of the subject at hand would also consider the effects of the preexisting social and economic frameworks on the reaction to population growth. A flexible framework may enable population growth and economic growth to facilitate each other, whereas a rigid framework may mean that population growth leads only to immiseration and eventually the cessation of the population growth. As Weir (1984, 48) noted in a comparison of French and English history: "If . . . we allow that some societies may be more successful than others at generating productivity growth in response to population growth, then a new set of research questions will emerge to integrate economic and demographic history."

Most historians (e.g., Gimpel 1977) agree that the period of rapid population growth from before 1000 B.C.E. to the beginning of the middle of the 1300s was a period of intellectual fecundity. Chaunu's remarks are not atypical.

> The increase in population which both caused and accompanied these developments, the spread of human settlement, and technical progress, all were greater from the tenth to thirteenth centuries than at any other time. . . .
>
> The plague can be seen as a permanent debunking of the Malthusian model: it was far from resolving the problems of a world which people have supposed to have been over-populated. On the contrary, the great season of death brought fifty years of dreadful misery in its train, with repeated fresh mortality such that the population in 1400 was smaller everywhere than it had been in 1350. . . .
>
> The crucial influence, we must remember, was the fantastic impetus achieved after the process of absorbing the south began. During and after gaining 174,000 square kilometres in thirty-nine years, Christian Spain's whole population doubled between 1240 and 1340, a rate comparable to that during the eighteenth or twentieth centuries. It was caused by the surplus of births over deaths. Before the Black Death the population had reached a level higher than at any time until the new peak in 1580. It cannot be too often repeated that the start of any great period of innovation always coincides with a sharp increase in population. (Chaunu 1979, 59, 62, 88)

Cameron viewed this period as a specific case of his general observation.

> It is virtually certain that each accelerating phase of population growth in Europe was accompanied by economic growth, in the sense that both total and per capita output were increasing. . . .
>
> The hypothesis of economic growth accompanying the growth of population is strongly supported by the unquestioned evidence of both physical and economic expansion of European civilization during each of the accelerating phases of population growth. During the eleventh, twelfth, and thirteenth centuries European civilization expanded from its heartland. (1989, 17)

It was also a period of great dynamism generally, as seen in the extraordinary cathedral building boom. Cameron continues: "[T]he acceleration phases of each period of population growth in Europe witnessed outbursts of intellectual and artistic creativity, followed by a proliferation of monumental architecture" (1989, 18). But around the period of depopulation due to the Black Death and perhaps also the major famines of 1315–17 and climatic changes starting with the 1300s, intellectual and social vitality waned until perhaps the 1500s.

These are very slow-moving phenomena, of course, despite terms like *fecundity*. Changes during the period starting about 1750 continued and extended population-related changes that began centuries before in Europe. For our own time, we finally have decisive statistical evidence from comparisons of centrally planned versus market-directed economies of the importance of the political and economic structure in economic development in general and of property rights in particular (Przeworski and Limongi 1993). Earlier I mentioned comparisons of pairs of countries with the same history, language, and culture divided after World War II: Korea, Germany, and China (see table 1 in chap. 2). Further evidence lies in Scully 1992; Scully and Slottje 1992; Gwartney, Lawson, and Block 1996; Holmes, Johnson, and Kirkpatrick 1997; and references in Przeworski and Limongi 1993. These contemporary data help us infer the effects of population growth in causing greater openness, diversity, and decentralization in earlier centuries.

Evolved Patterns of Culture, Values, and Customs

The processes of evolutionary growth extend into technical knowledge, social institutions, language, law, morals, rituals, and practices; all of these "cultural" patterns, which affect human productive capacities as much as the evolving stocks of land, tools, shelter, and other physical capital, constitute one of the most interesting aspects of this subject.

Evolved cultural patterns include voluntary exchange among individuals and also include the markets that function to provide resources in increasing quantities, as discussed earlier; institutions that pass on knowledge, such as schools; libraries and legends and storytellers, all of which store knowledge; and monasteries, laboratories, and research-and-development departments that produce knowledge.

It is plausible that these cultural, nonmaterial aspects of human life have changed only under the pressure of necessity, as represented by increased population, and that in turn the new conditions then influenced the growth of population. If humankind had not developed patterns of behavior and association that increased rather than decreased the available physical resources, we would not still be here. If, as humankind's numbers increased (or even as numbers remained nearly stationary), behavior patterns had led to diminished supplies of plants and animals, less flint for tools, and disappearing wood for fires and construction, I would not be writing these pages, and you would not be reading them. At least for now, these processes cannot be documented for prehistory, of course, but we have begun to develop knowledge about the operation of similar processes in recent decades and the present, for example, changes in institutions for agricultural research (see Hayami and Ruttan 1987 for a review), that corroborate this assessment.

Humans have evolved into creators and problem solvers to an extent that people's constructive behavior now outweighs their destructive behavior, as evidenced by our increasing life expectancy and richness of consumption. And in recent centuries and decades, the positive net balance of each generation has been increasing rather than decreasing. This view of the human as builder conflicts with the view of the human as destroyer, the latter a view that underlies the thought of many other writers on the subject.

Rules and Customs about Having Children

Paradoxically, *rules and customs that lead to population growth* rather than to population stability or decline may be part of our inherited capacity to deal successfully with resource problems in the long run, though the added people may exacerbate the problems in the short run. Such rules and customs probably lead to long-run success of societies in two ways. First, as noted earlier, high fertility leads to increased chances of a group's physical survival, other things being equal. For example, though the Parsis of India have been, as individuals, very successful economically, as a people they seem headed for disappearance in the long run due to their marriage and fertility patterns. Second, high fertility leads to resource problems, which then evoke solutions that usually (eventually, though there may be suffering until then) leave humanity better off in the long run than if the problems had never arisen — the fundamental process of civilization's progress as discussed earlier. In a more direct chain of events, rules and customs leading to high fertility yield an increased supply of ingenious people, who respond productively to the increased demand for goods.

The Persistence of "Culture"

Hume and more recently Hayek (1989; see many references there to Hume) emphasize the importance of deeply ingrained customs whose functions we cannot rationally understand yet whose rejection can cause severe damage. But this does not imply that values and "culture" have a life of their own that is transmitted from generation to generation resistant to external conditions and that has a crucial role in determining economic success. Indeed, as Jones quotes Fenoaltea, in the spirit of Petty in the epigraph that precedes the preface to this essay, part of the economic historian's "cast of mind is the refusal to recognize systematic differences in casts of mind" (1988, 186).

My own view is close to that which sociologist Ronald Freedman has expressed. Values have an effect on behavior, says Freedman, but only for a matter of years; they are mainly an intermediate variable between objective conditions and behavior; they transmit the impulse from the former to the latter with something of a lag. In the case of fertility, for example, it apparently takes perhaps half a generation for the fertility pattern of an immigrant's place of origin (say, a poor Catholic farming village in Poland) in the early 1900s to be replaced with the fertility of the place of destination (say, the United States; for details, see Simon 1974, 104–7).

The Effects of Population upon Psychology

The most difficult effect to pin down is the influence of population growth and economic development, and their proximate effects discussed earlier, upon individual psychology and small-group sociology. Adam Smith remarks that "The progressive state is in reality the cheerful and the hearty state to all the different orders of the society. The stationary is dull; the declining melancholy." And it was a commonplace during the earlier part of the industrial revolution that industrial work discipline, including attention to the daily time schedule for work hours, was both important and slow to develop.

Many writers have discussed the mentality of progress and the notion of systematic scientific progress (e.g., Kuznets and his "epochal innovation" discussed in chap. 5); both ideas were concomitants of the industrial revolution. Though these observations about psychological and small-group effects may be accurate, however, they do not stand on the same level of demonstrated fact as do the phenomena discussed in the earlier parts of this essay. Yet the brevity of this treatment here should not be taken as suggesting that these factors may not be of great significance.

CHAPTER 5

The Enigma of China, India, and Europe

Chapter 5 constitutes a defense against a possible criticism of this essay. Because the chapter is not an element in the central argument, it combines some materials used elsewhere in the essay with some additional materials.

The following issue is frequently raised: If more people generate more ideas and knowledge, stimulate growth of markets and cities, and, hence, produce higher productivity and income, why did the modernization revolution not begin in India and China? Why did China and India lag further and further behind Europe even though their population sizes and densities were greater? The same answer fits both forms of the question.

Mokyr makes this a central question in understanding the history of world population growth. He speaks of "The immense difficulty of the question of why China fell behind" (1990a, 224). He also says that "The Chinese experience is a powerful counterexample to the Boserup-Simon theory that population pressure leads to technological progress."[1] So the topic certainly must be addressed here, though I argue that it is a nonproblem for present purposes.

It was noted earlier that in accord with the simplest supposition about population size, China was indeed a technological leader, apparently by a wide margin, until perhaps 1400. China also led economically. Differences in education explain much of the huge difference between the West and the East at present, but educational differences probably do not explain what happened starting five centuries ago. At that time printing had barely begun to be practiced, and formal education was too sparse in both continents for any difference to explain the activities that produced the inventions and adoptions of innovations that occurred.

The response to the China-Europe question offered here is that the question cannot be answered scientifically, at least at present. There are three major elements in that response: (1) There indeed were structural differences in the *political-institutional systems,* as mentioned earlier, but the standard analysis based on those differences does not constitute a satisfactory answer to the question at hand. (2) Both Asia and Europe were *parts of the same larger system,* and hence the question of why they differed is not a question that matters for this book; the question addressed here is why Sudden Modern Progress began *anywhere in the world* in 1750–1800. (3) An answer to the question set forth previously *cannot be given scientifically* because there is only one pair of entities to be compared, and not a larger sample, without any evidential saving grace — that is, there is an econometric problem. The rest of this section will expand on these three elements.

Structural Differences in the Political-Social Systems

In Europe there occurred concurrently, along with population growth, a nexus of interconnections between loosening of feudal ties, growth of cities, increases in personal economic freedom, political freedom, greater openness of societies, competition among the various European states, economic advance, popular government, and general economic advance. Hume ([1977] 1987), McNeill (1963), Jones (1981), and others have suggested that over several centuries the relative looseness and changeableness of social and economic life in Europe, compared to that in China and India, helps account for the emergence of modern growth in the West rather than in the East. Change implies economic disequilibria that (as Schultz [1975] reminds us) imply exploitable opportunities that then lead to augmented effort. (Such disequilibria also cause the production of new knowledge, it would seem.)[2]

More specifically, the extent to which individuals are free to pursue economic opportunity and the extent to which there is protection for the property that they purchase and create for both production and consumption, together with the presence of diversity and competition at all levels, seem to make an enormous difference in the propensity of people to develop and innovate. Clough (1951, 10) discussed the importance for the "development of civilization" of

a social and political organization which will permit individuals to realize their total potential as contributors to civilization. What is implied here is that in a system where social taboos or political restrictions prevent large segments of a culture's population from engaging in types of activity which add most to civilization, the culture cannot attain the highest degree of civilization of which it is capable. Thus the caste system in India, restrictions on choice of occupation in medieval Europe, and the anti-Semitic laws of Nazi Germany curtailed the civilizing process.

This factor seems to be the best explanation of Europe forging ahead in comparison to the recent centuries' histories of India and China.[3]

As Jones puts it, "[T]he Qing economy, impressively expansible though it proved, failed to move from *extensive to intensive* growth because its political structure did not establish a legal basis for sufficient new economic activity outside agriculture" (1981, 20). That observation, together with the mobility and political competition in Europe, and the closure of China, seems convincing explanation for the European miracle and the lack of a comparable Chinese miracle. This is the way Hume put the same idea sometime before 1777:

> Here then are the advantages of free states. Though a republic should be barbarous, it necessarily, by an infallible operation, gives rise to LAW, even before mankind have made any considerable advances in the other sciences. From law arises security: From security curiosity: And from curiosity knowledge. . . .
>
> GREECE was a cluster of little principalities, which soon became republics; and being united both by their near neighbourhood, and by the ties of the same language and interest, they entered into the closest intercourse of commerce and learning. . . .
>
> EUROPE is at present a copy at large, of what GREECE was formerly a pattern in miniature. . . .
>
> In CHINA, there seems to be a pretty considerable stock of politeness and science, which, in the course of so many centuries, might naturally be expected to ripen into something more perfect and finished, than what has yet arisen from them. But CHINA is one vast empire, speaking one language, governed by one law, and sympathizing in the same manners. The authority of any teacher, such as CONFUCIUS, was propagated easily from one corner of the empire to the other. None had courage to resist the torrent of popular opinion. And posterity was not bold enough to dispute what had been universally received by their ancestors. This seems to be one natural reason, why the sciences have made so slow a progress in that mighty empire.
>
> If we consider the face of the globe, EUROPE, of all the four parts of the world, is the most broken by seas, rivers, and mountains; and GREECE of all countries of EUROPE. Hence these regions were naturally divided into several distinct governments. And hence the sciences arose in GREECE; and EUROPE has been hitherto the most constant habitation of them. . . .
>
> The next observation, which I shall make on this head, is, That

nothing is more favourable to the rise of politeness and learning, than a number of neighbouring and independent states, connected together by commerce and policy. The emulation, which naturally arises among those neighbouring states, is an obvious source of improvement: But what I would chiefly insist on is the stop, which such limited territories gives both to power and to authority ([1777] 1987, 118, 120–3, 427–8).

Arguments against the Humian Explanation

The Humian explanation cannot be considered a complete answer and a stopping point to the discussion, for some of the following reasons.

The Failed Record of Explanations of the Rises and Falls of Nations

It is sobering to reflect on the long history of now-rejected informed opinions about the success and failure of countries: Protestant work ethic; Anglo-Saxon and European race; natural resources (or the lack of them); temperature and climate; north-south location; cultural explanations by the bushel; and on and on. This record of failures should warn us against any monocausal explanation.

Other Possible Explanations

One might also adduce such other possible explanations as the diffusion of printing in Europe. This might have occurred because of the importance of the written Bible in Christianity and/or the character system of writing. But whatever the reason, Western-style printing (including newspapers, which are very important for a modern economic society) did not arrive in Japan and China until the middle of the nineteenth century;[4] the interrelated absence of Western printing and of literacy could by themselves have exerted a huge drag on the development of China.

Concerning "the availability of journals" and other printed media, which surely are a crucial element in development: DeVries (1976) tells us that "London's first daily newspaper, the *Daily Courant,* was established in 1702; by 1709 eighteen dailies appeared in the city. For Europe as a whole newspaper sales have been estimated at 7 million copies per year by 1753" (189). These observations should be compared to the lack of any newspapers at all in China for another century and half, as noted earlier in this chapter.

One might also mention such other possible explanatory factors as the probable absence of the Arabic number system in China (the abacus continued to be used there even though it had disappeared before the eighteenth century in Europe [Dantzig 1954, 35]); higher life expectancy in Europe than in India and China, where well into the twentieth century the death rate was higher than that in Europe perhaps as early as 1600; and the greater possibility of migration within Europe than in India and China.[5] None of these factors can be shown to be decisive, alone or in combination with one or more other factors.

Was an Appropriate System "Inevitable" in China and India?

The reader might ask whether the very existence of a counterproductive legal-political structure (such as that of China) is consistent with the argument here that such phenomena are endogenous. But endogeneity does not imply immediate response; if history is clear on any one point it is that an appropriate political-economic system does not appear immediately when circumstances change. It is hope enough that even a rough approximation of such a system will appear sometime short of the very long run.

Should Poverty Not Have Induced Progress?

Elsewhere (Simon 1987a) I have systematically developed the hypothesis that the combination of a person's wealth and opportunities affects a person's exertion of effort, which may seem to contradict the thrust of this essay. Ceteris paribus, the less wealth a person has, the greater the person's drive to take advantage of economic opportunities. The millions of villagers in India and China certainly have had plenty of poverty to stimulate them. But they have lacked opportunities because of the static and immobile nature of their village life. In contrast, villagers in Western Europe apparently had more mobility, fewer constraints, and more exposure to crosscurrents of all kinds. Hence they were more easily able to loosen their rural ties and join in the changes that led to Sudden Modern Progress.

Multicausality

Mokyr comments that "The problem seems so huge that it is tempting to resort to some exogenous but relatively simple theory to explain a massive societal behavior change" (1990a, 226). He examines many such simple explanations that have been proposed and finds them all wanting. He implicitly endorses an entire complex of causes, as does Kuznets. Kuznets does suggest that the "epochal innovation" of a scientific attitude may have been crucial.

[M]odern economic growth, as observable for a substantial number of currently developed countries, could best be viewed as a process based on an epochal innovation — a complex of additions to useful knowledge which raises sharply the stock of technological and social knowledge in the world, and which when exploited is the source of the high rate of aggregate increase and of the high rate of structural shifts that characterize modern economies. Whether this basic source is best described as the increasing application of science to problems of economic production and organization — with the stimulus coming from the exogenous growth of science, basic and applied — or whether the emphasis should be on changes in men's views and social institutions which, at one and the same time, stimulate the growth of science and of its useful applications is an important question, but it need not concern us here. Whatever the source, the increase in the stock of useful knowledge and the extension of its application are of the essence in modern economic growth; and the rate and locus of the increase in knowledge markedly affect the rate and structure of economic growth. (1966, 286)

The process may be understood, I think, in light of a contemporary analogy: the difficult and relatively unproductive professional lives led by economists and other researchers who work in universities in poor countries. This analogy is developed at length at the end of this chapter.

Indeed, there is some reason to think that the entire intellectual infrastructure was much more fruitful in Europe than in China, as evidenced by the vibrant atmosphere in the major cities of Europe in the 1600s. Why, then, should one not think that ingenious Chinese individuals were hampered by more of the ordinary difficulties of lack of development than Europeans were around the 1600s?

And though China and Europe may (or may not) have started off with equally propitious situations for agents of progress to operate in, an unpredictable shock such as the death of a benign ruler and the onset of a disastrous regime, or a war and invasion, or a climatic shift could have set off a cumulative process wherein the circumstances were progressively more different for prospective agents of progress.

The Ecumene of Asia and Europe

The emergence of the ecumene encompassing both Asia and Europe was mentioned earlier. This concept suggests that the question of why the entities within the ecumene differed — as if they were separate, disconnected entities—is not the proper question for this essay; rather, the key question here is why Sudden Modern Progress began *somewhere* about 1750 or 1800.[6] Though he focuses on the differences between Europe and Asia, Jones notes that "European economic history is a special case of the economic history of all Eurasia" (1981, 3). He adds that attempting to analyze why the two continents differed is not profitable in this context.

Additional evidence that it is reasonable to consider the continental entities part of the same system for the purposes of the present analysis is that early advances in Asia (such as printing, paper, and gunpowder) fed into later developments in Europe and therefore should get part of the credit for the overall development. And a complicated interrelatedness, referred to earlier, was the trade-based division of labor between India and Great Britain; an increase in the standard of living of the latter led to a decrease in the standard of living of the former.

Trade in textiles and cotton between India and Great Britain was so great that because of the decline in Indian textile production, Indian urban income fell sharply, cities shrank, and the level of urbanization fell. Hard as it is to believe, income in Indian cities at the turn of the twentieth century is said to have been only half or a quarter of what it was in the second half of the sixteenth century (Bairoch 1988, 401). And the (proportional) deurbanization at that time was not restored until 1930. This suggests a division-of-labor process between urban and agricultural areas similar to that which spontaneously occurred between the U.S. South and North in the nineteenth century and to that which was forced on Indonesia by the Dutch after 1830.[7] (We should note, however, that there also was deurbanization in China over much the same period, and Bairoch says that the decline was "in no way imputable to colonization," which casts some doubt on his trade explanation of India's decline.)

One may think of the overall process as follows: The total population in Eurasia taken as a whole (plus the state of technology) became great enough to support one or more successful forays into SMP. As with multiple research-and-development teams working on the same problem, one does not expect all of them to succeed or even that the biggest one with the highest potential will succeed. In hindsight one might offer the informed opinion (as in the "Structural Differences in the Political-Social Systems" section of this chapter) that team China did not make it because of too strong a structure of authority (perhaps induced by a high density of population, together with pride), compelling inwardness, no international trade, and no colonies. Similarly, one can speculate that

India failed for many of the same reasons, though perhaps also because of the caste structure rather than because of excessive central authority.

Additionally, Woodruff (1973) makes a good argument for the importance of trade and imported treasures in the rise of the West after 1700. China and India lacked this element.

China certainly had at least reached the status of being a candidate for success half a millennium ago, as Jones makes clear. Its standard of living rivaled that of Europe as of 1500 (see fig. 71). Perhaps a complete change in the form of its government could have made a difference, as perhaps Hume thought. For perspective, could one imagine that low-population-density Africa or South America was a candidate at that time — let alone North America or Australia?

As with a drug company being large and strong enough to afford a set of three research teams that includes one that is eventually successful, we can say that by two or three centuries ago, the ecumene of Eurasia had became capable of producing three "laboratories," one of which succeeded — and only that was necessary for Sudden Modern Progress to become a fact.

In explaining the slowness or nondevelopment of horology in China, Landes again and again mentions the absence in earlier times of sufficient human talent.

> Needham . . . remarks that from Chang Heng (78–142), astronomer royal, mathematician, and engineer, the first in Chinese history to build a water-driven armillary sphere, to Matteo Ricci, the Jesuit missionary of the sixteenth century who first brought mechanical timepieces to China — that is, over a span of fifteen hundred years — only a half-dozen, perhaps only four, astronomer-clockmakers kept the great tradition alive in China or, more accurately, revived it at intervals. Needham presents this fact as something of a wondrous economy: "It is well worth noting how few men it took to span all the centuries of clockwork drive mechanisms." He might have written that nothing better illustrates the constraints on experiment and the impediments to diffusion of knowledge in this domain than the paucity of successful practitioners over time. (Landes 1983, 35)

This accords with the general remark by Jewkes, Sawyers, and Stillerman, cited earlier in connection with contemporary science in note 7 of chapter 1, that there "are always too few minds of the highest calibre and there is a limit to the help that can be afforded them in their original thinking" (Jewkes, Sawyers, and Stillerman 1958, 162). Reinforcing this

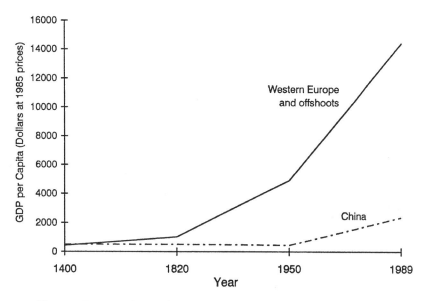

Fig. 71.   Comparative performance of Western Europe (and its offshoots) and China, 1400–1989. (From Maddison 1991, 10.)

point in discussing the search for a clock that would solve the longitude problem, Landes says that in the 1600s "Spain simply did not have the pool of knowledge and talent to solve the problem" (1983, 112).

China obviously had enough human beings at the time of which Needham and Landes write, by comparison with the raw talent pool of Europe. But it did not have enough *trained* persons working in *congenial settings.* A larger total population would have been likely, ceteris paribus, to have increased that pool, as also was the case in Spain. But again, let us put this problem aside by focusing on the Eurasian ecumene as the relevant unit and on the sudden leap a few hundred years ago as the key event, rather than trying to explain the details of the past couple of hundred years.

The Dominating Econometric Problem

One might say: If China had for exogenous reasons come to have a different set of political institutions than it actually did in (say) 1300, it might have entered into intensive growth and thereby speeded up the entire progress of humanity. But can one be *reasonably sure* that even if it had had the "optimum" institutions, China would have moved to a faster path and to intensive growth? Even if the structural analysis in the earlier part of this chapter is correct, there still must be much uncertainty. That is, an answer to the question set forth in this section cannot be given scientifically because there is a sample of only one pair of entities to be compared. In other words, the intellectual roadblock is placed there by sound econometrics and statistical inference rather than by the absence of penetrating historical analysis.

It would seem nearly impossible to explain a single such comparison with any surety because of the tiny difference in growth rates between the successful and the unsuccessful examples. The difficulty is illustrated by the large number of major outliers in any cross-sectional regression analysis of growth; this shows that even a proven important variable — such as economic freedom, nowadays — fails to be dominant in many cases; indeed, it fails in enough cases that correlation coefficients are not high.

Who can claim to offer a conclusive explanation of why southern Italy has done so much worse economically than has northern Italy? Or why French Canada has done worse than English Canada? Yet in those cases the political-legal structures were the same for both regions within the countries, which ought to make the comparison easier than the China-Europe situation.

This is the nub of the econometric problem: When the difference in the dependent variable is large, and there is only one big difference in independent variables, one can sometimes draw a solid conclusion. One could fairly decide that the Communism-capitalism structural difference explains postwar differences in economic growth between East and West Germany, even if we did not have corroborating evidence for North and South Korea, and for Taiwan and mainland China, because the prior conditions were much the same for each pair in the comparisons and because the growth-rate differences were very large.

In contrast, the yearly growth-rate differences between China and Europe were small. Yes, they cumulate to a lot. But the yearly differences in the period we are talking of surely were not independent of each other; rather, they depended upon past achievements — the cumulativeness emphasized by Kuznets.

[A]ggregate growth benefited from the easily *cumulative* character of modern tested knowledge. Handicraft skills embodied in mortal human beings cannot be accumulated as easily as modern technological knowledge embodied in quantitative formulations and innovations based on overtly measurable and testable characteristics of natural and social processes. It is the very overtness and easy embodiment of tested knowledge and of its scientific base in a variety of durable forms independent of the personal skills of human beings that make both for its easy communicability and worldwide availability, and for the steadily cumulative results. (Kuznets 1966, 290)

The model of cumulative stochastic growth is strengthened by the saga of the intertwined development of mechanical power and machine tools in Europe starting in the eighteenth century, as told by Usher and in chapter 3. The process comprises one advance following another after the latter was made possible by the former. For example, the saga of the cylinders in the steam engine is familiar. At first the gap between piston and cylinder walls was a loose enough fit that a smaller finger could be inserted, and rags were used to make it tighter. Then boring machines were improved, themselves driven by steam. And other improved tools were produced that contributed to the process.

Another example: There are differences in economic growth rates among U.S. states. But would one feel confident in explaining a Massachusetts-Indiana differential? One would feel more confident if several New England states moved together and moved differently than several Midwestern states — unless there were common regional elements; tax differences are somewhat independent from state to state and might offer a satisfactory explanation.

Similarly, the cumulative differences in population growth in the nineteenth century between the UK and France were large, but the yearly differences were small. And who would now claim to be able to explain those trend differences with surety? True, many have offered explanations, such as the inheritance system. But would you consider any such explanation to be more than an informed opinion? There are so many differences between the two countries that one might adduce, and the rate differences are so small — even the completed-family fertility differences are not huge — that doubt must continue. If one were to array 100 countries, one might test one's hypothesis about the France-UK difference, but even then there surely would be many exceptions and a low (multiple) correlation coefficient.

One has better basis for a before-after comparison of the same country — say, the birthrate in East Germany before and after the fall of the Berlin Wall — because so much else was the same (language, culture, etc.). It also helps when the event is sudden. But a China-Europe comparison does not have these favorable characteristics.

An analogy: Black squirrels seem to be displacing brown squirrels in my part of the world. But I doubt that any ecologist would bet much on any explanation of the phenomenon. In contrast, the total squirrel population seems to vary over the years, and the number of squirrels killed on the streets seems to rise and fall. That variation over time might be reasonably explicable in terms of changes in the food supply, breeding patterns, and so on.

Still another reason for seeing the entire matter as chancy rather than determined is the small numbers of persons involved, as noted in the preceding quotation from Landes. Nowhere does chance operate with a more fickle hand than in the adoption of inventions where adoption decisions are confined to a few persons — as often is the case. Was it not possible that Savery could have failed to find an adopter for his steam engine and that the entire course of invention following from that adoption could have not taken place?[8]

Despite the healthy scientific tendency to focus on statistical aggregations of microevents — see the epigraphs by Petty and Kuznets at the beginning of the preface to this essay — I will now reverse course and remind us that there always is the possibility that one of Jonathan Hughes's "vital few" can make a crucial difference, even for entities as large as a subcontinent. Might not a Chinese emperor who decided to close China — then, out of inertia, was followed in this policy by his successors, backed by those who acted from their own interests — have made a decisive decision whose consequences then cumulated?

Analogy to sports results may help bring out the econometric problem at hand. Preliminary work with Manouchehr Mokhtari on the outcomes of Olympics games from 1956 to 1984 finds that total population and the level of average income explain much of the ranking of countries in medals counts. Nevertheless, there are some far-out outliers — for example, India, which has scored far below its statistically expected results as well as far below China and even below many smaller poor countries; and East Germany, which scored far above its statistically expected results. If the only data that were available were for India, China, and a few other poor countries, it would not be possible to arrive at a sound conclusion about the roles of population size and the standard of living. And the role of political system might therefore receive disproportionate weight.

Here is another sports analogy. The countries competing in the Olympics may be presumed to be very different in many ways. This might well produce large discrepancies between actual and statistically expected performance. The performances among high school basketball teams in a given U.S. state — say, Indiana — may be expected to be more regular. And indeed, schools with larger student bodies usually beat schools with smaller student bodies, so much so that the winning of the championship by a smallest-category school was sufficient occasion for a Hollywood movie. But apparent anomalies do happen, and if one did not have available a large pool of such schools as context, those anomalies would be mysterious and challenging to the imagination, as in the case of the small school just mentioned. There are other cases where one school wins against another of the same size and character for many years in a row. Is it the coach that matters? Is it just the workings of chance? These are among the true mysteries of a world filled with variability.

Of course there also exist cases that are quite explicable — such as a few tiny private high schools that have national-caliber basketball teams year after year. The obvious explanation is that they recruit talented players from far and wide. This is the sort of case to which historians liken the China-Europe comparison, but that comparison seems not at all analogous.

A somewhat more ambiguous case is the small Minnesota town that has produced many Olympic medal winners in speed skating. Is the water better in Minnesota? Is the town just a suburb of a big city? Or is this just chance? Similar questions apply to the Australian dominance of tennis in the decades after World War II and the predominance of major-league baseball players from a single small town in the Dominican Republic.[9]

The point of the sports analogies is that any single comparison of China and Europe is attempting to explain more than can possibly be explained by the evidence — probably even any evidence that can be accumulated in the future.

Kuznets (1966, 462–68), too, suggested a stochastic approach to what he called the "restricted locus" problem: the problem of explaining why the industrial revolution occurred in Great Britain rather than in larger France or Germany and why in Europe and not in China. He first speculated that smallness of political unit may have been an advantage, by which we may assume he meant that a given large entity of land and people (Europe or China) would do better if it proceeded in several separate units rather than a single unit. He then mused that one of the smaller among the separate units might be the "winner" not just because it was small but also for undetermined stochastic reasons. He refers to this argument as "purely formal." "There are many more small countries than large — given the usual skewness in the distribution of politically independent units by size — and hence, other conditions being equal, there is a greater chance that the pioneer will be small rather than large" (467). So ultimately Kuznets suggests that we should not try to explain, or consider explained, the actual causes of Great Britain and Europe being the locuses of the breakthrough. Rather, he says, we should simply consider the matter unexplained, as the present essay suggests.

Interestingly, in the very essay in which Hume offers his discussion of the China-Europe differential — "Of the Rise and Progress of the Arts and Sciences" — he begins with an excellent statement of the econometric problem of too-small samples and statistical variability.

> Nothing requires greater nicety, in our enquiries concerning human affairs, than to distinguish exactly what is owing to chance, and what proceeds from causes; nor is there any subject, in which an author is more liable to deceive himself by false subtilties *[sic]* and refinements. To say, that any event is derived from chance, cuts short all farther enquiry concerning it, and leaves the writer in the same state of ignorance with the rest of mankind. But when the event is supposed to proceed from certain and stable causes, he may then display his ingenuity, in assigning these causes; and as a man of any subtilty *[sic]* can never be at a loss in this particular, he has thereby an opportunity of swelling his volumes, and discovering his profound knowledge, in observing what escapes the vulgar and ignorant.
>
> The distinguishing between chance and causes must depend upon every particular man's sagacity, in considering every particular incident. But, if I were to assign any general rule to help us in applying this distinction, it would be the following, What depends upon a few persons is, in a great measure, to be ascribed to chance, or secret and unknown causes: What arises from a great number, may often be accounted for by determinate and known causes. . . .
>
> For the same reason, it is more easy to account for the rise and progress of commerce in any kingdom, than for that of learning; and a state, which should apply itself to the encouragement of the one, would be more assured of success, than one which should cultivate the other. Avarice, or the desire of gain, is a universal passion, which operates at all times, in all places, and upon all persons: But curiosity, or the love of knowledge, has a very limited influence, and requires youth, leisure, education, genius, and example, to make it govern any person. (Hume [1777] 1987, 111–13)

The econometric problem we face here is related to the concept of path dependence[10] as expressed in the cumulative random growth models of Herbert Simon. If one assumes that two or more entities start out at the same size (or level of wealth), and each is incremented by a random percentage of its size in the prior period, the entities are likely to arrive at very different sizes after any given number of periods. Incrementing by a proportion rather than by an absolute amount expresses the path dependence, in that the size in the previous state influences the absolute amount of change; a higher state of technology, say, induces a greater change in technology. In such a random fashion, China, India, and Europe could have arrived at very different states of wealth even if there were no "real" nonrandom economic or other force at work.

This sort of random growth model runs counter to the natural human propensity to assume order and causality and consequently to search for an explanation for an observed outcome. But if one lacks a very solid agreed-upon explanation, a random growth model seems the most modest and defensible approach.

Landes (1994) provides additional references to writers who have viewed the China-versus-Europe and Britain-versus-France outcomes as "accidents." He views some as holding this view on ideological grounds, and he himself rejects this view on the grounds of "a golden rule of historical analysis: *big processes call for big causes*" and "all these things have their reasons" (653). But he does not, I think, come to grips with the possibility of a *cumulatively large* random process whose first step may have been a *small* "accident."

The extent of path dependence may be much greater than we suppose at first. In fact, it may cast light on all of human progress and not just the China-Europe comparison. Consider as an example the development of the process of statistical inference. There is nothing in the arithmetical techniques of statistical analysis that in principle could not have been invented much earlier. But the first analyses of census data apparently were done by John Graunt in 1662. Graunt's work was based on the London Bills of Mortality, and the collection of these first vital statistics predictably was done in London, a very large city in a period of unprecedented wealth and growth. The availability of these data then stimulated Graunt to collect new data on his own in the town of Romsey, which he would not have done if he had not wished to compare some such data with the London data. And the first published formal test of a hypothesis seems to have been made by John Arbuthnott in 1718 (concerning the greater probability of a male than a female human birth). Arbuthnott's inference was based upon the existence of 80 years of vital statistics containing data on the sexes of children born, which apparently grew out of the Bills of Mortality, and his work probably was stimulated as well by Graunt's famous study. Arbuthnott's work, together with the work on probability that had been done by Parisian savants such as Pascal (though some of the work was done at Port Royal) and by European mathematicians such as Bernoulli and Gauss, came together in Thomas Bayes's theorem and then moved into the stream of work passing through the beginning of modern statistics by Francis Galton. All this was "organic" growth, and it is nearly unthinkable that the endpoint of this process should have been suddenly produced all by itself in some other place, especially a rural place or a place where census data had not been collected (such as China through the years). This is so, even though all the necessary mathematical devices were readily available.

There also seem clear links from the developments just described to John Snow's statistical discovery in London in 1854 that cholera was caused by polluted water. Snow had to collect voluminous data on each death. "Snow and his assistant systematically . . . went up and down the streets listing for each household, the age and sex of all residents, the address, and the name of the company that supplied their water" (Gehan and Lemak 1994). Snow's work could in principle have been done earlier, in any place where there had been cholera, requiring as a condition only that there had been water supplies from several wells that differed in whether or not they were polluted.[11] But his work was preceded by Francis Bissett Hawkins's *Elements of Medical Statistics* in 1829, the first, and very remarkable, tract in epidemiology. Though I have not dug into this history (my knowledge of it comes from Gehan and Lemak), it seems plausible that Hawkins linked backward to Graunt and forward to Snow.

Many of the other great discoveries about the prevention of infectious diseases, the main early killers in human history, also took place in the large cities. For example, Semmelweiss discovered the cause of childbed fever in the 1840s in Vienna, then the large capital of the Austro-Hungarian empire (Semmelweiss 1983). The large hospital in which he worked contained many cases for observation; such a hospital could only be found in a large city. And it is not likely that the sort of mortality data Semmelweiss used would have been available in earlier centuries or in smaller places.

According to Mokyr, inventions may not require that the conditions become right for them but rather simply that no one thought of them earlier. He may certainly be correct about *some* inventions. Here is an example that would seem to fit his description: Across the back of the wider part of men's ties is a one-inch strip of material — usually containing the brand name — through which passes the narrower end, to hold it in place unexposed. This innovation first appeared sometime in the 1940s or 1950s and completely replaced tie clips, but it could have been invented decades earlier. I assume that it was diffused soon after the invention. But for such advances as taking a survey of the affected population for data on disease incidence, surely many people were forced to think about the situation at some earlier time, and many must have thought of gathering such information; that idea comes too naturally not to have been thought of by anyone.

Another example of such path dependence in the development of practical concepts: in its discrete form, dynamic programming requires no more than multiplication and can be taught to middle-school students. Why, then, was this most powerful of all decision-making engines first invented by a mid–twentieth-century mathematician, Richard Bellman, culminating in a 1957 publication? This invention might be one of Mokyr's cases of no one thinking of it first, though the conditions for invention were much the same facing many people in the past. But the better explanation[12] may be that this was the first time in history that a group of the persons who would be likely to produce this innovation — mathematicians and operations researchers — was employed by organizations such as the Rand Corporation and was then exposed to the sorts of problems that would evoke such developments as dynamic programming. Hence this discovery may be seen as a result of the demand for better decision making by the military, by government, and by business firms, as well as by the supply of the various concepts that went into the discovery and the supply of trained persons in the United States and in the world who might have produced the discovery. The reader will notice the attention here to the existing stock of knowledge in a society rather than to the culture of the society as it relates to the spirit of discovery and the encouragement of intellectual activity.

Figure 14 (in chap. 1) brought out the nature of path dependence in rail travel. A large proportion of railway track laid before 1920 was in Europe or was built by Europeans. This construction was an outgrowth of European wealth as well as of familiarity with the steam engine in Europe. In the same way, it was no accident that until well into the twentieth century most of the world's oil reserves and production were in the United States, even though there were other areas of the world that were as well endowed with potential production as the United States (see fig. 72).

This discussion of path dependence was intended to show that a random growth model can explain the "European Miracle" even without some dominating explanatory factor being present in Europe rather than in China.

Conclusion

The prudent response to the question of why Europe forged ahead of China is that an answer is beyond the scope of scientific analysis at present. But this does not imply that the question is an enigma. It should

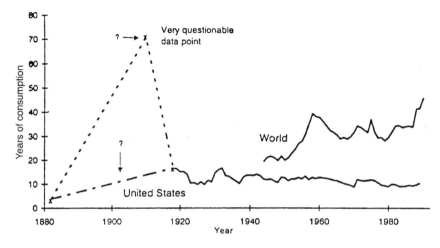

Fig. 72. Crude oil, United States and world known reserves/annual production. (From Simon 1996.)

not be allowed to trouble us any more than the fall of a coin onto its head, or the last-minute victory of one team rather than another.

In order to make more vivid and understandable the difficulty of making new inventions and having them adopted in a country such as China or India circa 1600, consider this contemporary analogy that many readers will understand from their own firsthand and secondhand experiences: the professional lives led by economists and other researchers employed by the universities in poor countries. The data show clearly that these people produce little new science, though the very same people (or people indistinguishable from them) can be very productive when working in universities in developed countries. The causes are many and varied but almost all related, directly or indirectly, to the overall standard of living.

Researchers in a poor country lack modern instruments and have available only primitive tools, perhaps nowadays not having computers (in Israel in 1968 three professors usually shared one desk, meaning that only one could be there at a time); sometimes they are without light and heat for many hours every day or for days and weeks at a time (as in the early and mid–1990s in many former Soviet countries); they lack research funds to hire assistants; war (including military service) and other social disturbances cause work disruption (as in several African countries); graduate students are poorly trained; interested colleagues may be in short supply; there are no funds to travel abroad and meet colleagues who will bring one up to speed on recent developments and provide mutual reinforcement; the administrators may have little interest in the production of research and do not reward it with status and salary, reducing incentive; recent journals and books may not be held by the university library or, indeed, be found anywhere within the entire country; patent and copyright law may not protect one's intellectual property; inadequate support staff, including lack of English-skilled word-processing and secretarial help; heavy teaching loads; pay may be so low that the researcher must moonlight to eke out a living; and if the product of research is locally oriented, the researcher may find insuperable barriers against having his or her work adopted into practice. An unbelievably strong will is required to overcome these obstacles.

Even with the most well-situated institutions in poor countries — such as foreign companies who invest in building poor-country factories in order to take advantage of what they consider to be a favorable wage situation — the lack of physical and human infrastructure often is enough to defeat these efforts and force firms to pull up stakes and return to producing in the developed country.

A researcher has a much better infrastructure for productive work even at the typical third-level North American university, despite teaching loads much heavier than at first- or second-level universities, than does a researcher even in the elite institutions in poor countries. Yet the heavier teaching loads at those third-level North American universities, together with an intellectual climate and a general culture that are not very congenial, and perhaps even hostile, to high-quality research, constitute enough of a barrier to slow or halt even some dedicated and capable scholars who must work in such places.

Seen this way, through the eyes of individuals who might contribute to progress, the issue does not seem so mysterious or difficult as it is often made out to be.

CHAPTER 6

Summary and Conclusions

This essay outlines a theory of the role of population size and density in determining the observed very-long-run trends in the progress of material human welfare and the date of the onset of Sudden Modern Progress.

This is the central question: What conceivable difference in conditions in the past might have had a significant impact on the timing of the breakthrough in material human welfare? The level of technology reached as a result of the accumulation of knowledge throughout human history clearly is crucial. But what produced the accumulated knowledge?

The answer offered is that the size of humanity (and the nexus of human numbers with technology) has been the main driving force. Starting at any particular moment in the past, the length of time it took to reach the modern breakthrough depended on the number of people endowed with intellect and training who lived thereafter, together with the amount of technology in existence at the particular moment about which the question is being asked. It follows that the only possible decisive differences would have been the introduction of knowledge of how to reduce epidemic disease — knowledge of the transmission of cholera and typhoid fever by polluted water, of plague by rats and fleas, and of malaria by mosquitoes. With this knowledge in hand, steps could have been taken to reduce mortality thousands of years ago; no complementary elements of technique or resources were necessary. This cannot be said of other kinds of knowledge or interventions.

The subject of this essay is *material consumer welfare* and not *productive capacity* or *productive knowledge;* this accounts for the kinked time path of the central element studied in this book, as opposed to the gradual time path of the central element studied by such writers as Kuznets.

Another way to put the central point of this essay is that population size was both necessary and sufficient for the history that occurred, whereas no other variable among those that were necessary was also sufficient to determine the path of the resulting progress. Population size was a sufficient force because increasing population would eventually bring about the other necessary conditions for progress. A thought experiment may help explain the point: If the course of population size had been at all points (say) half or double what it actually was, Sudden Modern Progress would have occurred later or earlier than it did. But the same cannot be said of any other variable.

The essay emphasizes some of the elements that affect the *speed of adjustment* to population change, conditions that are different at different times in history and vary from place to place:

1. The state of technical knowledge is clearly the dominant variable in the long run. It is affected by population growth and density, as technology in turn affects population growth and density.
2. Interrelated with changes in knowledge and production technique are changes in social structure. Structural changes are influenced by population variables and vice versa. There has been increasing recognition among historians of the importance of political and economic structure in economic development in even the short run. And population affects these structures in the long run.
3. The growth of markets, with their many associated phenomena, has been a function of population size and density. More people implies more buyers and more sellers and hence less monopoly and more competition and competitive effort.
4. Slowest-changing are the habits, rituals, language, law, morals, and various other social institutions, including sexual and child raising practices. All of these elements are subject to processes of evolutionary change. They not only are affected by population variables but in turn they influence population growth and — differentially — the likelihoods of survival of different human groups. Disease and population density also are mutually influential. Here the argument moves all the way to full biology-like evolutionary thinking, which is at the other end of the methodological spectrum from the sort of physicslike thinking appropriate to very-short-run analysis when the relevant elements are known and fixed. But the evolutionary processes in question are social and cultural rather than biological.

We may conclude with this quotation from Kuznets, which agrees in spirit with the view of the development process offered here, though he wrote more guardedly than I write here, perhaps because less evidence was available to him:

We do not argue that the population of a nation can increase indefi-nitely; it may well reach some nearly stable limit because the birth rate may decline to so low a level as to produce a slight rate of natural increase. Or other factors, such as preference for more leisure or low long-term elasticity of demand for economic goods, may permit and warrant only minor increases in per capita product once it has reached certain high levels. Or international relations may be charac-terized by conflicts which necessitate the expenditure of increasingly larger proportions of national resources on items that are not part of final product. None of these factors which may set a finite limit to the economic growth of a nation is denied by the hypothesis. But it emphasizes the point that *the growth potential that follows from progress in science and technology has no upper limit.*

Two distinct reasons can be advanced in support of this hypothesis. First, additions to knowledge are largely the product of the free inquiring mind. If there is no effective restriction — either prohibi-tion or complete lack of support — on the curiosity-motivated explo-rations of the mind, the search for new theories, new data, and new applications will continue. In other words, since the search is continu-ously self-propelled and aimed at no fixed goal, there is no *internal* source of a limit. This assumption of the *free* mind is both a qualifica-tion of the hypothesis and a partial explanation of the impressive development of tested knowledge during the last two centuries.

Given this continuous play of the free mind, the second reason for an unlimited economic growth potential becomes relevant. And that reason is simply the vastness of the observable universe; or, which is the same thing, the quantitative insignificance of mankind in that universe. (Kuznets 1965, 88; italics added)

The prospect for material human progress is bright. We can count on ever-diminishing constraints, indefinitely.

Other Difficult Matters Requiring Discussion

Will Population Size Matter in the Future?

If the negative population growth (NPG) movement were to have its way, and populations became smaller in the future than now, would it matter to the welfare of future humans? From the standpoint of material human welfare on Earth, I answer: No and yes.

From one point of view, population size in the future will matter very little. There already exists technology to provide food and energy and all other raw materials for vastly larger numbers of people than now exist, indefinitely. Furthermore, the greatly improved and increased communications among nations and individuals all over the world somewhat reduce the effect of its population size on a given nation or continent.

From another point of view, however, population size in the future may matter considerably. As of the end of the twentieth century, we have already gone most of the way from the set of conditions typified by the average life expectancy prevailing only (say) 200 years before. Nevertheless, the speed of the progress from here on with mortality reduction will depend on how many talented minds there are to work on the problems of health. Even if all the people now alive were to have access to as much education as they could use, the pool of skilled and talented people might only be increased by (say) a factor of four. (The principles discussed in the earlier measures suggested for calculating potential inventive power in the past are appropriate here, too.) As with health, much the same is true of the development of fusion power, say knowledgeable persons such as Hans Bethe. So there is still much to do even on Earth, let alone in space. And in the development of grand projects such as peopling the universe, population size will matter. Many people dismiss such possibilities, but remember that many Europeans in the fifteenth century dismissed the possibility of peopling continents other than their own. A larger population size will make these grand works happen sooner rather than later.

The sizes of *particular* countries are outside the scope of the discussion here, which focuses on total world population (or total educated world population). Nevertheless, it is worth raising a question that arises from time to time about whether individual countries can ride on the coattails of other countries with respect to technology — that is, whether there is a free-rider problem. This may be less of a problem than one might think. For one thing, knowledge is not always easily applied locally in a straightforward sense. As a case in point, soybean seeds developed in the United States did not grow well in India until the strains were modified because of the difference in angles of the sun. Additionally, countries like Japan have found that a policy of simply grabbing on to the latest knowledge produced elsewhere can have shortcomings. There is an analogy here to the common idea among U.S. legislators that they need not support research at their own state university. They reason that their state can take advantage of the research done at other universities and therefore have their faculties teach four courses and do no research. The professorial reader of this essay knows why this simply does not work even though it is difficult to explain to nonresearchers.

Do Multiple Discoveries Mitigate the Main Argument?

The only way for population size to have no influence on the (absolute) change in technology is for there to be so many multiple discoveries that additional people would only mean more multiplicate discoveries. But this degree of multiplication does not seem to have been the case throughout history. One telling piece of evidence is that entire continents have long continued without the presence of immediately beneficial practices that have at that time been engaged in elsewhere.

Mortality Reduction as a Counterfactual Proposition

Previously it was stated that even if any particular branch of knowledge had been developed earlier than it was, the course and speed of development could not have been changed much. The conquest of premature mortality in rich countries may be a counterexample (though it is not an exception in the sense that its effect is on human numbers). If the knowledge of the transmission of cholera, plague, childbed fever, and malaria had been discovered earlier, and if sanitation systems and vaccination had been invented earlier, the available knowledge of food production probably would have supported much more rapid growth of population centuries before these events occurred, thereby speeding the breakthrough to Sudden Modern Progress. Unlike most other technology, these discoveries did not require the availability of power other than human or animal muscles for adoption. But even if this medical technology had been available earlier, it would have been difficult to transmit the knowledge because of the lack of development of society at large, including lack of communications (see Winslow 1943; and Cipolla 1981 on epidemic disease). Furthermore, the low educational level of the populace would have limited the rate of adoption (as was still the case with vaccination and even putting raised rims on village wells in India as late as the 1960s and 1970s). Transmission of this knowledge would also have been difficult because rational reception of discoveries until the modern period, and indeed to this date of writing, has remained very slow (see the painful case of Semmelweis and childbed fever [1983]).

Rent Seeking and Future Growth

Jones (1988) suggests that promising bursts of intensive growth were in the past cut short by rent-seeking despotism. That leads one to wonder whether the same could happen in the future.

The likelihood of such an event would seem to have drastically declined because of the increased difficulty of *obtaining* the rents that are sought by the despots. Economic monopoly has declined as transportation, communications, and market sizes have increased; evidence may be found in the increase in labor's share of output from only a little over half in Petty's time to perhaps 80 percent now, and the (riskless) interest rate has declined over the centuries. Moreover, political monopoly has suffered the same fate for much the same reasons, as dramatized by the impact of the fax machine in China during the Tiananmen Square massacre and by the vast emigrations from Cuba and Eastern Europe. It simply is harder to be an effective despot now than in the past — one of the great gains of humanity during the period of Sudden Modern Progress.

CHAPTER 7

Epilogue

At the start of the essay these questions were asked: What governed the speed of progress through the ages? And, why did modern growth begin when it did and not centuries or millennia earlier or later? Let us return to those questions with a metaphor.

Consider a large community of people who are blocked by a wall from crossing over into the land of milk and honey. Only an occasional person, by dint of superior strength, is able to scale the wall. And ladders are too rickety and necessarily too few to allow most of the community to pass over. So the community embarks on the only feasible route—building a ramp of earth to the top of the rampart and then another ramp down on the other side.

So the community embarks on the project with primitive digging tools and carrying vessels, the way the Grand Canal was built in China. The job takes very, very long, but eventually it is done. Some people immediately jump over from the top of the rampart, with a few suffering injury or death; hence most await the completion of the ramp down. Eventually it, too, is completed, and the community passes over the wall to the promised land.

Please note that if the community had been larger, there would have been more hands to dig and carry earth. The process of building ramps would then have been faster, and the community would have passed earlier over the wall to progress.

Let us note that as critical a new element as any in Sudden Modern Progress was (and is) inanimately powered transport and agricultural machinery. With only animal-powered vehicles and agricultural implements, it would have been impossible to free up nearly as many people to produce other goods; most of humanity's labor would still be required for agriculture. Evidence for this may be seen in the trends in total farm population and in the numbers of draft animals and tractors in the United States after 1880 (see fig. 73). (Even the North American Amish who farm with animals benefit from mechanical transport off the farm.) And before about 1700 or even 1800 there did not exist the knowledge

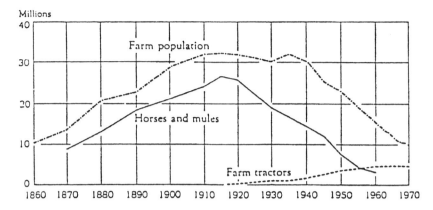

Fig. 73.   U.S. farm motive power, 1860–1970. (From Clawson 1972, 104.)

and tools for working with metals that enabled efficient and long-lasting engines and other machinery parts to be constructed. So the breakthrough into Sudden Modern Progress had to wait until those technical problems had been solved.

Colin Clark has remarked that for premodern farmers in many parts of the world, four hectares of land is as much as a man and his family could farm. With the mechanization in use circa 1997, families in the U.S. Midwest routinely farm 800 acres. Sometimes they do so while both spouses also hold city jobs.

The data in figure 73 on the rise in the use of tractors fit together with the data in figures 40, 41, and 42 (in chap. 3) that show the sped-up decline in the proportion of persons in agriculture starting in the last part of the nineteenth century and going ever faster in the twentieth century. It was the improvements in machine tools and the skills in using them, starting in the eighteenth century, that made possible the new power machinery in agriculture (the steam engine) and in industry (water and steam turbines, as well as steam engines); this entire saga could not have happened earlier.

The data show clearly that roads — a vital adjunct of modern transport vehicles (and hence of modern agriculture — are only built when there are sufficiently high levels of population density and of income (Glover and Simon 1975). This is one economic relationship that one can see clearly with one's eyes alone — as from an airplane flying over Iran even today; it is not hard to imagine that it was much the same in West Virginia in the United States a century ago. Indeed, the Tennessee Valley Authority only finished electrifying its part of the United

States in the 1930s or 1940s, though the technology was known long before then.

If China and India had opened their political and social systems more than they did, it is entirely possible that new knowledge would have been produced at a much faster rate there and then exchanged with new European knowledge, with the entire process of progress being speeded. If they had been able to join in the knowledge-creation process in the centuries after 1400, it might well be that steam- and internal-combustion-powered implements would have been developed before they actually were. And that increment of human beings would therefore have enabled humankind to move ahead faster.

It is with agricultural machinery as it is in the parable of building a ramp over the ramparts: A larger effective population available to join in the work might well have meant earlier breakthrough than actually occurred. Hence the central question may be answered as follows: Population size governed the speed of progress. And the takeoff occurred when it did simply because it was only at that date that (in addition to the accumulation of knowledge up to that point and the existence of a political system that enabled it to happen) there were enough people to finish the work and reach the critical level of the top of the ramparts.

One might suggest that even if Greece and Rome and other high points of past progress of civilization could not have embarked directly on the course that led to the state of contemporary material welfare, it would have been possible for them to have continued to create new technology and raise the standard of living at least somewhat. Perhaps. But there is first the question whether a mostly agrarian country can reasonably be considered to be in a state of advanced intensive growth. And second, there is the question whether such a continued course was possible. Perhaps it is more likely that societies with middle classes smaller than found in modern rich societies are inherently unstable economically, and the endpoint of most instabilities when a society is mostly poor and underdeveloped (though containing brilliant sectors) is likely to be the loss of those brilliant sectors. One might also speculate that until societies are largely urban they are particularly susceptible to attack from outside or to revolution. But such speculation leaves the known facts far behind.

Notes

1. Eric Jones writes that I am interpreting him too narrowly. So I'll let him speak for himself, as he wrote on September 29, 1994:

> Contrary to your impression, I am not in the least opposed to a biological, almost deterministic, style of history. . . . You are representing my views only from *Growth Recurring,* which flew a kite and is not my sole nor most recent piece.
>
> Unlike general historians, then, I believe there are *cumulative* trends as well as cycles. . . . I would characterise many societies as "close to growth" in that the innumerable and constant investment decisions needed, say to keep Qing China fed, shows that such societies weren't *inert.* The question is, what would return their growth to the *intensive* path—something more than breeding more people, in my view. . . .
>
> Furthermore, speaking in long units, the result of economic growth since 1750 *may* still turn out to be transient. I don't expect it to be so, the present cumulative forces are clear enough, but a reaction cannot be ruled out, given the minute length of the growth experiment, the anti-growth greens, and the number of soon-to-be nuclear nutters in the world.

2. Though aside from time indications, no shorthand notation will be used in the text itself, in footnotes and appendixes that state the argument more formally for the purpose of clarity, the following notation will be used: diff = indication of an incremental value indicating a rate of absolute (not proportional) change during a period and intended *not* to mean a difference for the period *as a whole* but rather a rate *during* the period—a "flow" in contrast to the "stock" variable that follows the "diff"; P = population size; P/Lnd = population density; A = level of technology; Y = standard of living, production, or income; K = physical capital; $L = l_0$ = life expectancy at birth; R = natural resources; C = climate; D = disease prevalence; H = health; S = political and social institutions. Infrequently mentioned variables such as law, human biology, and markets will be written fully or abbreviated economically.

3. The relationship of time series and cross-sections here is reminiscent of the relationship in biology between the ladder of the species and the development of the human fetus, prompting the famous expression "*xx* recapitulates phylogeny."

4. The broad brush with which this essay is painted inevitably fails to recognize some important exceptions and details. For example, many Europeans had incomes well above subsistence when few in Asia did; Jones (1981, 4) tells us that late Manchu China had only 2 percent nonproducers of food, whereas at the start of the fourteenth century almost 15 percent of the population of France, Germany, and Britain was not engaged in agriculture. "[T]he real wage tended to be high since at least the thirteenth century, compared with India even in the twentieth century," he writes (3). "Commentators in the seventeenth century were clear that a higher standard of living was enjoyed by a majority of Europeans" than by Asians (5). "By preindustrial times . . . Europe had the edge over other parts of the world in education and literacy" (6).

5. Though Mill is speaking of work rather than consumption in the narrow sense, this essay considers the pain or pleasure of one's breadwinning efforts to be an important aspect of one's standard of living, which is a truer measure of the concept being considered here than is consumption in the narrow sense.

6. *Washington Post,* December 20, 1993, p. A3.

7. There "are always too few minds of the highest calibre and there is a limit to the help that can be afforded them in their original thinking" (Jewkes, Sawyers, and Stillerman 1958, 162).

8. The rapidity of progress within the period since perhaps 1850 is illustrated by the fact that up through the nineteenth century, people would will to their inheritors the staples of everyday life, such as hand tools, cooking utensils, clothing; those were the main elements of value passed on through the generations in many or most families. Nowadays, the value of those items is so small relative to other assets that they are seldom mentioned in wills unless they are valuable heirlooms.

9. This essay might be called "Why Was the Whole World Poor until 1750, but No Longer?" by comparison with Easterlin's "Why Isn't the Whole World Developed?"

10. Bairoch writes:

> Though the use of camels marked progress at one stage of development, it also led to a neglect of the wheel that unquestionably had negative consequences at later stages. . . . as late as the 1920s . . . wheelbarrows are still used very little, if at all, on the work sites of present-day Tehran; and carts are as a rule rare in rural districts in the Middle East. (Bairoch 1988, 377)

11. The term *control variable* is chosen to go along with the term *endogenous* for other variables because *control* does not imply exogeneity; a control variable may well be affected by other variables. The term implies that an exogenous change in the control variable would affect the outcomes in which we are interested, but not all such changes are exogenous.

12. Population growth and size are affected by almost all the other variables mentioned in the course of the discussion, as well as affecting them; most espe-

cially, the standard of living influences both death rates and birthrates, the latter in nonmonotonic and complex fashion. This simultaneous determination would require careful and perhaps sophisticated treatment if the topic were to be framed in a fully realized formal model. I think that it could successfully be considered a recursive system with population growth being the highest-order variable.

There also is a saving grace: The feedback loop from the standard of living to fertility and even to mortality has only become marked in the centuries after 1750 or 1800, which is after the phenomenon that is the focus of the essay: the timing of the takeoff into Sudden Modern Progress. Hence the matter of simultaneous determination of population growth and other variables is not crucial here. (There also was a sharp effect of household economics on population growth at the time of the agricultural revolution and the transition from hunting-gathering to settled agriculture; perhaps this matter deserves more thought.)

13. This statement leaves aside the issue of whether there would also have been knowledge of how to reduce epidemic disease by preventing its transmission by polluted water, mosquitoes, and other vectors.

14. It is commonly believed that long-run prediction is more difficult than short-run prediction. Martin Gardner, famous for his writings about mathematical puzzles and scientific fallacies, says that prediction "is like a chess game. You can predict a couple of moves ahead, but it's almost impossible to predict 30 moves ahead." Or, "If it's so hard to be right about a decade, imagine the howlers in store a century hence," says the *Wall Street Journal.* The *Wall Street Journal*'s columnist Lindley H. Clark put the matter thusly: "Economists have a great deal of trouble predicting the future, and it's unlikely that this unhappy situation ever will change."

It is true that economists cannot predict *short-run* trends of interest rates, exchange rates, and security prices. The incapacity to forecast short-run economic events is well established scientifically, and there is sound reason *in principle* for the incapacity. It is, however, possible to forecast many *long-run* trends with great reliability. Indeed, the most important long-run economic predictions are almost a sure thing, subject only to the qualification that there be no global war or political upheaval.

15. Fire and stone tools are Malthusian "invention-pull" rather than Boserupian "population-push" technology—that is, inventions whose adoption does not require an increase in labor and that therefore are of immediate utility rather than having to wait on further population growth to make them profitable (see Simon 1977, chap. 8; 1978a; 1992, chap. 3).

16. When I was five years old in 1937, my life was saved from scarlet fever by the first new wonder drug, sulfanilamide; the physician had just read about it in the newspaper because it had saved the life of one of the Roosevelts. Until then, hot compresses and prayer were the only available therapies. Until then, people died of infected fingers or ruptured appendixes.

17. Formally, in earlier epochs $dP/P > dL/L > d$(various speeds and powers), whereas in the most recent period $dP/P < dL/L < d$(various speeds and powers).

18. Usher (1988, 10–11) traces this idea back to Ver Hulst in 1846, who attempted "to give an adequate formulation to the simpler generalizations of Malthus," and then through the later work of Raymond Pearl; Alfred Lotka and more recently Paepke (1993) and Ausubel, have worked in the same line. Usher criticizes the idea scathingly: "The entire conceptual framework of Pearl's logistic-analysis is inconsistent with any concept of evolutionary process or with any adequate interpretation of the empirical data" (11). I agree with Usher; the logistic curve is only appropriate when there is a clear upper limit, as for example the upper limit of 100 percent for adoption of an innovation, or when a technology is superseded by another technology, or where a species is limited by the food supply of a given niche. A somewhat more benign view of the logistic curve is held by Cameron (1989, 16–18).

19. In other words, Eric, give me a break.

CHAPTER 2

1. As to the opposite of progress, particular societies certainly have been capable of retrogression in the face of population growth, suggesting that the absolute change in population is not a sufficient condition for growth. The analysis suggests—though it cannot constitute more than a speculation on the matter—that conditions of twentieth century transportation and communications have rendered such long-term retrogression progressively less likely, however.

2. It is interesting and perhaps instructive that economic historians almost uniformly view population growth and increasing density as positive stimuli to the economy in the long run, in Europe and elsewhere within the past millennium. Komlos is not atypical when he writes: "Thus the upsurge in population growth in the 1730s was the proximate cause of the industrial advances made during the second half of the century" (1990, 84–85). The few exceptions I have run across are Fernand Braudel, LeRoy Ladurie, and Carlo Cipolla. Referring to India after 1945, Cipolla writes, "It is a typical case of the Malthusian trap. One who has seen poverty and its concomitants in rural areas in India, China, or Egypt does not doubt the reality of Malthusian checks" (1960, 105). In contrast, biologists even more uniformly see increasing population as having ill effects. So one wonders: Is there a basis on which to judge whose assessments are the more believable on the basis of the types of evidence they adduce? On the side of the economic historians, evidence consists mostly of broad historical analyses and statistical time series; on the biologists' side, laboratory and field observations of animal populations, casual observations of human living conditions, and a model of exponential or logistic growth until a constraint and then oscillatory growth. In this light, it is interesting that in the preceding quote from economist-historian Cipolla, he relies on casual observations of human living conditions rather than the more usual sort of evidence that historians use.

"Malthusian" in the preceding paragraphs refers to the central idea in the *first* edition of Malthus—before he radically changed his ideas in the second and subsequent editions — that income (food) and mortality constitute a "grand dynamics" (Baumol's term); mortality is determined by the supply of food, and increases in the supply of food are exogenously determined by weather and fortuitous new knowledge. There seems broad agreement that for much of human history since the beginning of agriculture, this pattern well describes much of human life in the very short run, after crops are planted each year. This pattern applies particularly well to subsistence agriculture, where bad weather can produce hunger; it also applies to situations prior to modern transportation, when the cost of moving grain was so high that transport was out of the question more than a dozen miles away.

William Petty, Simon Kuznets, and Colin Clark certainly were among the greatest economic statisticians, if not *the* greatest. Among other achievements, they shared the accomplishment of being the three greatest pioneers of national income accounts. They all also were interested in the economics of population and are among the greatest workers on the subject. It is interesting, then, to note that all three of them believed that more people are generally beneficial economically. If one doubts this about Simon Kuznets, who was typically very guarded in his statements on the matter, one may note his assertion that he would lose credibility if he were to be frank about the matter. When Kuznets first addressed the issue squarely in 1960, he assumed that the prevailing professional thought was pessimistic. "My impression is that recent professional (and popular) literature has emphasized the disadvantages and dangers of population growth" (1965, 124). And even with all of Kuznets's prestige, he worried that he would be considered ridiculous for emphasizing the positive aspects. "The concluding remarks are addressed primarily to qualifications, to avoid dismissal of this discussion as an expression of exuberant but unfounded optimism" (137).

3. This distinction is in the spirit of a distinction made by Herbert Simon (1991) in his autobiography, wherein he writes that he uses mathematics for discovery rather than for proof.

4. $P_{-1\,\text{mill}} = f(C_{-1\text{mill}}, \text{human biology})$,   (1a)

   $A_{-1\,\text{mill}} = 0$ and $S_{-1\text{mill}} = 0$.

5. $P_0 = f(C_0, \text{human biology})$.   (1a)

6. $dP_{-1\,\text{mill to}-80\text{m}} = f(P_{-1\,\text{mill}}, C_{-1\text{mill}}, D_{-1\text{mill}}, \text{biology})$.   (1b)

7. $A_{-1\,\text{mill}} = f(\text{genetic knowledge, imitation of animals})$.   (2a)

8. $dA_{-1\,\text{mill}-1} = f(A_{-1\text{mill}}, P_{-1\text{mill}}), A_{-1\text{mill}} = 0$.   (2b)

9. $R_t = f(A_t)$.   (3)

10. $K_t = f(A_t, P_t, Y_t, K_{t-1})$.   (4)

11. From (2a) and (2b) we get

$$A_1 = f(A_{-1\text{mill}}, P_{-1\text{mill}}). \tag{2c}$$

12. $dA_{1-2} = f(P_1, A_1, P/Lnd_1, dP_{1-2}, \text{needs}).$ (2d)

13. By substituting (2c) and then (2b) into equation (2d) we get

$$dA_{1-2} = f(P_1, P_{-1\text{mill}}, P/Lnd_1, dP_{1-2}, \text{needs}), \tag{2e}$$

which makes A_2 a function only of population and land (plus needs, as well as original genetic knowledge and imitation of animals, which can henceforth be ignored.) This substitution is the prototype for the entire analysis to come.

14. So we write

$$A_{\Rightarrow 3} = f(A_{t-1}, P_{t-1}, dA_{t-2\text{to}t-1}, S_t),$$

$$d_{A\Rightarrow 3} \text{ to } t = f(P_{-1\text{mill}}, P_1, \ldots P/Lnd_t, dP_{t-2\text{to}t-1}, S_{t-1}, \text{needs}).$$

15. $dS_{-1\text{mill}-1} = 0.$ (5a)

16. $dS_{-10\text{M to 0 c.e.}} = f(Y_{-10\text{M}}, P_{-10\text{M}}, A_{-10\text{M}}),$ (5b)

where Y is an index not just for income but for the entire system of production.

17. $\text{Mkts}_t = f(P_t, Y_t).$ (6)

18. $dP_{-1\text{ mill}-4} = f(P_t, A_t, D_t).$ (1c)

19. $dP_{>1000 \text{ or } 1750 \text{ c.e.}} = f(P_t, A_t, D_t, S_t, Y_t).$ (1d)

20. $D_{-1\text{ mill to } 1750 \text{ c.e.}} = f(P_t, P_{t-1} \ldots).$ (7a)

21. $D_{>1750 \text{ c.e.}} = f(P_{tP^{t-1}} \ldots P^0, Y^t, A^tS^t).$ (7b)

22. $Y_t = f(A_t, P_t, K_t, S_t, D_t, K_t),$ (8a)

where population size is here a proxy for the labor force size.

23. $Y_{1750} = f(A_{1750}, P_{1750}, K_{1750}, S_{1750}, D_{1750}).$ (8b)

24. $Y_{1750} = f(P_{t=1750}, P_{t-1}, P_{t-2}, P_{t-3}, P_{t-4}).$ (8c)

25. They go on to say, however, that "it is controversial whether democracies or dictatorships better secure these rights" (51). "Dictatorship" here clearly does not include Communist regimes, because there are no individual property rights for producers in true socialist states.

26. North's general vision and that of this essay coincide: "The major source of changes in an economy over time is structural change in the parameters held constant by the economist — technology, population, property rights, and government control over resources." (1981, 57).

27. The term *warranted* comes from the Harrod-Domar discussion of economic development, which otherwise has fallen by the wayside long since.

28. It is true that the first element identifiable as chicken must have been the egg, because the first chicken egg was produced by an animal that was not a chicken, but this is of little matter here.

29. The simplest approach is cumulating population — equivalent to integrating under the curve of population size — up to the event in question.

30. U.S. Bureau of the Census 1976, 808; and U.S. Department of Commerce, *Statistical Abstract, 1985*, 225. These data should reward some study. During the economic depression from 1930 to 1940, there was the expected stagnation and also during the years of World War II. But to my eye, the number of publications during the 1920s seems surprisingly flat, a gain of only about 15 percent. The number of new books, rather than the number of total publications (including new editions), may be the better series to look at, but it is difficult to come by. Interestingly, these data were dropped from the *Statistical Abstract* in the mid-1980s. R. R. Bowker's *Publisher's Weekly* is the original source.

31. Study of the citations in the Royal Academy journals should be productive and easy to do.

32. This need not be only a benign trend; the confinement of interest to recent literature may be counterproductive in the social sciences, where a long historical perspective is often crucial; it may also mean a loss of valuable earlier knowledge in the physical sciences.

33. David Hume asserted in "The Rise of Arts and Sciences" ([1977] 1987, 111 ff.) that the progress of arts and sciences is much more predictable than are the actions of rulers on grounds that are essentially the law of large numbers: The mean tendency of a large sample is more stable than is the tendency of a sample of one. On the other hand, he noted that predicting the course of commerce is much more feasible than predicting the course of the arts and sciences, for the very same reason.

34. This is not intended to suggest that all problems can be tackled successfully. Rather, the point is that if an R&D laboratory does select a problem to work on, the outcome often is reasonably predictable.

CHAPTER 3

1. The reader may notice that I often refer with respect to the work of Simon Kuznets. The fact that Kuznets said that something is so does not constitute proof, of course. But he was an unexcelled observer of the matters under discussion here and especially of the data concerning them. So, if my interpretations were wholly inconsistent with Kuznets's conclusions, that would be troubling, at least to me. There are some times when authority is relevant in science, dislike it

though we may. Indeed, this is the basis of the NAS-NRC system of issuing consensus reports.

2. Great Britain is an exception; see Wrigley and Schofield 1981.

3. "Retired government statistician Emmett 'Skip' Dye . . . completed a 189 day, 3155-mile cross-country trek . . . on foot . . . walking about 20 miles per day" (*Washington Post,* October 31, 1993, p. 35).

4. One can obtain the wrong impression by thinking of major highways—for example, comparing the Roman world to China. Most of the world's roads have always been farm-to-market roads.

5. Smith (1776) emphasized the importance of the division of labor and used the example of pinmaking; his predecessor William Petty made the same point when talking of the advantages of a large city like London over a small city, and he cited a more vivid example than did Smith

> [T]he Gain which is made by *Manufactures,* will be greater, as the Manufacture it self is greater and better . . . each *Manufacture* will be divided into as many parts as possible, whereby the Work of each *Artisan* will be simple and easie; As for Example. In the making of a *Watch,* If one Man shall make the *Wheels,* another the *Spring,* another shall Engrave the *Dial-plate,* and another shall make the *Cases,* then the *Watch* will be better and cheaper, than if the whole Work be put upon any one Man. And we also see that in *Towns,* and in the *Streets* of a great *Town,* where all the *Inhabitants* are almost of one Trade, the Commodity peculiar to those places is made better and cheaper than elsewhere. (Petty [1899] 1986, 473)

6. Keyfitz's estimate (1965) was 69 billion people up to 1960. This also is one of the same general magnitude as the other estimates. A more recent estimate is 3.8 billion before 40,000 B.C.E., 39 billion from 40,000 B.C.E. to the start of the common era, and 22.6 billion from the year 1 up until the year 1750, plus another 10.4 billion from then until 1950, and 4.3 billion from then until 1987, for a total of perhaps 80.3 billion (Bourgeois-Pichat 1989, 90). Even though Bourgeois-Pichat did not make reference to Desmond or Keyfitz, all the estimates are close to each other, which lends confidence to them. But Keyfitz has expressed some unease with the accuracy of all such estimates (correspondence, January 23, 1994).

7. Thanks to Kathy Rochelle for reminding me of this wisdom.

8. Kuznets offers this interesting related observation.

> [A]ggregate growth benefited from the easily cumulative character of modern tested knowledge. Handicraft skills embodied in mortal human beings cannot be accumulated as easily as modern technological knowledge embodied in quantitative formulations and innovations based on overtly measurable and testable characteristics of natural and social processes. It is the very overtness and easy embodiment of tested knowledge

and of its scientific base in a variety of durable forms independent of the personal skills of human beings that make both for its easy communicability and worldwide availability, and for the steadily cumulative results. (Kuznets 1966, 290)

9. It is relevant that the first great burst of cathedral building ended with the population decline of the black plague, resuming only with the rapid increase in population about 1500. This statement is based only on a causal review of the data; a formal analysis would be difficult due to obstacles to fixing dates for cathedrals.

10. The appropriate production function for the technology in a given industry—let us call it a_i—may involve the states of technology in other industries and be written

$$a_i = F(A,P,a_{i,t-1}),\tag{9}$$

where A = summation over a_i.
This may be a nonlinear (perhaps multiplicative) function, say,

$$a_i = F([P * a_{i,t-1}] * a_{1,t} * a_{2,t} * \ldots]\tag{9a}$$

11. Having said all the preceding, however, it still seems mysterious that the discovery of the connection between polluted water and cholera was not made before the nineteenth century. No complementary knowledge or skills were needed; no more than one individual was needed to make the discovery; and there was a demand for such knowledge. Perhaps the juxtaposition of two wells, one polluted and the other not, was an unusual accident, but that is a bit hard to credit.

12. In discussing an analysis of the optimum level of airline overbooking, a colleague once suggested a model that embodied a continuous function for the number of seats on a plane. When I pointed out that this does not accord with the fact that the number of seats is decidedly lumpy, he insisted on assuming that fact away because it made the mathematics intractable.

13. North goes on to say: "The classical model provided no escape from its dismal implications, although as Ester Boserup has persuasively argued (1965) population sometimes acted as a spur to induce [actually, *adopt* rather than *induce,* in her model] new techniques (but she provides no theoretical bridge to account for the overcoming of diminishing returns to a fixed factor)."

14. The best quick index to a country's economic development probably is the proportion of the population employed in agriculture; it also is an excellent index of average consumer welfare at a given moment. Life expectancy is probably the best single index of lifetime consumer welfare. In the past, the amount of coal burned per capita (as a replacement for household firewood as well as for use in industry) and the quantities of metals used per capita, and (later on) the use of all energy, may also be good rough indexes to consumer welfare. They

understate progress, of course, because of the increasing efficiency of use of materials over time. If one were to examine such measures more closely, one should keep in mind (based on a comment by Stanley Engerman, correspondence, August 22, 1997; see also Engerman 1997 for a general discussion of indices of the standard of living) that these and related indices work better for ordering nations at a given time than they do in indicating the cardinal distances among countries. These measures also do not do well in comparing nations in different periods.

15. Econometric analysis would not be easy here because the results of any analysis would depend very largely on (1) the time period (the long run of two centuries or more, or a much shorter period); (2) the set of countries in the sample, (all nations, or European nations, or twentieth-century less-developed nations); and (3) such technical decisions as the inclusion or exclusion of trend.

16. Of course there may also have been important or even decisive noneconomic elements in the decline of plague, such as climate, changes in the nature of the disease, other diseases that affect the propensity for leprosy, and so on.

17. Easterlin's article was published in the *Journal of Evolutionary Economics*. This economic history illustrates particularly well the evolutionary nature of this long-run developmental process and the inappropriateness of a resource-allocation framework in this context.

18. In conversation (January 1997) Preston says that now he also places weight upon the new knowledge that unseen organisms borne by water and air could cause disease. Certainly knowledge on this matter has become more precise with the passage of time. But this observation does not seem to take much away from his earlier conclusion quoted here and my interpretation of it. Nor does it make "technology" the prime mover.

CHAPTER 4

1.

"[T]he tighter the communications net binding each part of Europe to the rest of the world, the smaller became the likelihood of really devastating disease encounter. Only genetic mutation of a disease-causing organism, or a new transfer of parasites from some other host to human beings offered the possibility of devastating epidemic when world transport and communications had attained a sufficient intimacy to assure frequent circulation of all established human diseases among the civilized populations of the world. Between 1500 and 1700 this is what seems in fact to have occurred. Devastating epidemics of the sort that had raged so dramatically in Europe's cities between 1346 and the mid-seventeenth century tapered off toward the status of childhood diseases, or else, as in the case of both plague and malaria, notably reduced the geographic range of their incidence." (McNeill 1977, 197, 198)

Of course increased intercourse also raises the probability of infection by contact. But McNeill assesses an improvement on balance.

2. "It has been suggested that because they [the !Kung] do not have to work
every day they can be said to have an 'affluent society.' This is a *bon mot* but
does not add to the understanding. . . . The !Kung we worked with are all very
thin and . . . constantly expressed concern and anxiety about food" (Truswell
and Hansen 1976, 190, quoting Marshall 1968, 94).

3. Questions may be raised about this connection by the fact that life expectancy stayed as low as it did in rural areas, where it might be presumed that
people could increase their food output through harder work. But sound nutrition in the countryside was hardly omnipresent. Yes, Slicher tells us that "In
1573, on the Swedish royal farms [Gripsholm, I assume], the required amount of
calories, some 3,000 to 3,300 per person per day, was easily reached" (1963, 84).
But he also gives us this time series of daily calories per person at Gripsholm:
1555, 4,166; 1638, 2,480; 1653, 2,883; 1661, 2,920 (85). He also provides data
showing that "the diet of some English farm-labourers' families at the end of the
eighteenth century gives an impression of woeful inadequacy. . . . The food in
Germany in the eighteenth century was no better." And Clark and Haswell
(1967, 8) show a large difference in calorie intake between the worst-fed and the
best-fed castes in an Indian village—a spread from 1,580 to 2,720 calories per
day—though they question whether this had a large effect on height (and,
therefore, presumably on health).

Even where agricultural families had plenty of calories much of the average
year, food supply was less assured prior to the harvest and in bad years, and
there may not have been well-varied diets; the proportion of starchy foods was
too high for good nutrition even in poor countries in the second half of the
twentieth century.

4. The sharply increased death rate during the period 1877–80 (see fig. 62) is
explained, Harrison tells us (1994, 173), by the fact that the troops were in the
field rather than in cantonment during this period. And the higher death rate
among native than among British troops is particularly interesting. It suggests
that in the absence of cantonment discipline, Indian cultural practices had more
opportunity to affect mortality negatively.

5. The complexity of the issue may be exemplified by the case of cholera and
John Snow. Why did that event happen in one of the then-rich countries and not
in a poor one? Why did it happen then and not hundreds of years earlier when
England was poorer? Some suggested answers are given in chapter 5. But is the
subsequent mortality decline to be considered a result of technology or of
wealth? And why did (and does) cholera continue to plague poor countries? If
wealth is the prior causal factor here, it should get the credit, in my view.

6. This section draws even more heavily from my previous books, Simon
1977 and Simon 1996, than does the rest of this essay.

7. Surprising confirmation of the importance of political and economic organization comes from North's analysis (1968, 953) of the sources of productivity change in ocean shipping for 1600 to 1850. Rather than technological

development being preeminent, "The conclusion which emerges from this study is that a decline in piracy and an improvement in economic organization account for most of the productivity change observed."

8. More generally, it seems reasonable that the power of landowners must be reduced by increasing job opportunities for unskilled and semiskilled in the cities. This would seem to explain why one does not hear of rapacious agricultural landowners in developed countries. And it suggests that contemporary China need not worry about ownership of farmland despite the production system shifting to free enterprise in 1979–81. Through its role in promoting cities and markets, population growth may be seen as promoting this element of freedom.

9. This line of research, pioneered magnificently by Otis Dudley Duncan, Fenton Keys, and others in the 1930s, seems to have come to a complete dead end at that time. It is a topic worthy of further inquiry.

CHAPTER 5

1. I don't think that Boserup can be saddled with this criticism, because she did not write at all about invention. Rather, she focused entirely on the adoption of known techniques in response to increased population density. And in my own defense, I have always tried to carefully include a ceteris paribus clause: More people lead to more invention and progress, assuming that all else including stocks of knowledge, levels of education, and standards of living, is equal.

2. McNeill's discussion is illuminating.

[M]erchants were disreputable in China. Confucius had ranked them at the bottom of the social scale. . . .

The nub of the difference between the Far East and the Far West lay in the fact that despite the development of great cities, of a significant regional specialization, and of a highly skilled artisan class, these features of "modern" Chinese life were successfully encapsulated within older agricultural social relationships. The commercial and artisan classes of China never developed a will and self-confidence to challenge the prestige and values of the bureaucracy and landed gentry; whereas in northwestern Europe the evolution of merchant communities from the pirate bands of the ninth–tenth centuries gave them from the start a sense of independence from—indeed of hostility toward—the landed aristocrats of the countryside. European merchants did not cater to anyone: they sought to become powerful in their own right and soon succeeded in doing so. Indeed, by the thirteenth century in Italy, and by the sixteenth century in critically active centers of northern Europe, merchants had captured the state and bent it to their own purposes to a degree utterly inconceivable in Confucian China.

The net effect of the weakness of the Chinese mercantile class was to

blunt (or control?) the social and political impact of a number of important technological developments in which China conspicuously led the
world during the period before 1000 A.D. Inventions like paper and porce-
lain, printing and gunpower, were not entirely without effect upon Chinese society as a whole; but the full and reckless exploitation of these
inventions was reserved for the looser, less ordered society of western
Europe, where no overarching bureaucracy and no unchallengeable social
hierarchy inhibited their revolutionary application. (McNeill 1963, 514)

3. It must be noted that change and social stability are not opposites. Change
is not the same as instability or chaos. And according to Jones (1981, 149):

[T]he rise of the nation-state . . . seem[s] to account for . . . the establish-
ment of the stable conditions necessary for expanding development and
growth, for the diffusion of best practices in technology and commerce,
and in several countries for the actual founding of manufactories where
there had only been handicrafts. The self-propulsion of market forces
explains much, at least in the less authoritarian parts of north-west Europe. A full explanation of the generalisation of novelty must also take the
nation-state into account.

4. My authority for this statement is John Pierson, author of a book on the
first major Japanese newspaper (Pierson 1980); And "In Korea, where . . .
fifteenth-century printers invented a phonetic alphabet . . . which could have
made printing far easier . . . vested interests insisted on clinging to the old
Chinese characters, and consequently few books were printed in Korea until the
nineteenth century" (Mokyr 1990a, 221, referring to Volti 1988, 141).

5. Anecdotes tell much about the effect of migration, often accidental, upon
individuals. Philip Hitti was a poor boy born into a family of shepherds in the
Lebanese hills. Because at an early age he broke a bone that would not heal
properly, he was thought to need to get some schooling to make a living. Hence
he stayed in town and went to school. This put him on the track to become a
renowned scholar of Arab studies and a professor at Princeton, whereas otherwise he might have remained an illiterate shepherd.

6. This approach may indeed, "wash . . . out all the interesting differences
between regimes," as Jones has commented (correspondence September 29,
1994). That may make this essay less interesting, but the topic of differences
between regions simply is outside of the scope of the essay and a distraction from
its main theme.

7. "By the first years of the nineteenth century, and more intensely after
1830, these regions were forced by the Dutch to become major producers of
sugar, coffee, and so forth, and they lost all of their craft industries" (Bairoch
1988, 404).

8. I can personally attest to the high probability of failure of new ideas (to be
sure, mostly social rather than physical ideas, though including mechanical ideas)

to be adopted, even in a modern society and even when the idea has the advantage of being entirely costless. My one out-and-out success depended upon an entirely chance event — for the first time in a fairly long history, an economist rather than a lawyer being appointed to head the relevant government agency, and a person who could appreciate the idea in question. The idea referred to here is what has become the volunteer system of choosing people to be bumped from oversold airline flights (and later, from oversold ship cruises). During 12 years starting in 1966, every U.S. airline refused to try the scheme even for one day at one airport at one counter, even though the trial would be almost costless and success could produce an advertising bonanza ("You will never be kicked off one of our flights involuntarily"). Every relevant bureaucrat refused to take any action. Hundreds of letters were written back and forth to and from every group that might have any influence — airlines, bureaucrats, trade associations, financial analysts, advertising agencies, journalists, legislators — and finally to ex-presidents of the American Economic Association, who were almost the only persons to understand the value of an auction system. If economist Alfred Kahn had not been appointed to head the Civil Aeronautics Board in 1978, the scheme would almost surely still not be adopted. Interestingly, even after more than two decades of total success for this Pareto-optimal scheme, almost no non-U.S. airline has adopted it, giving the same sorts of reasons that U.S. airlines gave pre-1978. The British airlines were almost the sole exceptions as of 1993, and it is likely that the force of the greater competition they face compared to most world airlines can explain their adoption.

I have proposed other (including some similar Pareto-optimal auction schemes) over the years with remarkable lack of success. The most glaring failure has been the inability, even after decades of effort and research starting in 1967, to have the resampling method adopted widely in elementary statistics classes, despite a large heap of unequivocal data showing large benefits for the method. Resampling threatens the intellectual capital of formula-skilled mathematical statisticians, just as the alphabetical *hangul* system of Korean writing was said to have threatened vested interests in Korea after 1500.

The notion that there is something unusual or pathological about a situation where inventions do not become innovations in practice is a dreamworld. The realistic view is that the adoption of a new idea is a rare and chancy event, even in a society that tries to institutionalize adoption of promising new ideas; anyone who was offered a simple and even cost-free Pareto-optimum idea in a large corporation, armed force, or university, in the absence of a crisis atmosphere requiring some change, knows how unlikely it is that anyone will even take notice. It is not China that needs explaining but rather Europe — as Kuznets tries to do with his "epochal innovation" of a scientific attitude.

Another anecdote: At a furniture store in a market of the city of Jubalpur in 1971, I watched an Indian artisan carve bed legs on a lathe. The four legs for a single bed were not at all identical because the latheman worked by eye rather than using a patterned guide. When I suggested using a guide — even of wood, which (unlike metal) would cost almost nothing — the lathe operator (who may also have been the proprietor) said that it was a good idea. "Maybe in the future," he said. But he added apologetically that the shop was still new. "How new?" I asked. "Nine years old," I was told. If it is difficult to get a sound idea adopted in a rich country toward the end of the twentieth century, think how difficult it must have been in the China of 1500.

9. Thanks to Stanley Engerman for the latter two examples.

10. Mokyr (1990a, 162–64, 285), following Paul David and others, emphasizes the path-dependent nature of the process, but he does not bring to bear a random-cumulation model such as that of Herbert Simon.

Acemoglu and Zilibotti (1997) model a related process in which variability in growth diminishes (improving the rate of growth) as growth proceeds; this is an acceleration of path dependence, even stronger than Herbert Simon's process. They suggest that this fits various chunks of historical evidence.

11. The outbreaks in England starting in 1817 may have been more severe and more visible than most in the past (see Colwell 1996).

12. Saul Gass suggested this in discussion, December 1996.

Bibliography

Abramovitz, Moses. 1956. "Resource and Output Trends in the United States since 1870." *American Economics Review Papers and Proceedings* (May): 5–23.

——. 1989. *Thinking about Growth.* Cambridge: Cambridge University Press.

Acemoglu, Daron, and Fabrizio Zilibotti. 1997. "Was Promotheus Unbound by Chance? Risk, Diversification, and Growth." *Journal of Political Economy* 105 (August): 709–51.

Bairoch, Paul. 1988. *Cities and Economic Development.* Trans. Christoper Braider. Chicago: University of Chicago Press.

Barnett, Harold, and Chandler Morse. 1963. *Scarcity and Growth.* Baltimore: Johns Hopkins University Press.

Basham, A. L. 1954. *The Wonder That Was India.* New York: Grove Press.

Baumol, William J., Sue Anne Batey Blackman, and Edward N. Wolff. 1989. *Convergence of Productivity.* Cambridge, MA: MIT Press.

Beach, William W., and Gareth Davis. 1997. "The Index of Economic Freedom and Economic Growth." In *1997 Index of Economic Freedom,* ed. Kim R. Holmes, Bryan T. Johnson, and Melanie Kirkpatrick, 1–13. Published by the Heritage Foundation and the *Wall Street Journal.*

Bengtsson, Tommy, Gunnar Fridlizius, and Rolf Ohlsson, eds. 1984. *Pre-Industrial Population Change.* Stockholm, Sweden: Almquist and Wiksell International.

Boserup, Ester. 1965. *The Conditions of Economic Growth.* London: Allen and Unwin.

Bourgeois-Pichat, J. 1989. "From the 20th to the 21st Century: Europe and Its Population after the Year 2000." *Population,* English Selection no. 1 September: 57–90.

Braudel, Fernand. 1972. *The Mediterranean and the Mediterranean World in the Age of Philip II.* 2 vols. London: Harper and Row.

Brems, Hans. 1980. *Inflation, Interest, and Growth.* Lexington, MA: Lexington Books.

Burke, James. 1978. *Connections.* Boston: Little, Brown.

Burnett, John. 1991. "Housing and the Decline of Mortality." In *The Decline of Mortality in Europe,* ed. R. Schofield, D. Reher, and A. Bideau, 158–76. Clarendon Press: Oxford.

Cambel, Ali Bülent. 1993. *Applied Chaos Theory: A Paradigm for Complexity.* Boston: Academic Press.

Cameron, Rondo. 1989. *A Concise Economic History of the World.* 2d ed, 1993. New York: Oxford University Press.

Campbell, John. 1996. "Perpetual Uncertainty: The Emergence of Technologies." *Federal Reserve Bank of Boston Regional Review* 8 (fall): 6–14.

Chapman, Stanley D. 1972. *The Cotton Industry in the Industrial Revolution.* London: Macmillan.

Chaunu, Pierre. 1979. *European Expansion in the Later Middle Ages.* Amsterdam: North-Holland.

Cipolla, Carlo M. *The Economic History of World Population.* 1962. Penguin Books: Baltimore.

———. 1981. *Fighting the Plague in Seventeenth-Century Italy.* Madison, WI: University of Wisconsin Press.

Clark, Colin. 1957. *The Conditions of Economic Progress.* 2d ed. New York: Macmillan.

Clark, Colin, and Margaret Haswell. 1967. *The Economics of Subsistence Agriculture.* New York: St. Martin's Press.

Clawson, Marion. 1972. *America's Land and Its Uses.* Baltimore: Johns Hopkins University Press.

Clough, Shepard B. 1951. *The Rise and Fall of Civilization.* New York: McGraw Hill.

Colwell, Rita R. 1996. "Global Climate and Infectious Disease: The Cholera Paradigm." *Science* 274 (December 20): 2025–31.

Court, W. H. B. 1954. *A Concise Economic History of Britain—From 1750 to Recent Times.* Cambridge: Cambridge University Press.

Curtin, Philip D. 1984. *Cross-Cultural Trade in World History.* New York: Cambridge University Press.

———. 1989. *Death by Migration.* Cambridge: Cambridge University Press.

David, Paul A. 1975. *Technical Choice, Innovation, and Economic Growth.* Cambridge: Cambridge University Press.

Deane, Phyllis. 1973. "The Industrial Revolution in Great Britain." In *The Fontana Economic History of Europe—The Emergence of Industrial Societies, Part 1,* ed. Carlo M. Cipolla, 161–227. London: Fontana/Collins.

Deevey, Edward S. 1960. "The Human Population." *Scientific American* 203: 195–204. Reprinted in *Man and the Ecosphere,* ed. Paul R. Ehrlich, John P. Holdren, and Richard W. Holm. San Francisco: W. H. Freeman, 1971.

De Vries, Jan. 1976. *The Economy of Europe in an Age of Crisis, 1600–1750.* New York: Cambridge University Press.

Desmond, Annabelle. 1975. "How Many People Have Ever Lived on Earth?" In *Population Studies,* ed. Kenneth C. W. Kammeyer. 2d ed. Chicago: Rand McNally.

Domar, Evsey. 1970. "The Causes of Slavery or Serfdom." *Journal of Economic History* (March): 18–32.

Duncan, Otis Dudley. 1949. "An Examination of the Problem of Optimum City-Size." Ph.D. diss., University of Chicago.

———. 1956. "Optimum Size of Cities." In *Demographic Analysis: Selected*

Readings, ed. Joseph J. Spengler and Otis Dudley Duncan, 372–82. Glencoe: Free Press.

Easterlin, Richard A. 1995. "Industrial Revolution and Mortality Revolution: Two of a Kind?" *Journal of Evolutionary Economics* 5:393–408.

———. 1996. *Growth Triumphant.* Ann Arbor: University of Michigan Press.

Economist. Various issues.

Engerman, Stanley L. 1997. "The Standard of Living Debate in International Perspective: Measures and Indicators." In *Health and Welfare during Industrialization,* ed. Richard H. Steckel and Roderick Floud, 17–45. Chicago: University of Chicago Press.

Fellner, William. 1970. "Trends in the Activities Generating Technological Progress." *American Economic Review* 60:1–29.

Flinn, Michael W. 1981. *The European Demographic System, 1500–1820.* Baltimore: Johns Hopkins University Press.

Flora, Peter, Jens Alber, Richard Eichenberg, Jurgen Kohl, Franz Kraus, Winfried Pfenning, and Kurt Seebohm. 1983. *State, Economy, and Society in Western Europe, 1815–1975: A Data Handbook.* Vol. 1, *The Growth of Mass Democracies and Welfare States.* Chicago: St. James Press.

Floud, Roderick, Kenneth Wachter, and Annabel Gregory. 1990. *Height, Health, and History: Nutritional Status in the United Kingdom, 1750–1980.* New York: Cambridge University Press.

Fogel, Robert William. 1989. "Secular Trends in Mortality, Nutritional Status, and Labor Productivity." Mimeo, February 2.

Fredericksen, Peter C. 1981. "Further Evidence on the Relationship between Population Density and Infrastructure: The Philippines and Electrification." *Economic Development and Cultural Change* 19:749–58.

Gehan, Edmund A., and Noreen A. Lemak. 1994. *Statistics in Medical Research: Developments in Clinical Trials.* New York: Plenum Medical Book Co.

Gimpel, Jean. 1977. *The Medieval Machine.* New York: Penguin.

Glover, Donald, and Julian L. Simon. 1975. "The Effect of Population Density upon Infrastructure: The Case of Roadbuilding." *Economic Development and Cultural Change* 23, no. 3.

Goubert, Jean-Pierre. 1984. "Public Hygiene and Mortality Decline in France in the 19th Century." In *Pre-Industrial Population Change,* ed. Tommy Bengtsson, Gunnar Fridlizius, and Rolf Ohlsson, 151–59. Stockholm, Sweden: Almquist and Wiksell International.

Grantham, George. 1995. "The World's Rising Food Productivity." In *The State of Humanity,* ed. Julian Simon, p. 361 Oxford: Blackwell.

Grigg, David B. 1993. *The World Food Problem.* 2d ed. Oxford and Cambridge, MA: Blackwell.

Gwartney, James, Walter Block, and Robert Lawson. 1992. "Measuring Economic Freedom." In *Rating Global Economic Freedom,* ed. Stephen T. Easton and Michael A. Walker, 153–229. Vancouver, BC: Fraser Institute.

Gwartney, James, Robert Lawson, and Walter Block. 1996. *Economic Freedom of the World, 1975–1995.* Vancouver, BC: Fraser Institute.

Harrison, Mark. 1994. *Public Health in British India: Anglo-Indian Preventive Medicine 1859–1914.* Cambridge: Cambridge University Press.

Hayami, Yujiro, and Vernon W. Ruttan. 1987. "Population Growth and Agricultural Productivity." In *Population Growth and Economic Development: Issues and Evidence,* ed. D. Gale Johnson and Ronald D. Lee, 57–104. Madison, WI: University of Wisconsin Press.

Hayek, Friedrich A. 1960. *The Constitution of Liberty.* Chicago: University of Chicago Press.

———. 1989. *The Fatal Conceit.* Chicago: University of Chicago Press.

———, ed. 1954. *Capitalism and the Historians.* Chicago: University of Chicago Press.

Hicks, John. 1969. *A Theory of Economic History.* London: Oxford University Press.

Higgs, Robert. 1971. "American Inventiveness, 1870–1920." *Journal of Political Economy* 79:661–67.

Holmes, Kim R., Bryan T. Johnson, and Melanie Kirkpatrick, eds. 1997. *Index of Economic Freedom.* Washington, DC: Dow Jones/Heritage Foundation.

Hume, David. [1777] 1987. *Essays Moral, Political and Literary.* Indianapolis: Liberty Classics.

International Bank for Reconstruction and Development. (IBRD). 1980. *World Tables.* Baltimore: Johns Hopkins University Press for the World Bank and IBRD.

———. 1985. *World Development Report.* New York: Oxford University Press.

Jacobs, Jane. 1969. *The Economy of Cities.* New York: Random House.

Janelle, Donald G. 1968. "Central Place Development in a Time-Space Framework." *Professional Geographer* 20, no. 1:5–10.

Jewkes, John, David Sawyers, and Richard Stillerman. 1958. *The Sources of Invention.* London: Macmillan.

Jones, Eric L. 1981. *The European Miracle.* New York: Cambridge University Press.

———. 1988. *Growth Recurring.* New York: Oxford University Press.

Kates, R., and I. Burton. 1986. *Geography, Resources, and Environment.* Vol. 2. Chicago: University of Chicago Press.

Kelley, Allen. 1972. "Scale Economies, Inventive Activity, and the Economics of American Population Growth." *Explorations in Economic History* (fall): 35–72.

———. 1976. "Demographic Change and the Size of the Government Sector." *Southern Economic Journal* 43, no. 2: (October).

Kelley, Allen C., and Robert Schmidt. 1995. "Aggregate Population and Economic Growth Correlations." *Demography* 32:543–55.

Keyes, Fenton. 1942. "The Correlation of Social Phenomena with Community Size." Ph.D. diss., Yale University.

Keyfitz, Nathan. "How Many People Have Lived on the Earth?" *Demography* 3, no. 2: 581–82.

Klein, Herbert Arthur. 1974. *The Science of Measurement—A Historical Survey.* New York: Dover.

Komlos, John. 1990. "Nutrition, Population Growth, and the Industrial Revolution." *Social Science History* 14 (spring): 69–91.

Kremer, Michael. 1993. "Population Growth and Technological Change: One Million B.C. to 1990." *Quarterly Journal of Economics* (August): 681–716.

Kunitz, Stephen J., and Stanley L. Engerman. 1992. "The Ranks of Death: Secular Trends in Income and Mortality." *Health Transition Review* 2, supplementary issue.

Kuznets, Simon. 1957–60. *Population Redistribution and Economic Growth: United States, 1870–1990*. Philadelphia, PA: American Philosophical Society.

———. 1965. *Economic Growth and Structure—Selected Essays*. New York: W. W. Norton.

———. 1966. *Modern Economic Growth: Rate, Structure, and Spread*. New Haven: Yale University Press.

Lal, Deepak. 1990. *Cultural Stability and Economic Stagnation: India, 1500 B.C.–1980 A.D.* London and New York: Oxford University Press.

Landes, David S. 1983. *Revolution in Time*. Cambridge: Harvard University Press.

———. 1994. "What Room for Accident in History? Explaining Big Changes by Small Events." *Economic History Review*, 2d ser., 4:637–56.

Leakey, Richard E. 1981. *The Making of Mankind*. New York: Dutton.

Lee, W. R., ed. 1979. *European Demography and Economic Development*. New York: St. Martin's Press.

Lichtenberg, Frank R. 1994. "Have International Differences in Educational Attainment Levels Narrowed?" In *Convergence of Productivity*, ed. William J. Baumol, Richard R. Nelson, and Edward N. Wolff, 225–42. New York: Oxford University Press.

Livi-Bacci, Massimo. 1991. *Population and Nutrition: An Essay on European Demographic History*. New York: Cambridge University Press.

———. 1992. *A Concise History of World Population*. Cambridge, MA: Blackwell Publishers.

Machlup, Fritz. 1962. "The Supply of Inventors and Inventions." Comment by Jacob Schmookler. In *The Rate and Direction of Inventive Activity: Economic and Social Factors*, 143–69. A Conference of the Universities—National Bureau Committee for Economic Research and the Committee on Economic Growth of the Social Science Research Council. Princeton: Princeton University Press.

Maddison, Angus. 1982. *Phases of Capitalist Development*. Oxford: Oxford University Press.

———. 1991. *Dynamic Forces in Capitalist Development*. Oxford: Oxford University Press.

———. 1994. "Explaining the Economic Performance of Nations, 1820–1989." In *Convergence of Productivity*, ed. William J. Baumol, Richard R. Nelson, and Edward N. Wolff, 20–61. New York: Oxford University Press.

McEvedy, Colin, and Richard Jones. 1978. *Atlas of World Population History*. New York: Penguin Books.

McKeown, Thomas. 1976. *The Modern Rise of Population.* London: Edward Arnold.

———. 1983. "Food, Infection, and Population." *Journal of Interdisciplinary History* 14:2. Reprinted in Rotberg and Rabb, 1986, 29–50.

McKeown, Thomas, and R. G. Brown. 1955. "Medical Evidence Related to English Population Changes in the Eighteenth Century." *Population Studies* 9:119–41.

McNeill, William H. 1963. *The Rise of the West.* New York: Mentor.

———. 1977. *Plagues and Peoples.* Garden City, NY: Anchor Books.

Meguire, Philip. 1993. Correspondence with author, August 26.

Mill, John Stuart. 1848. *Principles of Political Economy.* London: n.p.

Mitchell, B. R., and Phyllis Deane. 1962. *Abstract of British Historical Statistics.* New York: Cambridge University Press.

Mitchell, B. R. 1973. "Statistical Appendix." In *The Fontana Economic History of Europe—The Emergence of Industrial Societies, Part 2,* ed. Carlo M. Cipolla, 738–820. London: Fontana/Collins.

———. 1978. *European Historical Statistics, 1750–1970.* New York: Columbia University Press.

Mokyr, Joel. 1990a. *The Lever of Riches: Technological Creativity and Economic Progress.* New York: Oxford University Press.

———. 1990b. *Twenty-Five Centuries of Technological Change: An Historical Survey.* New York: Harwood.

Moore, Thomas Gale, with the Assistance of Cassandra Chrones Moore. 1993. "On Progress." Photocopy of draft.

Morley, S. G. 1946. *The Ancient Maya.* London: Oxford University Press.

Motor Vehicles Manufacturers Association of the United States. *World Motor Vehicle Data.* Various years.

Murrell, Peter. 1985. "The Size of Public Employment: An Empirical Study." *Journal of Comparative Economics* 9:424–37.

Normile, Dennis. 1997. "Yangtze Seen as Earliest Rice Site." *Science* (January 17): 309.

North, Douglass C. 1968. "Sources of Productive Change in Ocean Shipping, 1600–1850." *Journal of Political Economy* 76, no. 5:953–70.

———. 1981. *Structure and Change in Economic History.* New York: W. W. Norton.

Ogburn, William F., and Otis Dudley Duncan. n.d. *City Size as a Sociological Variable in Urban Sociology.* Ed. Ernst W. Burgess and Donald J. Bogue, 58–75. Chicago: Phoenix Books, University of Chicago Press.

Paepke, C. Owen. 1993. *The Evolution of Progress: The End of Economic Growth and the Beginning of Human Transformation.* New York: Random House.

Petty, William. 1986. *The Economic Writings of Sir William Petty.* Ed. Charles Henry Hull. Fairfield, NJ: Augustus M. Kelley.

Phelps, Edmund. 1966. "Models of Technical Progress and the Golden Rule of Research." *Review of Economic Studies* 33 (April): 133–45.

Pierson, John D. 1980. *Tokutomi Sohúo, 1863–1957: A Journalist for Modern Japan.* Princeton: Princeton University Press.

Pirenne, Henri. [1925] 1969. *Medieval Cities.* Princeton: Princeton University Press.

Pound, Roscoe. 1921. *The Spirit of the Common Law.* Boston: Beacon Press.

Preston, Samuel H. 1975. "The Changing Relation between Mortality and Level of Economic Development." *Population Studies* 29, no. 2:231–48.

———. 1980. "Causes and Consequences of Mortality Declines in Less Developed Countries during the Twentieth Century." In *Population and Economic Change in Developing Countries,* ed. Richard A. Easterlin, 289–341. Chicago: University of Chicago Press.

———. 1995. "Human Mortality throughout History and Prehistory." In *The State of Humanity,* ed. Julian L. Simon. Boston: Blackwell.

Price, Derek de Solla. 1961. *Science since Babylon.* New Haven: Yale University Press.

Przeworski, Adam, and Fernando Limongi. 1993. "Political Regimes and Economic Growth." *Journal of Economic Perspectives* 7 (summer): 51–60.

Puranen, Bi. 1991. "Tuberculosis and Decline of Mortality in Sweden." In *The Decline of Mortality in Europe,* ed. Roger Schofield, David Reher, and A. Bideau. Oxford: Clarendon Press.

Rescher, Nicholas. 1978. *Scientific Progress: A Philosophical Essay on the Economics of Research in Natural Science.* Oxford: Blackwell.

Robinson, C. 1992. *Making a Market in Energy.* London: Institute of Economic Affairs.

Rosen, George. [1958] 1993. *A History of Public Health.* Baltimore: Johns Hopkins University Press.

Rosenberg, Nathan. 1976. *Perspectives on Technology.* Cambridge: Cambridge University Press.

———. 1982. *Inside the Black Box.* Cambridge: Cambridge University Press.

Rosenberg, Nathan, and L. E. Birdzell Jr. 1986. *How the West Grew Rich.* New York: Basic Books.

Rostas, Leo. 1948. "Comparative Productivity in British and American Industry." Occasional Paper no. 13. NBER, Cambridge.

Rotberg, Robert I., and Theodore K. Rabb, eds. 1986. *Population and Economy.* New York: Cambridge University Press.

Rotemberg, Julio J., and Garth Saloner. 1987. "The Relative Rigidity of Monopoly Pricing." *American Economic Review* 77:917–26.

Schofield, Roger, and David Reher. 1991. "The Decline of Mortality in Europe." In *The Decline of Mortality in Europe,* ed. Roger Schofield, David Reher, and A. Bideau. Oxford: Clarendon Press.

Schultz, T. Paul. 1981. *Economics of Population.* Reading, MA: Addison-Wesley.

Schultz, Theodore W. 1951. "The Declining Economic Importance of Land." *Economic Journal* 61 (December): 725–40.

―――. 1975. "The Value of the Ability to Deal with Disequilibria." *Journal of Economic Literature,* 827–46.

Science. Various issues.

Scully, Gerald W. 1992. *Constitutional Environments and Economic Growth.* Princeton: Princeton University Press.

Scully, Gerald W., and Daniel J. Slottje. 1992. "Measuring Economic Liberty." In *Rating Global Economic Freedom,* ed. Stephen T. Easton and Michael A. Walker, 255–79. Vancouver, BC: Fraser Institute.

Semmelweis, Ignaz. 1983. *The Etiology, Concept, and Prophylaxis of Childbed Fever.* Madison, WI: University of Wisconsin Press.

Sigerist, Henry E. 1942. *Civilization and Disease.* Chicago: University of Chicago Press.

Simon, Herbert A. 1991. *Models of My Life.* New York: Basic Books.

Simon, Julian L. 1967. "The Effect of Competitive Structure upon Advertising Expenditures." *Quarterly Journal of Economics* 81 (November): 610–27.

―――. 1974. The Effects of Income on Fertility. Chapel Hill, NC: Carolina Population Center.

―――. 1977. *The Economics of Population Growth.* Princeton: Princeton University Press.

―――. 1978a. "An Integration of the Invention-Pull and Population-Push Theories of Economic-Demographic History." In *Research in Population Economics.* Vol. 1, ed. Julian L. Simon. Greenwich, CT: JAI Press.

―――. 1978b. "The Effect of Population Size and Concentration upon Scientific Productivity." In *Research in Population Economics.* Vol. 1, ed. Julian L. Simon. Greenwich, CT: JAI Press.

―――. 1981. *The Ultimate Resource.* 2d ed., 1996. Princeton: Princeton University Press.

―――. 1987a. *Effort, Opportunity, and Wealth.* New York: Basil Blackwell.

―――. 1987b. "Population Growth, Economic Growth, and Foreign Aid." *Cato Journal* 7 (spring/summer): 159–86.

―――. 1992. *Population and Development in Poor Countries.* Princeton: Princeton University Press.

Simon, Julian L. (under the pen name Lincoln Pashute), and Douglas Love. 1978. "The Effects of Population Size, Growth, and Concentration upon Scientific Productivity." In *Research in Population Economics,* vol. 1, ed. Julian L. Simon. Greenwich, CT: JAI Press.

Simon, Julian L., and Edward Rice. 1983–84. "The Theory of Price-Changing and Monopoly Power." *Journal of Post-Keynesian Economics* 6, no. 2 (winter): 198–213.

Simon, Julian L., Guenter Weinrauch, and Stephen Moore. 1994. "The Reserves of Extracted Resources: Historical Data." *Non-Renewable Resources* (summer): 325–40.

Simon, Julian L., and Gunter Steinman. 1981. "Population Growth and Phelps' Technical Progress Model." In *Research in Population Economics,* vol. 3, ed. Julian L. Simon and P. Lindert, 239–54. Greenwich, CT: JAI Press.

Simon, Julian L., and Paul Burstein. 1975. *Basic Research Methods in Social Science.* 3d ed. New York: Random House.

Simon, Julian L., and Richard J. Sullivan. 1989. "Population Size, Knowledge Stock, and Other Determinants of Agricultural Publication and Patenting: England, 1541–1850." *Explorations in Economic History* 26:21–44.

Simon, Julian L., and Roy Gobin. 1980. "The Relationship between Population and Economic Growth in LDC's." In *Research in Population Economics,* vol. 2, ed. Julian L. Simon. Greenwich, CT: JAI Press.

Slicher van Bath, B. H. 1963. *The Agrarian History of Western Europe,* A.D. *500–1850.* London: Arnold.

Smith, Adam. [1776] 1980. *The Wealth of Nations.* New York: Viking.

Sobel, Dava. 1995. *Longitude.* New York: Penguin.

Solow, Robert. 1957. "Technical Change and the Aggregate Production Function." *Review of Economics and Statistics* 39:312–20.

Spengler, J. J., and Otis Dudley Duncan. 1956. *Demographic Analysis.* Glencoe, IL: Free Press.

Steinman, Gunter, and Julian L. Simon. 1981. "Phelps' Technical Progress Model Generalized." *Economic Letters* 5:177–82.

Stevenson, Robert F. 1968. *Population and Political Systems in Tropical Africa.* New York: Columbia University Press.

Thompson, Wilbur R. 1962. "Locational Differences in Inventive Effort and Their Determinants." In *The Rate and Direction of Inventive Activity: Economic and Social Factors, 253–71.* A Conference of the Universities—National Bureau Committee for Economic Research and the Committee on Economic Growth of the Social Science Research Council. Princeton: Princeton University Press.

Tinsley, B. A. 1980. "Technological Development and Colonization as Factors in the Long-Term Variation in Growth." *Cosmic Search,* Year End, 11.

UNESCO. 1963. *UNESCO Yearbook.* Paris: UNESCO.

UNESCO, Office of Statistics. 1990. "Comparison of Statistics on Illiteracy." Paris: UNESCO.

United Nations. 1984. "Report on *World Population.*" New York: The Fund.

U.S. Bureau of the Census. 1976. *Historical Statistics of the United States.* New York: Basic Books.

U.S. Department of Commerce. 1978. *World Population.* Washington, DC: Government Printing Office.

U.S. Department of Commerce. Various years. *Statistical Abstract.* Washington, DC: Government Printing Office.

Usher, Abbott Payson. 1988. *A History of Mechanical Inventions.* New York: Dover.

Vallin, Jacques. 1991. "Mortality in Europe form 1720 to 1914: Long Term Trends and Changes in Patterns by Age and Sex." In *The Decline of Mortality in Europe,* ed. Roger Schofield, David Reher, and A. Bideau, 38–67. Oxford: Clarendon Press.

Volti, Rudi. 1981. *Society and Technological Change.* New York: St. Martin's Press.

Washington Post. Various issues.

Weber, A., and E. Weber. 1974–75. "The Structure of World Protein Consumption and Future Nitrogen Requirements." *European Review of Agricultural Economics* 2:169–92.

Weir, David R. 1984. "Life under Pressure: France and England, 1670–1870." *Journal of Economic History* 44 (March): 27–48.

West, E. C. 1971. *Canada-United States Price and Productivity Differences in Manufacturing Industries, 1963*. Ottawa: Economic Council of Canada.

Williamson, T. 1987. "Common Land." In *The New Palgrave: A Dictionary of Economics*, vol. 1, ed. John Eatwell, Murray Milgate, and Peter Newman, 499–500. New York: Macmillan.

Wilson, E. O. 1995. *Naturalist*. New York: Warner Books.

Winslow, Charles-Edward Amory. [1943] 1980. *The Conquest of Epidemic Disease—A Chapter in the History of Ideas*. Madison, WI: University of Wisconsin Press.

Wittfogel, Karl. 1957. *Oriental Despotism: A Comparative Study of Total Power*. New Haven: Yale University Press.

Woodruff, William. 1973. "The Emergence of an International Economy, 1700–1914. In *The Fontana Economic History of Europe—The Emergence of Industrial Societies, Part 2*, ed. Carlo Cipolla, 656–737. London: Fontana/Collins.

Wrigley, Edward A., and Roger S. Schofield. 1981. *The Population History of England, 1541–1871*. New York: Cambridge University Press.

Young, Alwyn. 1993. "Invention and Bounded Learning by Doing." *Journal of Political Economy* 101, no. 3: 443–72.

Zinsser, Hans. [1935] 1960. *Rats, Lice and History*. New York: Bantam Books.